Flashes of a Southern Spirit

CHARLES REAGAN WILSON

Flashes of a Southern Spirit

Meanings of the Spirit in the U.S. South

The University of Georgia Press   *Athens and London*

© 2011 by the University of Georgia Press

Athens, Georgia 30602

www.ugapress.org

All rights reserved

Set in Berthold Baskerville by Graphic Composition, Inc., Bogart, Georgia

Printed digitally in the United States of America

Library of Congress Cataloging-in-Publication Data

Wilson, Charles Reagan.

Flashes of a southern spirit : meanings of the spirit in the U.S. South /
Charles Reagan Wilson.

p. cm.

Includes bibliographical references and index.

ISBN-13: 978-0-8203-3829-3 (hardcover : alk. paper)

ISBN-10: 0-8203-3829-X (hardcover : alk. paper)

ISBN-13: 978-0-8203-3830-9 (pbk. : alk. paper)

ISBN-10: 0-8203-3830-3 (pbk. : alk. paper)

1. Southern States – Civilization.

2. Regionalism – Southern States.

3. Group identity – Southern States.

4. Southern States – Religious life and customs.

5. Southern States – Religion – Social aspects.

6. Spiritual life – Social aspects – Southern States.

7. Spirituality – Social aspects – Southern States. I. Title.

F209.5.W55 2011

975 – dc22   2010043511

British Library Cataloging-in-Publication Data available

TO MY BROTHER

CONTENTS

PREFACE

Spirit and a New Southern Studies

The chapters in this book have all been previously published but in a diverse array of publications. Four of them were originally prepared for international southern studies conferences, and four more began at annual professional associations and symposia. All of those were published in volumes of essays or in journals; the remaining chapters also first appeared in journals or in collections of essays. The introduction and afterword appear for the first time here.

The essays reflect a common interest in the interdisciplinary study of the American South, with a special focus on cultural history. They reflect my graduate training in American history and American studies, and they draw from my later work in the southern studies curriculum at the Center for the Study of Southern Culture at the University of Mississippi. As editor of the *Encyclopedia of Southern Culture* and *The New Encyclopedia of Southern Culture*, I became interested in a variety of theories, methodologies, genres, and perspectives; in these chapters I cite evidence from the South's writers, musicians, folk artists, politicians, preachers, and policy makers, among others. The southern studies program at the University of Mississippi focuses typically on text and context, and this volume reflects those concerns, broadly understood. Most of the essays in this volume deal with the period from the post–Civil War era into modern times. One special concern throughout is the South's regional identity, and the essays in part 1 trace a rough development of that from the late nineteenth century to the late twentieth. A second special concern is how religion in the South has affected regional identity and cultural expression. The particular focus of this volume is on manifestations of "spirit" in the South, which include southern patriotic spirit, southern prophecy, and religious ecstasy. I argue that "southern spirit" is both constructed and performed, and the volume encourages further consideration of spirit as a dimension of a new southern studies.

In 2001, Houston Baker Jr. and Dana D. Nelson called for "a new Southern studies, an emerging collective already producing a robust body of work in current American studies scholarship," and since then a variety of publications and conferences have contributed to efforts to extend the long-standing scholarly interest in the interdisciplinary study of the U.S. South. Baker and Nelson suggested that a new southern studies should "reconfigure our familiar notions of Good (or desperately bad) Old Southern White Men telling stories on the porch, protecting white women, and being friends to the Negro." Indeed, nothing has been more fundamental to "re-visioning" the study of the South than the inclusion of blacks and women as formative figures in the southern cultural imagination. Baker and Nelson called the emerging new approaches to the South at the turn of the twenty-first century a "paradigm shift," with the potential to complicate "old borders and terrains" and "to construct and survey a new scholarly map of 'the South.'" They identified religion as a possible topic for a new southern studies when they used the term "thick" to describe "not only the heaviness of summer atmospherics" but also the "viscous dynamics of every day labor, politics, and religion that characterize life in the deep South."[1] Nonetheless, they did not explore matters of the spirit in their essay, nor did they include an article on religion in the special issue of *American Literature* that launched the explicit discussion of a new southern studies.

Literary critic Michael Kreyling responded to the Baker and Nelson essay with an analysis of works that might contribute to the reimagining of southern studies, also using the term "paradigm shift" and noting that the study of "southern literature" had evolved into "southern studies." He saw this field struggling to absorb several "new discourses," especially memory studies and interest in globalization. He concluded that a new southern studies "surrenders its traditional claim to regional and historical distinctiveness, finds a common language in public debates over globalization of identities, and takes its chances in the dangerous, new, postmodern world where construction replaces essence." However, Kreyling, too, failed to raise religion as an analytical category to explore in a new southern studies.[2]

Another early seminal text in the reinvigorated interdisciplinary study of the South was Kathryn McKee and Annette Trefzer's special 2006 issue of *American Literature*, "Global Contexts, Local Literatures: The New Southern Studies." They brought great clarity to the scholarly issues involved, recognizing the continued need to examine the South's relation to the nation and its centrality to American studies but emphasizing the "region's fascinating multiplicity and its participation in hemispheric and global contexts." Although they did not include a perspective on religion in the issue, their identification of the South's multiplicity and its global contexts has remained an accurate descriptor for the subject of a new southern studies. In imagining a broad intellectual movement, they concluded that the South of the new paradigm "emerges as an in-between space, a process, an agenda, an itinerary, a discourse, an idea, a relational concept in a global context." In a resonant image, they saw "a shape-shifting South" with fluid boundaries.[3]

Southern studies has a long history as a project that brings disciplines together to exchange theoretical and methodological insights. Renowned scholars such as C. Vann Woodward, Howard Odum, Louis Rubin, Cleanth Brooks, and later, John Shelton Reed, Michael O'Brien, Eugene Genovese, and David Potter read each other's work across genres and conversed with each other's interpretations. The Center for the Study of Southern Culture, which has influenced my thinking on the interdisciplinary study of the region so much, began its work in 1977, representing a new nationwide interest in regional studies. The *Encyclopedia of Southern Culture* appeared in 1989, an expression of an overarching interest in culture as the focus of what historian Richard Maxwell Brown called the "New Regionalism."[4]

The new southern studies of the last decade surely builds on that earlier movement, but the use of the term "new" suggests how widespread is the exploration of innovative ways of looking at the South. The titles of two influential collections of essays reference classic southern texts but take off from them. *South to a New Place: Region, Literature, Culture* consciously invokes black writer Albert Murray's *South to an Old Place*, a key volume in asserting the post–Jim Crow claim by southern blacks on southern culture, while *Look Away! The U.S. South in New World Studies* echoes the song "Dixie" and its association with white Confederate identity but indeed "looks away" from that nineteenth-century South by positioning the region in a global world. These volumes offered fresh perspectives on familiar literary works but also examined wide-ranging texts that went beyond literary productions. They broadened the canon of traditional southern literary studies and provided historical and cultural context. The titles of other recent scholarly books also suggest transformations, as in *Redefining Southern Culture, Bridging Southern Cultures,* and *Reconstructing Dixie.* The latter book, by Tara McPherson, was particularly significant in bringing a variety of mass-culture texts into the discourse of southern studies. She praised practitioners in the field for their focus on region and place as a way to "ground contemporary theory's generalizations and abstractions, allowing one to test the claims of theory in a site-specific frame." But she suggested that "southern studies, for its part, could also profit from an encounter with contemporary critical theory" to provide greater complexity to the idea of the South. Her stress on critical theory has been a crucial part of many efforts to establish a new southern studies.[5]

Two book series are explicitly dedicated to a new southern studies. The University of Georgia Press's The New Southern Studies, edited by Jon Smith and Riché Richardson, has produced studies on gender and blackness, "grounded globalism," the economics of southern identity seen in literature, and literary modernism's regional-national connections. The University of North Carolina Press's New Directions in Southern Studies, which I edit, has published studies of Memphis as a site of globalization, lynching and mass culture, women writers and the South's visual culture, and the persistence of slavery generated commodification of bodies in modern popular culture. In addition to these series, *The New Encyclopedia of Southern Culture,* projected to contain twenty-four volumes, extends the approach of its predecessor and includes much of the new scholarship in its conceptualization, framework, and choice of entries.[6]

Much of the energy for a new southern studies has come from literary studies and cultural studies, but fresh interdisciplinary work on the South has appeared in other disciplines as well. A new southern studies should be inclusive enough to reflect the breadth of such scholarship. Recent ethnographic studies challenge the dominance of cultural studies in interpreting southern cultural patterns. Celeste Ray's edited book *Southern Heritage on Display* gathers essays by scholars who "look at how people identify themselves through popular religiosity, musical spectacles, ethnic festivals and celebrations, exhibitions of material culture, and particular dress, and what they communicate about themselves verbally and non-verbally in public gatherings." This event-based fieldwork shares with others in southern studies a focus on the contested or oppositional nature of identity and power within a specifically southern context. Ray, who is an anthropologist, draws from theory, not the postmodernism of much of the new southern studies but rather the ritual theory of social science. Ray emphasizes how performance of ritual can produce a *communitas*, a sense of unity even in an otherwise divided society. At the same time, cultural celebrations can show what divides some members of a community from others who may have different memories of the same selected past. The ethnographic approach of Ray and her colleagues provides a model that differs from that of many of the works explicitly identified with a new southern studies but one that surely merits inclusion in the field. Like literary scholars and historians, she agrees that the South is "not a cultural monolith but a complex creole of multiple traditions." Her usage of the word "creole" to describe southern cultural identity reverberates with others in a new southern studies. Ray's approach gives a rich specificity to understanding this "blending of cultures after long exposure, coexistence, and interaction of two or more social groups" in the region.[7]

Sociologists have also made important contributions to a new southern studies. Wanda Rushing's study of Memphis as a site of globalization challenges the conventional wisdom that globalization diminishes the significance of place. Although rejecting the idea of southern exceptionalism, Rushing argues that cultural and economic distinctiveness persists in local places because global processes work themselves out in communities with particular histories and cultures. Her findings in Memphis reflect broad southern patterns, with a sense of place coming from particular embodiments of social relations and social processes more than simply from landscape. Rushing's eclectic approach combines sociological theory (especially theories of space-time compression), literary narrative, thick description, and a new historical sociology, which represents an alternative to the variables-oriented paradigm that dominates social science research.[8]

Historians have used the terminology of a new southern studies less frequently than literary scholars, but they have produced studies that surely contribute to this developing field, with its focus on the multiplicities of the South, theoretically grounded works, and explorations of new topics and materials for study. Edward Ayers's synthesis of late nineteenth-century history, written well before recent talk of a new paradigm, reflects postmodernist influences, with its multiplicity of voices existing in a contested terrain, and W. Fitzhugh Brundage's study of memory represents a major contribution to conceptualizing a new southern studies. Matthew Pratt Guterl's *American Mediterranean: Southern Slaveholders in the Age of Emancipation* (2008) places the U.S. South within the spatial zone of the Caribbean in the antebellum era, while Jack Temple Kirby's *Mockingbird's Song* draws from agronomy, archaeology, geology, sociology, and literature to enhance his model historical narrative about what he calls the poetics and politics of the southern environment. Ted Ownby, director of the Center for the Study of Southern Culture, has recently surveyed the "most notable developments" in southern historical writing over the last decade, and his list provides a useful guide to disciplinary work that is contributing to a new southern studies. "Perhaps nothing in the past decade or so has been as influential," he writes, "as the argument that concepts, ideas, arguments, assumptions about race, blackness, whiteness, gender, nation, region, and lots of other ideas are constructions," which people use "to support existing social relations, to try to make them seem natural or normal, or to subvert or at least complicate those social relations." He also lists the global South; gender studies and women's studies; respectability and uplift; Indians; the slave trade; memory; civil rights scholarship (local studies and white southerners' responses); the environment; and the end of social history, cultural history, and maybe political history as separate fields. These trends suggest a reinvigorated study of southern history that should be brought into discussions of a new southern studies. As McKee and Trefzer noted, new southern studies is surely a collaborative project of scholars working within disciplines contributing their perspectives to a broader framework.[9]

These essay collections, monographs, and book series, as well as other ongoing work within various academic disciplines, have produced a vibrant body of material that has invigorated the interdisciplinary study of the South. They have given, however, scant attention to religion, despite the continuing centrality in the South of its predominant evangelical Protestantism and despite the region's evolving religious context through the growth in the last decade of such "new" religions as Latino Catholicism, Islam, Buddhism, and Hinduism. Moreover, innovative works in southern religious studies that draw on theory – a major concern of a new southern studies – have not worked their way into recent discussions of interdisciplinary approaches to the South. Paul Harvey's exploration of religious interracialism between whites and blacks provides a rich source for understanding the South's "creolization" in spirituality. Donald Mathews's landmark study of the religious roots of lynching in the South draws on the work of a wide variety of theorists, such as Victor Turner on ritual, Mary Douglas on purity, and Rene Girard on violence and religion. Mathews's article appeared in the online *Journal of Southern Religion*, which regularly publishes wide-ranging reviews of films as well as texts that cross academic boundaries (scholars operating in new southern studies will hopefully be regular visitors to the site). *Southern Spaces*, another peer-reviewed Internet journal, is a storehouse of work in a new southern studies, including prominent visual, musical, and textual materials on religion.[10]

The chapters in this book, in truth, were largely written before talk of a new southern studies began, but my work has evolved with its ideas in mind. I have explored elsewhere some of the field's central concerns, such as the use of postmodern critical theory, globalization (in terms of religion in the South), and connections between the South and the Caribbean.[11] This volume makes its contribution to a new southern studies through its explorations of another thematic concern of the field – the region's multiplicities – and its incorporation of new texts (namely those of self-taught and visionary artists). It deconstructs the idea of tradition, through application, to the region, of Eric Hobsbawm and Terence Ranger's theory of the invention of tradition and through a general deconstruction of other ideological constructs. Social class may seem a topic of the "old" southern studies, but its relationship to issues of power that still animate the field should be highlighted, which I do in chapter 4, by engaging with the complex issues surrounding the poor white's sense of regional identity. Although the new southern studies moves beyond a racial binary of black-white, the region's biracial culture continues to be the focus of such central practitioners of the project as Houston Baker and Riché Richardson. Chapter 5 deconstructs the representation of the South as a biracial society in the 1970s, while other chapters explore the on-the-ground dynamics of the region's cultural interactions – its creolization – among its historically dominant populations from Western Europe and West Africa. This volume highlights issues that should be on the agenda of a new southern studies. One is creativity and the issues of aesthetics across genre. The chapters in part 2 examine the idea of a Southern Cultural Renaissance in the twentieth century, and the topic remains a fruitful one for the application of a variety of methods and theories associated with a new southern studies. This volume's underlying argument is that matters of the spirit are central to southern culture, and spirituality should be considered more centrally by scholars pointing to a new southern studies.

The chapters in this book came out of this transitional moment in southern studies, and they draw both from what sociologist John Shelton Reed congenially calls "Southern Studies Classic" and from an emerging new southern studies. I have learned much from reading the work of my colleagues who identify with this project and hope this volume will contribute to its conscious development as an approach that is new yet acknowledges its long interdisciplinary roots. I share literary critic Martyn Bone's belief that a new southern studies "should be marked by an expansive, intellectually generous sensibility," one that "has a sense of humility that at least matches its sense of inventiveness." My hope is that "the spirit" can provide an applicable framework for other scholars pursuing a new southern studies.[12]

ACKNOWLEDGMENTS

I am grateful to the original editors and publishers of these essays for permission to reprint edited versions of them. They appeared originally as the following: "The Invention of Southern Tradition: The Writing and Ritualization of Southern History, 1880–1940," *Rewriting the South: History and Fiction*, ed. Lothar Honnighausen and Valeria Gennaro Lerda (Tubingen and Basel: Francke-Verlag, 1993), 3–21; "The Burden of Southern Culture," *Bridging Southern Culture*, ed. John Lowe (Baton Rouge: Louisiana State University Press, 2005), 288–300; "Saturated Southerners: The South's Poor Whites and Southern Regional Consciousness," *The Many Souths: Class in Southern Culture*, ed. Waldemar Zacharasiewicz (Tubingen, Germany: Stauffenberg Verlag, 2003), 133–146; "Our Land, Our Country: Faulkner, the South, and the American Way of Life," *Faulkner in America*, ed. Joseph R. Urgo and Ann Abadie (Jackson: University Press of Mississippi, 2001), 153–166; "The Myth of the Biracial South," *The Southern State of Mind*, ed. Jan Gretlund (Columbia: University of South Carolina Press, 1999), 3–22; "Creativity and Southern Culture," *Visualizing the Blues: Images of the American South*, ed. Wendy McDaris (Memphis: Dixon Gallery and Gardens, 2001), 130–137; "Flashes of the Spirit: Creativity and Southern Religion," *Image* (Fall 1999), 72–86; "Self-Taught Art, the Bible, and Southern Creativity," *Sacred and Profane: Voice and Vision in Southern Self-Taught Art*, ed. Carol Crown and Charles Russell (Jackson: University Press of Mississippi, 2007), 3–20; "Apocalypse South: McKendree Long and Southern Evangelicalism," *Reverend McKendree Robbins Long: Picture Painter of the Apocalypse*, ed. David Steel and Brad Thomas (Davidson, N.C.: Davidson College and North Carolina Museum of Art, 2002), 10–19; "'Just a Little Talk with Jesus': Elvis Presley, Religious Music, and Southern Spirituality," *Southern Cultures* 12 (Winter 2006), 74–91; "Richard Wright's *Pagan Spain*: Reading Spain through the American South," *Transatlantic Exchanges: The American South in Europe – Europe in the American South*, ed. Richard Gray and Waldemar Zacharasiewicz (Vienna: Austrian Academy, 2007), 167–180; "My

Journey to Southern Religious Studies," *Autobiographical Reflections on Southern Religious History*, ed. John B. Boles (Athens: University of Georgia Press, 2001), 206–218.

The University of Mississippi is a stimulating environment for anyone interested in studying the South, and I want to acknowledge the many faculty members there whose classroom lectures, symposia and brown bag lunch presentations, and writings have helped shape my approach to the South, including especially Ted Ownby (my longtime friend and colleague and new director of the Center for the Study of Southern Culture), Nancy Bercaw, Katie McKee, Robbie Ethridge, Adam Gussow, Jay Watson, Annette Trefzer, Angela Hornsby-Gutting, Joe Atkins, Curtis Wilkie, Mark Dolan, Amy Wells, Charles Eagles, Chuck Ross, and Don Kartiganer. I want to especially note my gratitude to David Wharton for working with me on including his photographs in this book. Bob Haws always points me to interesting, or puzzling to him, aspects of the South that make me think. Ann Abadie and I have worked closely on collaborative projects for a long time now, and I always appreciate her support of my work. Joe Ward, chair of the Department of History at the University of Mississippi, has offered a congenial setting for me as I transitioned from directorship of the Center for the Study of Southern Culture to fulltime teaching. Sally Lyon, Betty Harness, and Nikki Bourgeois are a constant help and a delight to work with. I appreciate the helpful advice and suggestions of Derek Krissoff at the University of Georgia Press in final editing of this volume.

My wife, Marie Antoon, shares my interest in the South, and she has made major contributions to understanding the region, and especially the state of Mississippi, as director of Mississippi Public Broadcasting. More importantly for this manuscript, she has listened to my ideas, raised questions, and unfailingly encouraged me to pursue my research and writing. My dedication of this study to my brother reflects our long engagement with the South in which we grew up and our common interest in so many aspects of its history and culture.

Flashes of a Southern Spirit

"The Soul-Life of the Land"

Meanings of the Spirit in the U.S. South

Soul singer Al Green was born in Arkansas, moved to Michigan, and then returned to the South in 1970, noting later that "there's something here that makes it easier for that music of the soul, that feeling sort of music, to come out." In a 1986 essay on "The Southern Soul," Green saw history as the background to a distinctive spirit in the South, reminding readers that slaves "didn't have much of anything, but they had God, and when they sang, what they sang was for Him, and it had meaning, and it had feeling." He saw a "sweetness here, a Southern sweetness, that makes a sweet music." The South, he said, is "the home ground," the place that "can keep the real thing alive."[1]

Green's comments are only one example of the social construction of the spirit as a signifier of the South. Green's words primarily apply to African American music, but they appeared in *Southern* magazine, implying that the "soul" he spoke about was a specifically "southern" soul, part of the biracial regional culture that has been celebrated in the South since the 1970s. In the early twentieth century, W. E. B. Du Bois identified a similar working of the black spirit on the southern landscape in his classic *The Souls of Black Folk.* He noted the pain of black life in the South since the end of Reconstruction, "the burning of body and rending of soul" that made the region's way of life one that rested on the brokenness of the physical and spiritual black selves. He lamented that the materialism of the times, "the spirit of the age which was dominating the North," was affecting the South, "replacing the finer type of Southerner with vulgar money-getters." In this view, the South was a place of the spirit as distinct from the material, an idea that the creators of the Lost Cause myth had memorialized for several decades. He feared that a particularly African American spirituality was endangered by "the Mammonism of this South" that was "reinforced by the budding Mammonism of its half-wakened black millions." Du Bois used the striking phrase "the soul-life of the land" and noted that what blacks dreamed in his age was "unthought of, half forgotten" by the larger society. Du Bois's book was a testament to that black spirituality and its profound role in the South's "soul-life."[2]

A range of observers, in and of the South and from outside its boundaries, have found the region a place where the spirit has worked in a variety of ways. It has sometimes been a patriotic spirit, while at other times a prophetic one. The dichotomies of a hierarchical society appeared in uses of the spirit: the spirit could be wild and spontaneous, tapping into some primal quality, whether the blues or Pentecostal worship; or the spirit could be disciplined and orderly, a spirit that helped generations of people in the South survive the traumas of their history.

Spirit can be an abstract concept, of course, but dictionary definitions can help anchor the meanings that have taken particular configuration in the South. The first definition of spirit in the *New Oxford American Dictionary* (2001) says it is the "nonphysical part of a person that is the seat of emotions and character," or "the soul."[3] Elaborating on this definition, the dictionary says it is the part of a person "manifested as an apparition after their death; a ghost." It mentions that the spirit, this "nonphysical part of a person," can refer to a supernatural being, "the Holy Spirit." As we will see, this language rests comfortably with discourse about the spirit in the South. The second definition does as well: "those qualities regarded as forming the definitive or typical elements in the character of a person, nation, or group, or in the thought and attitudes of a particular period." So "the definitive or typical elements" forge one of the understandings of the "spirit" of a group, and in this case the group is a regional one. Such a definition works against contemporary realizations that there are not "essences" that define movements or places, but the definition captures the long-standing tendency of people to invest just such meanings in the South, understandings that are the focus for this study. In seeing a "spirit of the times" or "spirit of a movement," the dictionary elaborates that such a spirit is "a specified emotion or mood," suggesting that the spirit world is not a cerebral one so much as one of feelings and emotions, and indeed this study places the spirit of the South in the realm of social psychology.

Finally, the dictionary is helpful in providing meanings for a term related to spirit – spiritual. This word relates to "the human spirit or soul," making the two virtually synonymous, as opposed to "material or physical things." One of its definitions brings us to southern ground, namely the African American spiritual: "a religious song of a kind associated with black Christians of the southern United States." The third definition ends with an explanatory phrase that also resonates with regional culture: "one's spiritual home: a place in which one feels a profound sense of belonging." Exploring meanings of spirit in the South may help delineate ways that people in the American South created a sense of belonging as a particular social group – southerners. That social group was once assumed by scholars to refer only to whites, but this book argues that "southerners" were always a complex group and that blacks as well as whites were culturally southerners, even when they did not ideologically embrace a racist society.

Literary critic Lewis Simpson has shown how twentieth-century writers in the South created the idea of the "southern spiritual community," a "myth of the South as a spiritual nation" that represented "an assertion against the materialistic way of life." This concept of the South as providing a ground for nonmaterial ways has been an especially powerful one in associations of the South with "spirit" and with that spirit's grounding for a southern identity. Richard Weaver once wrote that "being a southerner was a spiritual condition," and he added that it was "like being a Catholic or a Jew; and members of the group can recognize one another by signs which are eloquent to them, though too small to be noticed by an outsider." Maurice Halbwachs, the theorist of collective memory, observed that when a collective remembrance has a material reality and a symbolic one, "or something of spiritual significance, something shared by the group that adheres to and is superimposed on this physical reality," then group identity results. Weaver's "signs" that resonate among members of a religious group and Halbwach's use of "spiritual significance" and its relationship to the physical provide a framework for the following chapters.[4]

"Spirit" has not received the same attention in southern cultural studies as two other defining human qualities, mind and body. W. J. Cash's classic work on southern mind made ideas about the South and identity key to structuring research on what made the South distinctive. James C. Cobb's recent history of the self-conscious southern identity, of ideas of the South, is a near definitive one. Susan Donaldson and Anne Goodwyn Jones have been at the forefront of recent efforts by literary critics to unravel meanings of "the body" in the South. They locate the body in southern sexuality – for example, in the southern lady's supposed transcendence of desire or in the black lynching victim accused of unrestrained desire. As Jay Watson notes, our understanding of the South "needs to be rematerialized, grounded in the activity and sentient experiences of southern bodies, and in the cultural values assigned to them."[5]

Consideration of spirit is naturally a part of the discourse of religious historians of the South, but they do not always relate their work to broader issues of southern cultural identity. Furthermore, their work is sometimes marginalized by other historians who study southern identity. The leading scholar of southern memory, W. Fitzhugh Brundage, has recently noted, for example, the paucity of studies of religion's role in defining the collective memories of the South. This study argues that "the spirit" needs to be placed at the center of efforts to understand what made southerners invest so much meaning in their social identity.[6]

The qualities of mind, body, and spirit should not be neatly separated in analyses because they have been intertwined in the functioning of culture in the South. "When people think more of their skin color than of their souls," wrote Lillian Smith in the 1950s, "something has happened to them." Her singling out skin color identified the key feature of the body that has to be juxtaposed with the spirit in the South. She added that "this is the point: none of the functions of the human personality can be safely split off or abandoned: they must work together."

Observers have often seen those functions not working well together in a region that was about separation more than unified personalities. White Virginian George W. Bagby looked around the devastation of the post– Civil War South and concluded that "the soul is fled." He did not refer to those black southerners liberated from their bondage but to the ruin of the region's plantations and traditional society and the spiritual destruc- tion accompanying that physical ruin. "With emancipation, the soul had indeed fled the Old South," writes historian Joel Williamson, "but the body lived on. The great fact about southern history since emancipation is that the body lived on, and the body must somehow be sustained – first with bread, and then with spirit. Bread came but the spirit required a new fabrication beyond slavery. To provide a soul to legitimate the presence of our bodies upon this American earth is what we 'thinking' southerners are all about and have been since 1865." Beyond "thinking" southerners, some in the region saw how, with God's help, the senses could work together. "When God gives you a vision your whole body kind of soaks up the message, like a biscuit soaks up red-eye gravy," said Charley White, an early twentieth-century Holiness preacher in Texas. "And sometimes you can hear the message as well as feel it. And some- times you can see it."[7]

The first human inhabitants of what would become the American South lived in a world alive with spirits. Religious belief systems gave coherence to all phases of Native American life, with little separation between the sacred and the secular. Mississippian culture had a world- view rooted in spiritual understandings of existence that emphasized respect for authority, the importance of kinship, and the centrality of animals and the environment. Southeastern Indians built temples and retained a priesthood to work with rituals that reminded Indians of the sacred nature of life. The later Cherokee were typical of other southeast- ern tribes, with several categories of spiritual beings. The spirits of the Upper World, such as the Sun, the Moon, Thunder, and Corn, rarely intervened in everyday life, but people could approach them in moments of special need, such as curing disease. Spirits of the Under World, by contrast, such as the Immortals, did assist tired hunters and lost children. The Little People, small in form and mischievous like European lepre- chauns, intervened in human affairs more often than other Cherokee spirits. Animals had spirits, too, and generally were beneficent, but they could bring suffering to a careless hunter who did not take proper ritual precautions that honored the animal. Whereas Indian spirituality was an initial source of conflict with European Christians, it slowly became a basis for interaction. Southeastern Indians accepted evangelical Protestantism partly through the ritual of water baptism, which they recognized as a nature ritual, with the Holy Spirit added to their pantheon.[8]

The antebellum and Civil War eras gave birth to many enduring uses of the spirit in the South. Historian Frank Owsley saw the term as useful in explaining social relations in the Old South, arguing that the yeomen identified with the "spirit" as well as the "manners" of the gentry. Writing in 1939, sociologist Wilson Gee claimed that "spiritual bonds are often stronger welding influences than any other kind." He made the case for the internal diversity of the southern states in the early nineteenth century and the close ties between an upper South state like Virginia and the Middle Atlantic states, which would seemingly work against South-wide unity. "In spite of this diversity, it has a closer spiritual unity than any other large part of the nation," he concluded. Despite "modern strains and stresses," he wrote "the mutuality of interests, ideals, and objectives has engendered a feeling of kinship and understanding." The dictionary definition of "spirit" noted the importance of feelings, and Gee's comments provided a southern context to those feelings at the base of a spiritual unity that he saw.[9]

The southern spirit became increasingly militant as the Civil War approached, and calls to a "southern spirit" justified secession and war and white efforts to overthrow Reconstruction governments. In a late nineteenth-century book on the Ku Klux Klan, Laura Martin Rose spoke of the Klan keeping "green the traditions of the Old South" and "its chivalrous spirit." Affirmation of the continuance of an Old South spirit into the New South era was part of the work of postwar builders of southern identity. A school history from the same period explained the southern reaction to the events leading to war this way: "No high-spirited courageous people could patiently submit to such a government." Commentators linked to postwar cultural institutions not just Old South traditions but also the regional spirit. Emily Herbert Glaze, in a United Daughters of the Confederacy history of the Confederacy, ended her book by not-ing that through groups like the Klan and the South Carolina Red Shirts "the Spirit of the South lived on." In 1844, C. D. Smith of Virginia pub-lished a poem, "The Southern Lyre's Waking Moments," exhorting the American muse to hear "ye fire in Southern soul," which was part of the effort to nurture a regional culture in an era of growing sectional divide. Sculptor Alexander Galt created a plaster bust of an idealized woman in response to the poem, evoking the sculpture of classical civilizations. No overtly "southern" dimensions characterized the piece, but Galt went on to serve as a Confederate army officer, and his bust became caught up in postwar Lost Cause sentiment. It would be known as the "Spirit of the South," though not until 1904, when it entered the collections of Rich-mond's Museum of the Confederacy and came to symbolize the iconic role of southern women and the region's identification with classical slave societies.[10]

The cult of the Lost Cause saw white southerners make a religion out of their history, with beliefs, creeds, myths, symbols, rituals, and orga-nizations that nurtured an authentic religious system of southern cul-ture. The southern experience was not unique in this regard. In a study of cultures of defeat, historian Wolfgang Schivelbusch entitled one sec-tion, "Losers in Battle, Winners in Spirit." He notes that societies expe-riencing the trauma of defeat in war often see loss as a purification rit-ual, leading to "their faith in their cultural and moral superiority over the newly empowered who have ousted them." The spirit underlying this movement survived into the twentieth century, as seen in the dis-play and aggressive defense of Confederate symbols in public contexts in the South. Writing in the 1950s, newspaper editor Hodding Carter noted that southerners would stand at required attention when the "Star-Spangled Banner" was played, but "play 'Dixie' and you had better stick cotton in your ears." He called such behavior "this emotional legacy," a "stubborn legacy." In his lifetime white southerners still relished hearing the stories of the Confederacy and the glories of an imagined southern past: "Let alone, the spirit of which these stories are symbols is harm-less enough; a little pathetic perhaps, and naïve and provincial." He decried "the politicians who subvert the Southern legacies to confuse their constituents and perpetuate themselves." The Lost Cause narrative represented a special destiny for white southerners, and they would continue to embrace that sense of mission in the twentieth century.[11]

At the same time that spirit could evoke a patriotic regionalism, the religious worldview that had settled on the South in the early nineteenth century became a major factor in uses of the spirit in the region. Religion functioned in differing ways in terms of southern spirit. Organized religion and elite theology blessed the slave society, the Confederacy, and the postbellum segregated South, becoming a key support for the system. Evangelical Protestantism also provided peculiar resources for an active spirit life among individual believers, offering the individual direct access to the divine, unmediated by institutions, creeds, theologies, or rituals. The inherent radicalism in this tradition took deep root in the rural South and has since provided a religious grounding for active workings of the spirit. Early evangelicalism in the late eighteenth- and early nineteenth-century South supported radical social attitudes, such as antislavery and empowerment of women, and when white and black Protestants became well institutionalized in the late nineteenth century, new movements of the spirit, such as Holiness and Pentecostalism, asserted new expressions of individualistic spirituality. In the contemporary South, regional visionary folk artists are inspired by the Christian Holy Spirit to make compelling art.[12]

Writing in the mid-twentieth century, newspaper editor Hodding Carter noted that the South was the last spot in the Western world where fundamentalist Christianity still prevailed among white Protestants, "the legatee of the spiritually zestful, mystic, and masochistic soul of its largely Celtic forebears." At its best, Carter saw this faith offering a "refreshment of the spirit." Carter's Mississippi contemporary, William Faulkner, was more skeptical, referring to the faith of the leading evangelical group in the South, the Southern Baptists, as "the human spirit aspiring toward something," but opining that this aspiration "got warped and twisted in the process." In any event, evangelical Protestantism would be important in providing an abiding sense of distinctive spirit-driven regional mission to generations of white southerners who sometimes had trouble seeing the difference between the values of their regional culture and the Christianity they affirmed.[13]

Black southern Christians brought their own resources to bear in claiming the South as a place of the spirit. African religions had bequeathed to African Americans a legacy of an active spirit world, seen in visionary experiences and spiritual journeys. A vivid vernacular religious tradition continued well into the twentieth century, with narratives of the soul's trip to the other world, where supernatural spirits struggled over the fate of those in peril and those who returned from the journey told of experiencing God's spirit. Spirits could be relied on to lead individuals through the difficulties of this life. The praise worship tradition of slaves allowed them to participate in spirit-filled communal worship, including the ring shout that defined slave religion. Voodoo was a system of African religious practice and belief, and its heritage became one source for a reconfigured African American religious system that highlighted the spirit world. Christian belief and survivals from African or rural folk belief were often evoked by the same people in different contexts.[14]

Robert Farris Thompson has shown the artistic and philosophical connections between African visual culture and black visual culture in the Atlantic diaspora, suggesting "the flash of the spirit of a certain people specially armed with improvisatory drive and brilliance." Thompson's book is important in showing ties between Kongo-Angola culture and black culture in the Deep South and the Caribbean. Dead spirits occupy a crucial role in African spirituality, and they have been central to African American vernacular faith as well. Part of the trauma of slavery was Africans having to leave the spirits of the dead, who they believed resided in their African homelands. Traditional grave decorating customs from Africa are especially revealing, such as leaving the last-used items of the dead at the burial spot, covering graves with seashells, and planting a tree on a grave.[15]

The Kongo-Angola influence is also seen in the continuance in the South of bottle trees – "trees garlanded with bottles, vessels, and other objects for protecting the household through invocation of the dead." Thompson found these trees from east Texas through the Deep South to the South Carolina coast, with concentrations in Virginia, southern Arkansas, northern Mississippi, and southeastern Alabama. Eudora Welty writes of them in a short story, noting "the way bottle trees keep evil spirits from coming into the house – by luring them inside the colored bottles, where they cannot get out again." African loas (spirits) were myriad in number and type. Benevolent spirits could be relied on to guide people through life; malevolent "haunts" could be seen and heard but were generally harmless, while murderous evil spirits could bring destruction to any one and bottle trees were indeed welcome to combat those spirits. Blues music became a repository of spiritual meanings, especially seeing evil spirits at work. Peetie Wheatstraw asked to be buried low, "so, now, that my old evil spirit, mama, now won't hang around your door." Robert Johnson mythically sold his soul to the devil at the Mississippi crossroads, with "me and the devil . . . walking side by side," and he asked to be buried by the roadside "so my old evil spirit can catch a Greyhound bus." Growing up a generation later in the Mississippi Delta that had produced the blues, Anne Moody recalls asking her mother at age seven about a lynching victim, and her mother replied that an "evil spirit" had killed him and "you gotta be a good girl or it will kill you too."[16]

If the spirit could be spontaneous and free, some southerners saw the need to discipline the spirit. Indeed, the term "breaking the spirit" is a troubling, recurring one in southern cultural history. An important part of the seasoning of new slaves from Africa was breaking their spirits, and the tools of plantation discipline were tangible expressions of not only disciplining the body but spirits as well. Richard Wright observed in his twentieth-century novel, *Native Son*, that whites who restricted black lives made those who violated racial codes "pay a terrible price. They were shot, hanged, maimed, lynched, and generally hounded until they were either dead or their spirits broken." Zora Neale Hurston's mother encouraged her children to "jump at the sun" and aim high in life, but her father's attitudes were more restrained. "It did not do for Negroes to have too much spirit," she recalled. "He was always threatening to break mine or kill me in the attempt." Her mother always protected her and did not want to "squinch [her] spirit."[17]

The need to discipline the spirit reverberated beyond race relations and African American culture. Mary Austin Holley, a northerner visiting the Deep South before the Civil War, was horrified to hear white southerners talk of child raising customs, including "whipping them, & breaking their spirits as you do horses and dogs." While planter families often indulged their children to encourage an aggressiveness in style, Robert E. Lee articulated a more moralistic attitude in an 1837 letter that warned against a child considered "hard to manage" because that indicated "self-will and obstinancy" that needed to "brought under his control." Evangelical parents throughout southern history were inclined to discipline children, sometimes harshly, to bring their wills and spirits in line with expectations. While evangelicals had the possibility of direct access to the divine and the spiritual spontaneity that implied, they also highly valued congregational order and individual self-discipline, which worked to contain the spirit. Virginia Baptist minister Jeremiah Jeter looked back on early Baptists in his state who "aspired to be grave, avoiding mirth and frivolity." Moral purity was highly prized and a disciplined will and spirit were important in achieving that goal. Women had special responsibilities in nurturing the spirit in southern families. Historian Ted Ownby sees a fundamental tension in southern culture between men's often rowdy recreational life and women's concern for spiritual order.[18]

Developments in denominational history after the Civil War provided another perspective on breaking the spirit that sometimes flowed freely in vernacular worship. Church leaders, among both white and black evangelicals, wanted to regularize worship, but their efforts often put them in opposition to local grassroots desires for a spirit-filled religion. Although revivals continued as central features of southern life, denominations increasingly devised more centralized and bureaucratized institutions that represented a modernization of the evangelical spirit. As they modernized, southern churches continued to see themselves as different from their northern brethren, with whom they had not reunited after the war. One local church leader complained about denominational efforts to systematize church finances, seeing this initiative coming from men who did not understand "the spirit and genius of Southern Baptist churches." He made clear regional lines between the South and "the New England policy," which "is to have a line of cleavage as clear and cold as ice between the spiritual functions and the administrative and finance." The local churchman made the southern spirit clearly distinctive from the South's traditional nemesis, New England. The Southern Baptist Convention justified production of its own Sunday school publications after the war, rather than relying on those coming from national Baptist agencies, because materials from outside the South would expose southern children to the "vitiated spirituality and rationalism of latitudinarianism of England, and the politic-religious mixture and doctrinal looseness of the North."[19]

Looking internally within the South, writers have given spiritual meanings to the region's natural environment. William Faulkner's story "The Bear" is about a spiritual initiation. Trappist monk Thomas Merton suggests it is the story of a disciple learning from "a spiritual Father," in this case the hunter Sam Fathers, who teaches the boy, Ike McCaslin, about mastery of life, "a certain way of being aware, of being in touch not just with natural objects, with living things, but with the cosmic spirit, with the wilderness itself regarded almost as a supernatural being." Old Ben is the monumental bear that is finally killed after a ferocious battle with its human pursuers, a battle that demonstrates the mutual respect the two species – the man and the bear – hold for each other. "It is as if the wilderness spirit were somehow incarnated in Old Ben – as if he were a wilderness god," Merton notes. McCaslin becomes aware of the bear "as a spiritual reality and as 'presence,'" and he experiences "the numinous mystery of the Bear as quasi-transcendent being." Merton concludes that young McCaslin's wilderness life is "a spiritual formation," the terminology for a disciplined cultivation of an awareness of a supernatural realm. The death of the bear and of Sam Fathers makes McCaslin "the 'child' and 'heir' of the wilderness spirit." Merton goes on to note that another way of "participating in the wilderness spirit" is through drinking whiskey. To return to the dictionary for a moment, we should note that a final definition of "spirit" is "distilled liquor such as brandy, whiskey, gin, or rum." The South has indeed been the bourbon belt, and drinkers and tee-totalers have defined differing identities around spirits in this sense. Merton's point regarding the environment, then, is that to hunters whiskey is a "condensation of the wild immortal spirit."[20]

Presbyterian churchman, social reformer, and author James McBride Dabbs told of an epiphany – an experience of rural life on the edge of the woods – that revealed to him the importance of place to spirituality. He confessed in his book, *Haunted by God*, that "it was through the imagination," not his church, that he found a "spiritual sense of completeness" and reconciliation and "related these basic attitudes to the culture and the church which produced it." Growing up in a culture that dwelt on southern loss and seeing the suffering of black people around him, he admitted to becoming aware as a child of the "potential sadness of life." But one day he sat on the back porch of his family's house in rural South Carolina, on the edge of the woods, and experienced a "spiritual and aesthetic and moral completeness," which nurtured thereafter a sensitivity to the mystery of life and God's presence. He consciously saw this experience as a meaningful one for himself as a southerner, one that he inculcated in his concept of "spiritual freedom," a freedom that rested in social order, which was not an order based in social justice so much as one based in place: "Though no social order can give to its members spiritual freedom – insure, that is, that through imagination they will live in the Spirit and the Spirit in them, and thus live freely in the world (for this would be the kingdom of God) – one social order can do more than another to this end. However we describe social orders, some, I am sure, take men further toward spiritual freedom than do others."[21] The South's flawed and unjust social order could still stir the spirit for Dabbs, providing a place-based inspiration.

The spirit figured into politics in the South in differing ways that reflect the complex uses of the concept. Speaking for one urgent meaning of the spirit was Sam Adams, an Alabama farmer and agrarian protestor who positioned the soul as part of broader human functioning, noting that "those Christians who believe in the freedom of the mind, soul, and body, will have to take hold of the politics of this country, or we will be enslaved by the rule of a class of men who have no regard for the souls of men." His righteous indignation links the spirit with protest against business exploiters. The underlying issue was freedom and its link to the spirit. Historian Paul Harvey argues that the holiness doctrines that crystallized in the 1890s represented in spiritual life much the same challenge that Populism represented in politics – "the use of southern evangelical forms for culturally or politically radical ends." Focusing both on the internal spiritual experience of the individual and on "the communal expression of spiritual emotion," holiness and Pentecostal churches could be culturally radical, especially when they allowed interracial worship and female preaching.[22]

The era of the civil rights movement represented a compelling spiritual renaissance in the South. Theologian James Washington noted the centrality of the "spirituality of the civil rights movement," but only recently have scholars begun paying increased attention to this dimension of the movement. John Lewis sees the movement as "a process, an unstoppable overflowing event." He noted that some people call it "the spirit of history but I believe the movement happened because we were in step with the Creator." Martin Luther King Jr. said the movement was about releasing "spiritual power" and "soul force" that would transform not only the South and the nation but also the world. The sense of a particular spirit at work in this era was not just limited to blacks. Douglas Hudgins, pastor of the powerful First Baptist Church of Jackson, Mississippi, and a defender of God-ordained segregation, said in a sermon at the beginning of the civil rights years that "now is the time to move the emphasis from the material to the spiritual." White writer Lillian Smith was, by contrast, one of the sharpest critics of Jim Crow segregation, and she wrote in the 1950s of "the spiritual crisis which the South and its people are facing." She argued that whites as well as blacks had been spiritually maimed by segregation, as whites learned to disrespect the same black people they had loved in childhood and to treat them meanly or with "warm cheap sentimentality instead of the dignity and courtesy due them." These were "stains on the soul." White southerners suffered from "spiritual deprivation," "the fear of the emptiness inside [them] that makes some of [them] cling to segregation." Commenting on black students' nonviolent protests, Smith saw the hope of "this spiritual renascence."[23]

Activists noted then and now the strong spiritual aspect of the movement. Victoria Gray saw activists as "spirit people" and the movement "as a journey toward the establishment of the kingdom of God." Student Nonviolent Coordinating Committee staff member Jean Wheeler Smith noted that organizational meetings "lit up [her] mind." "The religious, the spiritual was like an explosion to me, an emotional explosion," she explained. The emotions ranged from the joy of communal celebration of the cause to the dark nights of the soul when terror seemed to surround the activists, but they "were sustained by the spiritual energy radiating outward."[24]

Psychologist Robert Coles has written of the experience of black sharecroppers in Mississippi in the hard days of segregation, on the eve of its disappearance, with the goal of capturing "the animated spirit of the Spirit, as [he] happened to see and hear and feel that Spirit come alive, become an event." His fieldwork helps give context to the spiritual preparation that bore fruit in the civil rights movement. He writes of a Mississippi black woman named Sally who worked hard in the fields all week and then was in church each Sunday morning. "I kneel all week long with the beans," said Sally, "but on Sunday I kneel to speak with God, and He makes my knees feel better, much better." Coles thus sees the spirit and the body as related; as Sally says, "All of a sudden I know He's touched me and given me a little of His strength, so I can go on." Coles describes her "stubborn, quarrelsome spirit, which returns almost weekly to the struggle." Sally and others like her prayed long and hard, and they knew their Bible. They knew resignation to life's demands and estrangement from the community, as well as "a certain soreness of mind and body." They knew faith and doubt but also the sustaining joy that came, as Coles said, "with listening to music, with praying, with singing, with saying things." The black church had helped these suffering poor to keep their spirits whole. A North Carolina tenant farmer told Coles about his daddy's advice: "[He] used to tell me when I was a boy that he didn't want my spirit to break, and if I prayed to God, He'd keep me strong, and I'd never lose my spirit, no matter how bad they treat you, and no matter what words they call you, the bad words."[25]

Fannie Lou Hamer was one of those women whom the black church had long sustained when other institutions had failed her. Charles Marsh sees Hamer as having "one of America's most innovative religious imaginations," blending African American musical and spiritual traditions with prophetic religion and a passionate belief in Jesus as a redeeming figure of the poor and disfranchised, all of which prepared her for her unique role in embodying the workings of the spirit in the civil rights movement in the South. Marsh writes that the church "had sustained her wearied spirit when all other institutions had served contrary purposes." The black church "not only awakened spiritual energies but also inspired the exercise of political ownership through such practices as electing officers and organizing church programs." Contact with civil rights activists stirred a new spirit in Hamer in the early 1960s. As Marsh notes, "her imagination was charged by new moral and spiritual energies," and she felt "empowered to discern the signs of the times." Hamer is especially significant in embodying the relationship between singing and the spirit in the black tradition, particularly as part of the spiritual renaissance associated with the black freedom struggle. "Singing brings out the soul," she said, while in jail in Winona, Mississippi, after a savage police beating. She sang the old spiritual, "Paul and Silas," about those New Testament figures jailed unjustly but not abandoned by God, and her singing led others in jail to join her, nurturing a spiritual community by verbalizing, in her songs, the sufferings of herself and others. As Marsh notes, her singing "embraced the suffering, named it, and emplotted it in a cosmic story of hope and deliverance." White activist Sally Belfrage recalls that "she represented a challenge that few could understand: how it was possible to arrive at a place past suffering, to a concern for her torturers as deep as that for her friends."[26]

Historian and civil rights activist Vincent Harding links the "powerful creative spirit of the movement and its participants" to southern black self-taught artists, who are among the subjects for chapters in this book. He laments that scholars have undervalued the civil rights activists' "constant visionary surging toward new human possibilities, transformative hope, and democratic experimentation," and he believes "that such creative power could not be confined to political, economic, and traditional social domains." The visionary art of women like Mary T. Smith and Bessie Harvey expresses to him "another kind of freedom in the capacity to see the unseen and make it visible to others." They remind him of "the work of their sister artists, Fannie Lou Hamer, Septima Clark, and Bernice Reagon, and the prophetic political mysticism of the freedom movement." One recurring saying of the black freedom movement praised a God "who can make a way out of no way," and Harding sees black visionary artists working with few resources as making "art out of no art." He compares Alabama environmental artist Lonnie Holley's "audacity of spirit" and "grandeur of vision" with those same qualities of Alabama activists Fred Shuttlesworth and JoAnn Robinson.[27]

The contemporary South is increasingly homogenized with the nation, and talk of spirit in the region often takes place against a national backdrop, but one that still resonates with historical references. In July 1979, President Jimmy Carter gave what became known as his "malaise speech," referring to America's "crisis of confidence" and the need for "a rebirth of the American spirit." Carter spoke as a Georgian imbued with C. Vann Woodward's "burdens of southern history," even as one who had grown up saturated with the Lost Cause's Civil War fascination, as seen in his use of the war in negotiating with Israeli and Palestinian leaders at Gettysburg. Another southern president, Bill Clinton, struck a similar theme of spiritual prophecy in a speech to the national convocation of the Pentecostal Church of God in Christ, noting the "great crisis of the spirit that is gripping America today." He was summoning Americans "to reach deep down inside to the values, the spirit, the soul, and the truth of human nature." Carter and Clinton were both Southern Baptists who spoke with more ease on matters of the spirit than many American politicians of their eras, and the tendency was not just among Democrats. South Carolinian Lee Atwater was one of the architects of the Republican Party's southern strategy and a sometimes ruthless tactician, as exhibited in the distorted campaign advertisements against Democratic presidential nominee Michael Dukakis in 1988. In 1991, dying from a brain tumor, Atwater grasped for the southern evangelical hope of redemption, apologizing for what he had done to Dukakis and others he had once regarded as enemies: "My illness helped me to see that what was missing in society is what was missing in me: a little heart, a lot of brotherhood." He called on leaders to "speak to this spiritual vacuum at the heart of American society, this tumor of the soul."[28]

One of the most significant developments in the recent relationship between regional culture and identity and "the spirit" is the emergence of a specifically womanist spirituality. Of course, women have long played a key spiritual role in church life, and the image of the southern white women was key in defining a regional identity around their moral and spiritual purity. In the early days of evangelicalism, women were empowered spiritually for their gifts of prophecy and healing, but by the early nineteenth century evangelical churches proscribed any public leadership by women. After the Civil War, women dominated church life, in what was a gendered dimension of southern culture. Although limited to a supportive role in organized religious life, they were the majority of church members, served as church matrons, and became icons of yeoman culture as the source of the steady and harmonious spiritual life that was the evangelical ideal. Women's active spirit life was also seen in diaries and journals and family devotionals. Among African American women, revelations, visions, and prophecies were not unheard of through the twentieth century, and the emergence of the Pentecostal-Holiness tradition in the late nineteenth century empowered women through the gifts of the spirit that tradition affirms.[29]

Southern women, like those elsewhere in the nation, have embraced new forms of spirituality in the contemporary era. Georgia-born black writer Alice Walker is a leading figure in the womanist spiritual movement. She recalls that her mother showed a special radiance when working in her garden. Walker's mother was "involved in work her soul must have," providing order to the universe "in the image of her personal conception of beauty." Walker looks back on her women ancestors, affirming that "the majority of our great-grandmothers knew, even without 'knowing' it, the reality of their spirituality, even if they didn't recognize it beyond what happened in the singing at church – and they never had any intention of giving it up." Some of the explorations of women's spirituality have delved into nature religions, some with links to Native American spirituality. New Age spiritual practice gives a prominent role to women. A lesbian couple, Wanda and Brenda Henson, bought a farm in Ovett, Mississippi, in 1993 and named it Camp Sister Spirit. The 120-acre farm became a feminist education retreat and a center that worked with such causes as prisoners' rights, recovery for battered women, and reproductive rights, and they established a food pantry. Despite official and unofficial harassment, they achieved what they called "a haven from which their political and cultural vision could grow," a place for an "indigenous lesbian culture" but also a space of the spirit, "a place to work and care."[30]

The spirit in the South has obviously taken many forms, and the chapters that follow explore some of its expressions. Part 1, "Tradition," contains chapters that explore traditions that worked to construct the South as a distinctive place. "Tradition," though, is a term with many meanings that complicate, and enrich, our understanding of the South. Folklorists and anthropologists use tradition to suggest custom, while intellectual historians, philosophers, scholars of religion, and others use it to suggest a body of ideas. Charles Joyner's book *A Shared Tradition*, for example, comes from his historical-folkloristic effort to explore the South's biracial folk culture, while Eugene D. Genovese's *The Southern Tradition* examines the long-standing regional conservative philosophical and political outlook.[31]

Chapter 1, "The Invention of Southern Tradition: The Writing and Ritualization of Southern History, 1880–1930," applies Eric Hobsbawm and Terence Ranger's influential theory of invented traditions to the creation of a particular regional tradition at a particular moment in time – the definition of a "southern" tradition based on identification of regional history and cultural forms in the late nineteenth century. Chapter 2, "The Burden of Southern Culture," takes off from C. Vann Woodward's insights on the burden of southern history and suggests that cultural history is especially useful in understanding the region, arguing in particular that the sense of regional mission, perceived as divinely ordained, has been a tradition that has given an abiding moral framework for an evolving South. Chapter 3, "Saturated Southerners: The South's Poor Whites and Southern Regional Consciousness," considers the spirit of one of the South's most deracinated social groups, its poor whites, and one of its most self-conscious artists, James Agee. The chapter explores the relationship of the marginalized southern poor to the tradition of regional consciousness, which is often associated with the region's intellectual and social elites. *Let Us Now Praise Famous Men* is one of the iconic texts in southern studies, and Agee's artistically centered spirituality shaped his approach to the sharecroppers at the center of the book. The chapter juxtaposes Agee's sensibility with that of country singer Hank Williams, another of the South's creative giants, who spoke from within the working-class white community and used its evangelical worldview in his art.

Chapter 4, "Our Land, Our Country: Faulkner, the South, and the American Way of Life," looks at William Faulkner's post–World War II essays and other writings that reflect his understanding of the South's place in the nation and the world. It deals with such ideological constructions as Americanism, the American Dream, the American Way of Life, and the Southern Way of Life. His biting critique of the cold war American military-industrial complex noted that it promoted the "harassment of the private individual human spirit." Faulkner dismissed the idea of a Southern Way of Life rooted in white supremacy, but the chapter shows he was part of a group of writers and others who put forward the vision of a southern way that was based in biracial culture. The last chapter in part 1, "The Myth of the Biracial South," follows up on the previous chapter, taking the story of regional tradition into the 1970s, tracing the development of a mythic view of southern culture that became an important ideological underpinning of the move from a segregated society to one with new ideals in its public culture. The chapter argues that this view of the South as a place with the potential to achieve a truly integrated society was a long-standing liberal, if distinctly marginal, tradition in the South until social changes in the 1970s promoted its adoption as a dominant public ideal. The concept of a redemptive South weaves through many of the chapters in part 1, reflecting issues of the spirit that have been attached to aspects of tradition in the region.

Part 2, "Creativity," complicates issues of tradition in southern culture. "Traditionalism" is a prescriptive term that has been used ideologically in the South and elsewhere to suggest the benefits of an unchanging culture, but historians, folklorists, and cultural studies specialists make the case that what Hobsbawm calls "genuine tradition" (as distinct from "invented tradition") is an evolving condition. Vernacular culture is a dynamic, not a dichotomy, of continuity and change. Traditions die out if they do not adapt, and that is as true in the South as anywhere. African Americans have been a formative force in the South, and scholars note that black culture is especially oriented toward improvisation. Richard Westmacott puts it well that "adaptation itself is a tradition," in speaking of African American gardens in the South, and scholars of jazz, quilting, architecture, and other forms make the same point. Paul Gilroy sees a "nontraditional tradition" where forms can be retained "without needing to be reified," while Tara McPherson notes that the South's "innovation within tradition" has broad meanings as a "space of possibility within the common ground of southern cultures."[32]

Chapter 6, "Beyond the Sahara of the Bozart: Creativity and Southern Culture," looks at the social and cultural context for the highly honored creative expression in the twentieth-century South. It is a riff on an idea of Michael O'Brien's that putting southern writers and musicians together in the same analytical framework can extend our appreciation of creativity in the South. The chapter argues that a Southern Cultural Renaissance began in the interwar period, and it advances some significant, if not surprising, factors that likely promoted this creative efflorescence in a region whose socioeconomic problems made prolific creative expression seem in some ways unlikely. Chapters 7 and 8, "Flashes of the Southern Spirit: Creativity and Southern Religion" and "The Word and the Image: Self-Taught Art, the Bible, the Spirit, and Southern Creativity," build on the previous chapter, looking specifically at the relationship between the South's predominant religious tradition, evangelical Protestantism, and its role in discouraging certain kinds of creativity while still providing the spiritual resources for creative individuals to use the Bible and personal visionary experience to further their work. One purpose of these two chapters is to focus scholarly attention on the South's contemporary self-taught and visionary artists, who represent a recent expression of a new genre of regional creativity.

Part 3, "Spirituality," contains chapters relating to aspects of religious life in the South. The contemporary South, like other parts of the nation, has witnessed a privatization of religion that has affected meanings of the spirit. Religion scholars make a sharp distinction between religion and spirituality. Robert Wuthnow argues that Americans in general have departed from the idea that spiritual meaning is attached to "a spiritual dwelling" that can give clues to purpose in life, embracing now instead "the spiritual life as a journey, a quest, that traverses many paths." People in the American South today reflect the influences of a popular religion that includes such privatized dimensions as fascination with angels and watching televangelists in disproportionate numbers to other Americans (and producing some of the most prominent televangelists). Religious pluralism is growing rapidly, thanks to immigrants from, especially, South Asia and Latin America, who are bringing their Buddhism, Hinduism, Roman Catholicism, and other faiths into the region, providing new ingredients for the region's spirit world. The iconic Our Lady of Guadeloupe and the ritualistic presence of rosary beads have been added to the South's spirituality.[33]

Chapter 9, "Apocalypse South: McKendree Long and Southern Evangelicalism," studies a visionary artist who, unlike many other southern visionary painters, was not self-taught. Reverend McKendree Robbins

Long was from a prominent North Carolina Presbyterian family, but his conversion to evangelical faith led him not only to paint bold religious scenes of the end days but also to become a traveling revivalist. Revivals have been pervasive rituals of southern life for centuries, "seasons of refreshment of the spirit," as they were commonly known. The chapter briefly charts the changing context for Long's spiritual life, as the South moved from Victorianism to modernity. Long's most significant visionary paintings were from the 1950s, when the nuclear bomb gave a tangible new image of apocalypse. Chapter 10, "'Just a Little Talk with Jesus': Elvis Presley, Religious Music, and Southern Spirituality," addresses the South's evolving spirituality in the mid- and late twentieth century. Samuel S. Hill long ago noted the "relative absence of 'disciplined spirituality' in the church life of the region." The evangelical tradition, "a high-intensity form of faith," did not breed "a keener interest in cultivating personal piety, at least with regard to so-called spiritual formation and some variant of mysticism."[34] This essay argues that a white religious musical culture in the South included institutions and activities that made for a distinctive spiritual discipline that scholars have previously overlooked and that did come out of the "high intensity" evangelical tradition. Elvis Presley was a product of that culture, and the chapter examines how his spirituality developed in unorthodox ways from his upbringing as his career advanced.

Chapter 11, "Richard Wright's *Pagan Spain*: A Southern Protestant Abroad," suggests that Wright's portrait of the Spain that he visited in the 1950s reflected his experiences growing up in the American South. He made comparisons between Franco's authoritarian nation and the Jim Crow South, except that he saw race as a virtual nonissue in Spain. The chapter offers other underlying relationships between the two societies that surely influenced his view of Spain, even if he did not consciously acknowledge them. The essay argues for the importance of civil religion, which sacralized the nation-state, and popular religion, with its perceptions of the supernatural in everyday life, as defining connections. Religion was surely more important than race as the central issue for *Pagan Spain*. Suffering is the key trope in that book as well as in Wright's memoir, *Black Boy*. He writes that his observation of his mother's suffering shaped his life and writing, because "the spirit [he] caught gave [him] insight into the suffering of others." Chapter 12, "A Journey to Southern Religious Studies," is a dramatic change from the previous chapter, representing my spiritual autobiography, one that attempts to draw together my religious life and my academic study of religion. It discusses my mentors, the field of southern religious studies, and the places that have nurtured my engagement with spiritual issues.

PART ONE

Tradition

1 The Invention of Southern Tradition

The Writing and Ritualization of Southern History, 1880–1930

Like many other American small towns in the 1930s, Hazelhurst, Mississippi, presented its self-image to the world through a post office mural commissioned as one of Franklin Roosevelt's New Deal cultural programs. The scene the community chose captures our attention because it presents an image intended to evoke the Old South. The mural features a steamboat cruising the river country nearby. The only problem is that Hazelhurst is landlocked; no river nearby is large enough to support a steamboat. Partly the mural reflects nonsouthern attitudes – a federal government agency's judgment on an appropriate image for the community. But Hazelhurst selected the scene of the cotton-laden steamboat with the advice and counsel of its citizens, reflecting their perception of the way they wanted to be presented, through an image evoking the predominant southern cultural mythology.[1]

This was a classic example of the invention of southern tradition. Southerners of the 1950s and 1960s often talked about "the southern tradition," especially people who opposed racial integration, economic development, and general change in the region. But that "southern tradition" was itself the product of a certain time period in the South's history. The invention of tradition was a common occurrence in Western society in the nineteenth and early twentieth centuries. Although a familiar phenomenon, it took different shapes in different nations. The French Third Republic, for example, downplayed references in public ceremonies and publications to history, especially pre-1789 history, wishing to avoid memories of a French past that it did not want nurtured. Instead, it mass-produced public monuments to French culture in general; it nurtured primary schools as an alternative tradition to the loyalties of the church; and it fostered Bastille Day (the official public celebration, now so familiar, did not begin until 1880 with the full backing of the state). Bismarckian Germany, by contrast, combined overt appeals to German history with the myths and symbols of nineteenth-century liberalism. Bismarck's ideological problem was gaining public legitimacy for his version of German unification, and so appeals to German history were especially important.[2]

The peculiarity of the southern invention of tradition is that it developed as an alternative tradition to that of the nation. Americans in general were busy inventing traditions to bring greater social unity at a time of rapid economic development and social change, but many of these were aimed at incorporating the massive numbers of immigrants into the expansive American republic of the era. Southern whites worried about social unity, yet in a different sense, since few immigrants came south. Southern intellectuals and cultural leaders began the process of creating a regional identity before the Civil War, growing out of sectional division with the North. It was a long process, one that was surely incomplete before the Civil War began. D'Azeglio noted that "we have made Italy; now we must make Italians." Fighting for the Confederacy had helped to forge a strong regional identity: it was a large step toward creating southerners as a distinct group. But it had destroyed the dream of the South as a separate nation. So the southern problem involved inventing traditions to embody for southerners, in tangible ways, the concept of the South without nationality. To understand the penetration of the past into regional social psychology the formal writing of history is revealing, as is the perceived importance of the past in general and the belief in distinctive southern cultural ways. The regional context, moreover, was within a society deeply divided by social class and racial fissures in the period between the Civil War and World War I.

The American regional context offers a particular angle, then, on the phenomenon of inventing tradition.

Historian C. Vann Woodward made perhaps the first effort at isolating the phenomenon of invented southern tradition. In his classic book *The Strange Career of Jim Crow* (1955), Woodward argued that the rigid Jim Crow system of legal racial segregation that emerged in the South during the 1890s was something new in the region. He showed the considerable degree of cultural interaction and, at times even, intimacy between slave owner and slave. He also highlighted the "forgotten alternatives" in race relations after Emancipation, both the liberalism of George Washington Cable and the conservatism of the Redeemers who wanted racial accommodation to promote a harmonious society that would appeal to potential northern investors in the South. Historians since Woodward have qualified his argument, suggesting that belief in the separation of the races was in fact deeply entrenched in the folk mind of the South, that legal segregation existed much earlier than Woodward argued, and that indeed segregation was not even a unique southern problem but an expression of American racism in general.[3]

Woodward, nonetheless, correctly identified evidence of a larger phenomenon. Although de facto segregation was indeed deeply rooted in the South, the codification of laws in the 1890s, accompanied by a new virulence in race relations, suggests that white southerners were taking a new step in formalizing a restricted role for blacks in southern life. White southerners were inventing the tradition of rigid racial segregation as a constant in southern history, when in fact the history of race relations suggests that paternalism and brutality have characterized racial interaction in different periods. White southerners in the years between 1880 and 1930 defined a number of traditions that were part of a broader process of growing, not diminishing, self-awareness, of recognition that their identity as southerners meant something important to them in a period of perceived dramatic change and social disorder and at a time when Confederate defeat had seemingly put that identity in jeopardy.

While recognition of white supremacy as a fundamental basis of southern white tradition was crucial in this process, the identification of the Civil War as the central event for the southern people was essential to the attempt to make sense of the past, which is to say "tradition" in general, a supposed southern trait. The Lost Cause, the effort to preserve the memory of the Civil War, offers perhaps the best evidence for considering the uses of the past in this period. White southerners became increasingly attuned to the idea of regional history after the war. Historical writing in the South previously had focused on individual states, as did the work of historical societies. Before the war, no one wrote a southern history or founded a southern historical society. In May of 1869, however, "a number of gentlemen" founded the Southern Historical Society in New Orleans. The collecting and archiving of regional history materials was the task of the 1880s, and organizations like the Southern Historical Society devoted themselves to it with enthusiasm and single-mindedness. The results were significant in laying the basis for the future but represented only a small number of interested individuals of Confederate background.[4]

Those individuals who had been active participants in the Confederacy wrote their memoirs or battle accounts, giving rise to much overt fictionalization of history. Virginia general Jubal Early, in an 1872 address, charged, for example, that General James Longstreet was the cause of Robert E. Lee's loss of the battle of Gettysburg because Longstreet failed to carry out Lee's order for an early attack. Other Confederate generals from Virginia soon repeated the charge, collectively deciding to make Longstreet the scapegoat for the failure, exonerating Lee in the process. The generals coordinated their attack, utilizing the *Southern Historical Society Papers.* A key reason for the attack on Longstreet, and certainly for its severity and endurance, was that during Reconstruction he had become a Republican – he was a dreaded southern scalawag identified as a political betrayer of the South.[5]

Related to this demonization of Longstreet was the effort to make Robert E. Lee into the central southern hero. While Lee was certainly always respected during the war, he shared the spotlight with a number of other generals – J. E. B. Stuart, for example, and above all, Stonewall Jackson, who was clearly the great hero of the plain folk, a rough-hewn character, with a driven righteousness that was Civil War charisma. After the war, though, and after Lee's death in 1870, Virginians and the organizations they launched worked carefully to champion Lee's cause. He fit the southern legend of the cavalier far better than Jackson did, becoming a key ideological component in cultivating "southern tradition" as identified with elite ideals. Prominent writers and institutions deliberately nurtured the cult of Lee.[6]

Defeat in the Civil War did inspire an awareness of the effects of history in the post–Civil War South. Woodward identified the burden of southern history as the basis of an enduring southern distinctiveness, but his original argument was ahistorical, not identifying when the awareness of this supposed sense of history first appeared. White southerners after the Civil War often complained that the region's people were not doing enough to preserve history for posterity. Thomas Nelson Page, for instance, insisted, in an address published in 1892 but delivered earlier, that "there is no true history of the South," which was an urgent issue because "in a few years there [would] be no South to demand a history." Whatever real economic and social change occurred in the postbellum South, most white southerners believed that they were living in an era of dramatic, radical change that threatened their group identity. Defeat of the Confederacy might well lead to the dissolution of that identity; as a preemptive measure, Page proposed using history as a basis for preserving it.[7]

Page outlined the southern position regarding the need for historical writing. "By the world at large we are held to have been an ignorant, illiterate, cruel, semi-barbarous section of the American people," he complained, "sunk in brutality and vice, who have contributed nothing to the advancement of mankind: a race of slave-drivers, who, to perpetuate human slavery, conspired to destroy the Union, and plunged the country into war." Southerners "stand charged at the judgment bar of history with these crimes," he continued. The reason for this sorry state of affairs was that the North had written the history of the sectional conflict. To the North, heretofore "inherently incapable of comprehending her," the South had "left the writing of the history of her civilization." Page appealed to southern pride in regional achievement and its history. The South was the section of the nation "that largely has made America, governed her, administered justice from her highest tribunal, commanded her armies and navies, doubled her territory, created her greatness." Southerners had "crowded into two centuries and a half a mightiness of force, a vastness of results, which would have enriched a thousand years," but he now saw this civilization passing away, without leaving a "written record of its life. A civilization has existed more unique than any other since the dawn of history, as potent in its influence, and yet no chronicle of it has been made by any but the hand of hostility."[8]

Page then made a key correlation. "Reverence for the greatness of its past, pride of race," he said, "are two cardinal elements in national strength." These qualities "made the Greek; they made the Roman; they made the Saxon; they made the Southerner." The people of the South were in danger of losing those qualities; if one vanished, perhaps even more ominously the other would soon follow. The tie between a sense of history, precarious regional group identity, and racial pride became clear: "We are not a race to pass and leave no memorial on our time."[9]

Proponents of a new historical view of the southern past in this era explicitly rejected the idea that they wanted a history biased in their favor. They did not advocate any deliberate invention of history. Former Confederate General D. H. Hill, in an address on southern history, professed that he would not use a book just because it was by a southerner: "If a Hottentot or a Zulu wrote a better text-book on history than the one I was using, though mine were written by a composite epitome of all that is Southern, I would unhesitatingly adopt the Hottentot or Zulu book." The advocates of this position argued that northern historians did invent history: they wrote unfair pictures of the southern past either "through ignorance of thought or a willful perversion of truth." Southern children reading such books could never sort out the truth.[10]

The Lost Cause myth was about history, and the organizations that embodied its outlook were prominent supporters of southern historical writing. Southern veterans formed the United Confederate Veterans (UCV) in 1889, and the organization soon established a historical committee. The committee proclaimed its desire for fairness. Referring to existing histories, Stephen D. Lee noted in 1892 that "to select those which are partisan to the South would be as objectionable" as picking "those which are partisan to the North." Committee members refused to authorize Thomas Nelson Page to write a new history of the Civil War, fearing he would produce a book partisan toward the South. In its 1894 report, the committee insisted, though, that "justice to the South imperatively demands a different presentation" of history. While the

South had produced few competent historians of its own since the Civil War, "northern men . . . have . . . given undue prominence to what was done by their section to the omission and corresponding fair statement of what was done by the South." White southerners clearly did not see themselves as having a special tradition of expertise in historical interpretation at this point, as late as the 1890s.[11]

In its unofficial oversight of southern history, the UCV Historical Committee encouraged historical writing within circumscribed guidelines, in the context of seeking what seemed to be fairness. The historical committee protested the way schoolbooks, mostly written by northerners, presented states' rights, nullification, slavery, and secession. Committee members also stressed the need for accuracy in textbooks, but at the same time they insisted that school history texts show that white southerners in the sectional crisis were motivated only by a concern for independence and self-rule; that the war was a "conflict between the states" rather than a "rebellion"; and that the southern people had shown "unparallel [sic] patriotism" in accepting the results of the war. Every book the committee recommended as meeting these requirements was written by a white southerner.[12]

Northern and southern veterans waged a bitter literary war, in fact, struggling to ensure that as many schoolbooks as possible incorporated their views of the war. Each group believed that it was only seeking historical truth and accuracy, although each was self-serving. Publishers often kept two versions of the same textbook – one for the northern market and one for the southern. A look at one representative southern history textbook will suggest the nature of the historical writing and interpretation that, at the turn of the century, was being put to the service of nurturing a regional tradition in the schools. Susan Pendleton Lee, daughter of Confederate General and Episcopal priest William Nelson Pendleton, authored *Lee's Advanced School History of the United States*, which the UCV and the United Daughters of the Confederacy recommended and school boards throughout the South widely adopted. Lee devoted considerable attention to southern heroes, such as an extended treatment of the scientific work of Matthew F. Maury. Furthermore, she treated the sectional crisis at great length, expressing true puzzlement at northern behavior in the events leading to the war, and repeated the proslavery arguments verbatim in discussing abolitionist charges against the South. Forty percent of the narrative is on the Civil War and Reconstruction. It was history as vindication, focusing on the events that had been at the heart of the emerging sense of a regional tradition.[13]

Professional historians, trained in modern historical methods at the best American universities, also used historical writing to nurture the idea of a southern tradition. Edwin Alderman, John Spencer Bassett, William Trent, and William Dodd are examples of young southern historians who were involved in this practice in the 1890s and the next decade. They saw themselves as reformers questioning southern tradition, but many of them, after public controversies involving issues of southern historical orthodoxies, retreated from open criticism of the South and its history. They rarely criticized slavery openly or challenged traditional views of the legality of secession. Trent remained irreverent, to be sure, noting once that having served at a college with two Confederate generals did away with the mystery of the South's losing the war; but most young historians of the era fell into writing articles lauding Robert E. Lee and celebrating the Lost Cause. They had grown to maturity in the South between 1865 and 1890, and like other white southerners, they were a product of the increasing belief that the South had a regional tradition that could not and should not be questioned too carefully.[14]

The invention of tradition depends on its ritualization, as history becomes tradition through its dissemination to the public. The years after Reconstruction witnessed the ritualization of activities with symbolic dimensions for the glorification of the Southern Way of Life. Official recognition was given to a rich array of symbols that became self-consciously recognized as southern. The paraphernalia of nationalism associated with the South was even more emotion packed after the war than during it. Some symbols dated from the Civil War era itself. The song "Dixie," for example, became a patriotic Confederate air, and it did not vanish afterwards, capable of rousing southern sentiments as passionately in 1910 as earlier. The Confederate battle flag also was a wartime artifact with continued cultural meaning; not only was it on display at the public ceremonies of the Lost Cause, but it was also displayed during political campaigns, local parades, and recreational activities. Most significantly, perhaps, its design was incorporated into the new version of the Mississippi state flag in the 1890s, at a time when the state was pioneering measures for disfranchisement and racial segregation.[15]

Holidays with explicit regional dimensions embodied southern tradition. Confederate Memorial Day, celebrated variably from late April to June 3 (Jefferson Davis's birthday), was the key seasonal ritual celebrating the southern tradition. Whereas white Americans of the former Confederacy did not honor American Memorial Day until well after World War I, the separate Confederate Memorial Day was the center of community life in the typical small town after the Civil War. While Confederate Memorial Day began informally immediately after the war, the process of inventing tradition seems more clear in considering Robert E. Lee's birthday: it did not become a regional holiday until much later and was not an official holiday of southern states until 1900. In most southern states it still is a government holiday, although many places combine its celebration with that of Martin Luther King Jr. Day. You still cannot go wrong mentioning irony with the South.[16]

Even a truly traditional holiday, Christmas, took on ideological meaning it had not had before. Irwin Russell's dialect poem "Christmas in the Quarters," which dates from the 1880s, captured the belief in a distinctive plantation Christmas, a happy joyous time epitomizing the friendly race relations of the region. In ways not seen in the South earlier, Christmas now became a specifically southern festival in Russell's rendering and in that of other sentimental pieces about the plantation Christmas. This seasonal memory became a part of the larger southern plantation tradition, which writers were emphasizing as the South's shared past. Memoirs recalled such holidays in the past, in history, with nostalgic enthusiasm, as part of a time when life was better. Yet the implication was this was an ongoing tradition that southerners should honor in the future as well as the past.[17]

Ritual occasions, such as the dedication of Confederate monuments and the meetings of Confederate veterans groups, showed white southerners an image of their past not as Americans, nor as citizens of a state, country, or town, but as members of a southern regional group with distinct traditions. Communities erected hundreds of Confederate monuments across the South, mostly in the years from 1880 to 1920. The ceremonies attached to their dedications were dramatic social occasions.

Over one hundred thousand people showed up in Richmond for the dedications of major monuments, and thousands came to small towns for similar ceremonies.[18]

Why the devotion to such memorialization and why the response? The wartime generation had aged by 1900 sufficiently to fear that younger white southerners would forget the cause for which they sacrificed, and the erection of monuments became a way to mark the landscape with the visual image of the Lost Cause. As the Reverend Moses Drury Hoge noted in an address in Richmond, the monuments were a tangible form of history for people who did not even read. "Books are occasionally opened," he said, but "monuments are seen every day." The South put up more statues between 1900 and 1910 than at any time, evidence that the first decade of the twentieth century was a defining moment in the southern tradition. The prosperity of the first decade of that century enabled southern towns and cities to place more elaborate monuments. Prosperity and indeed increasing modernization in general in that era helped in the dissemination of the symbols of the defined regional tradition. Stephen D. Lee, who was chair of the UCV Historical Committee, suggested the meaning of this process, insisting that the South needed monuments "first for the sake of the dead, but mostly for the sake of the living, that in this busy industrial age these stones to the Confederate soldier may stand like great interrogation marks to the soul of the beholder." Supporters of this memorialization trend were not just backward-gazing, grizzled Confederate veterans; vigorous young Rotarian types associated with the New South supported the idea of a southern tradition, rooted in the Lost Cause, as a stabilizing force in an era of change, as a spiritual force countering the very materialism they were also promoting. The monuments stood as counterpoint to the general tendencies of the era looking toward progress.[19]

If the Lost Cause provided the crystallizing incentive and many of the most overt images of the southern tradition in this period, the process went well beyond glorification of the Confederacy. Cultivators of the southern historical garden showed interest in early southern history as well as in more contemporary events. From the Civil War, they read backward to develop a full history of the southern people. As one southern writer of a children's history text published in 1907 put it, "with romance and poetry, our Southern past is glorious." With the southern love for being the "first with the most," the author noted that Roanoke, "the first English settlement in the New World," was on what would be southern soil. St. Augustine, Florida, despite the taint of Spanish and Catholic influence, emerged as "another sacred shrine." But the writer reached his stride when he came to early Virginia: "Still dearer to us of English blood are the ruins of Jamestown. The feelings that stir our hearts as we stand under the shadow of the old tower are too deep for utterance, and we almost beg to be left alone with our awe and our solemn meditation." After reading that passage, one does want to leave him alone with his thoughts.[20]

Popular writers, professional historians, genealogists, historical preservationists, and anyone interested in the past ransacked southern history in the early twentieth century, gathering the pieces that would create a new vision of the South as a place with a special tradition rooted in its past. Remember Thomas Nelson Page who had complained how little white southerners had done to preserve their history and how soon there would be no South even to care; a generation later the South had an established tradition and, in the process, white southerners had preserved their regional identity as well.[21]

The years from 1880 to 1930 saw the definition of many concepts that came to be associated with the southern tradition, far beyond the Confederate aspects. The identification and ritualization of southern tradition included the encouragement of a southern style that emphasized the past, and tracing the emergence of a self-consciousness about southern style can perhaps clarify what was new about the invention of southern tradition in the years around the turn of the twentieth century. These years witnessed, for example, the identification by popular and academic writers of a southern style of public speaking, one typical supposedly of past orators and now approved as *the* southern style. The image of southern oratory first emerged, to be sure, in the early nineteenth century. In September 1840, the *Maine Cultivator*, a farm paper, noted that "stump oratory" was a "Southern Fashion." In June 1844, a contributor to the *Democratic Monthly Magazine* noted that a Virginia speaker was unlike his New England counterpart because he was "less complicated, with fewer apparent paradoxes, hospitable, generous, liberal and even profuse in his indulgences." Frederick Law Olmstead, in 1856, saw "southern legal oratory" exemplified by the "excessive use of metaphors and figures of speech, and of rodomontade." The term "southern oratory" likely appeared when white southerners began, after 1830, comparing themselves to the mythical Yankee and ascertaining ways in which they could claim a degree of cultural achievement. After the Civil War, school readers contained excerpts from southern speeches, but they did not stress southern distinctiveness in speech. Richard Sterling's 1872 compilation *Little Southern Orator*, for example, listed only one Confederate hero as a possible essay topic for students. Such readers would soon be far different.[22]

The tradition of a style of southern oratory, as a widespread cultural belief, did not gain acceptance until the first decade of the twentieth century. No anthology of southern speeches was published before 1900, but within ten years from that date many volumes and periodical articles appeared focusing explicitly on the southern orator. Three collections using the term "southern oratory" appeared between 1908 and 1910 alone. The intellectual and cultural awakening in southern universities and colleges in the period from 1890 to 1910 promoted identification of southern cultural traditions that would be incorporated into the idea of a general southern tradition. C. Alphonzo Smith was the scholar who championed the concept of a southern oratory style. An English professor who gave his first speech on "Southern Oratory Before the War" in 1895, his purpose was intentionally to stoke southern cultural pride and counter the belief that the South had been culturally insignificant. He mentioned such orators as Patrick Henry, John C. Calhoun, Henry Clay, John Randolph, Robert Hayne, Seargent Prentiss, Benjamin Hill, Alexander Stephens, Robert Toombs, Judah P. Benjamin, Jefferson Davis, and L. Q. C. Lamar. Smith himself had grown up after the Civil War, in an era when mythmaking and hero worship escalated in the South, and he saw in these statesmen not only a distinctive but a distinguished southern way of oratory.[23]

Southern literary critics in general promoted the idea of a tradition of southern oratory. William Trent said he wanted to show that southerners contributed "a large and a better share to the literature of the Republic than is generally admitted." To this end, he included statesmen and orators in his *Southern Writers* as a category of literature. Trent noted that "the fame of these old-time speakers" was still fresh but rather "through tradition than through much reading of their speeches." Note the self-conscious invoking of the idea of tradition as well as the acknowledgment that the tradition is not one of real continuity since the speeches remained largely unread. Carl Holliday's article on oratory in the *History of Southern Literature* (1906) suggested the end result of this creation of a southern oratorical tradition: he saw Robert Hayne's "fiery eloquence" as "the epitome of extremely Southern characteristics." Hence, not just oratory but "fiery eloquence" would now be recognized as the southern tradition.[24]

In architecture, the Greek revival style, which had certainly been popular for high-style houses in certain areas of the South before the Civil War, became in the late nineteenth century *the* building form that the culture sanctioned as the appropriate one for those striving to perpetuate past ideals associated with the region. The white-column tradition was recognized in this period as the popular embodiment of the plantation way of life, evoking sentimental emotions about the regional past. It became a familiar image by which white southerners saw themselves in aspiration, and it was an easy stereotype for nonsoutherners to use to evoke the South. What should be emphasized is the historical dimension of the incorporation of the Greek revival image as a core component of the southern tradition. Classicism was the first national style of the United States, not distinctively southern, and many American public buildings reflect this development. Southerners enthusiastically built in the Greek revival style, but southern architecture was diverse before the Civil War. The well-off families of the older Atlantic Coast South never embraced it, although the new plantation elite of the Deep South did employ it to augment their social prestige. Cotton snobs and sugar barons before the Civil War built Greek revival houses, yet it is doubtful that they viewed them as embodying a southern tradition. It was simply a fashionable style at the time and bolstered their self-presentation as a new elite.[25]

As a high-fashion style, though, Greek revival was on the decline in the South, as in other places, by the 1850s. Wealthy southerners increasingly built in an eclectic style, Victorian in look and coming under such names as Italian villa, neo-Gothic, and Moorish. More significantly, defenders of southern nationalism during the 1850s did not embrace neoclassicism but recommended that southerners build simple houses adapted to the environmental conditions of the region. An article in the southern farm journal *Soil of the South* advised southerners to build "not a gee-gaw palace, but a substantial, comfortable house," having an "airy porch for our hot summers, and yet close and comfortable rooms for our chilly, changing seasons." Little evidence suggests that southerners before the Civil War saw Greek revival, neoclassical architecture as a symbol of the Southern Way of Life.[26]

After the Civil War, southern residential building reflected the era's Victorian gingerbread styles, adapted with features appropriate to the region's hot climate. But southern ideology and mythology idealized the antebellum mansion. Popular writers such as Joel Chandler Harris and Thomas Nelson Page explicitly and repeatedly used "the stately house on a wooded hill, the huge white pillars . . . rising high enough to catch the reflections of a rosy sunset" as a central symbol of their new literary definition of the southern tradition. Their writings promoted a brief revival of neoclassical building in residential housing in the early twentieth century. As Mrs. Thaddeus Horton wrote in 1902, southerners turned "once more to the taste of their fathers." Most significantly, thanks to popular writers the symbol was now fixed in the American imagination, and it continued to be reinforced. The annual Natchez (Miss.) Pilgrimage began in 1932, the first of the now-ritualized house tours that nurture the Old South connection. When producers made the film *Gone with the Wind*, Margaret Mitchell had to fight Hollywood to keep its producers from making Tara an even more spectacular mansion, as distinct from the modest plantation house she knew was more typical of her north Georgia setting. Tradition dictated by then that the southern myth needed not only high cotton but high columns as well.[27]

As Hobsbawm has noted regarding the invention of tradition in Europe, ruling elites often manipulate the process in a time of change as a way to gain social legitimacy and validation. But those efforts can only succeed to the degree to which the process meets the needs of other social groups. In the South of the late nineteenth and early twentieth centuries, an elite group that represented the shared interests of planters identified with staple-crop agriculture and of businessmen-industrialists seeking changes in the region clearly initiated the invention of tradition. In addition, the intellectual-cultural elite increasingly associated with universities played the key creative role in nurturing the new vision of a southern tradition.

Women were also central to the invention of southern tradition, and white women found meaning in it for many of the same reasons that white southern men did. The experience of women suggests, to be sure, the tensions between the image and the reality; their diaries, journals, and letters show considerable private questioning of the defined public role of women in a tradition-dominated South. Moreover, women played diverse roles in this society, even participating actively in public life through churches, women's groups, and reform organizations. Nonetheless, they were well incorporated into ideas of a southern tradition. The southern lady was a variant of the Victorian lady, but the concept of true womanhood became especially entrenched in the South because it was tied in with racial issues. If the "true woman" of legend throughout the Western world was to be chaste and moral, her southern sister came to embody the need for purity with special significance: she was an artifact of white power, one who had to remain on a pedestal protected from black hands eager, in the southern white male mind, to gain symbolic power over southern civilization through possession of its purest icon.

Many elite white women welcomed this status and in turn became the most enthusiastic guardians of the southern tradition. Winnie Davis, who was Jefferson Davis's daughter, was honored throughout the South as "the Daughter of the Confederacy." Lost Cause organizations erected monuments to honor the Confederate lady. Mildred Rutherford, an energetic Georgia woman, was only the most famous of a legion of women who promoted the Lost Cause and the broader idea of a historically based southern tradition through speeches, collections of documents on southern history, books promoting southern literature, and extensive organizational work nurturing regional history in schools and colleges. For white women, the "southern tradition" offered prestige and status, a sense of importance rooted in a regional identity with distinct social class and racial dimensions.[28]

The yeomen of the region's rural folk culture and of the emerging textile villages had an ambivalent relationship to the newly invented sense of tradition after 1880. They criticized and aggressively fought attempts by the region's elite to use the tradition to reinforce their political and economic dominance. The Farmers' Alliance of the late 1880s initiated a major effort among southern plain folk to challenge the orthodoxies of the emerging southern tradition that placed cultural authority as well as economic power and political influence in the hands of a combined businessman-planter elite atop a hierarchical society that increasingly seemed sanctioned by the past. The plain folk were in the middle of modernization, and they created their own traditions, just as working-class people did as counterweights to the dominant traditions throughout Western culture in this era.[29]

But southern plain folk were very much a part of the ritualization of southern history, affirming the Confederacy and other aspects of the regional way of life in countless ways. Sheldon Hackney once wrote that the unhappy farmers who pressed for reform were tied only tangentially to the larger southern society by the myths of the Old South, the Lost Cause, and Reconstruction, but he underestimated the power of those myths. The participation of working people in the Confederacy and their validation of the Lost Cause after the Civil War nurtured cultural bonds with other white southerners. The same southern farmers who protested their economic plight would have likely slugged anyone who said anything against Stonewall Jackson; they voted into political offices the same captains who had led them during the Civil War; and they subscribed to a plain folk version of the Lost Cause, centered around Nathan Bedford Forrest and evoking its own symbols and activities. Racial grievance was a more pervasive part of this version of the southern tradition than that evoked in the larger regional activities of those dominating the Lost Cause movement. The myth of Reconstruction expressed fundamental racial fears of a black-dominated government, a tenacious fear that has reverberated throughout southern history among the plain folk.[30]

Ritual activities incorporated the plain folk into the cultural tradition. In 1894, Richmond dedicated its Soldiers' and Sailors' Monument to the nonelite veterans who bore most of the burden of the war. Over one hundred thousand people attended the ceremony, where they marched, prayed, sang, and listened to their heroes, lauded for their dedication to duty as common men who had defended their fellows. This ceremony was typical of ritual occasions in which society's norms are reversed; a special sense of community put the plain folk on top, making them the center of regional attention. When the ritual ended, normal society with its social class and other divisions resumed, but the presentation by the community of the plain folk as the southern regional hero acknowledged their important role and strengthened ties between social classes.[31]

Black southerners were a fundamental part of southern society, representing a third of the population, and yet their relationship to the region's public culture was even more ambivalent than that of the plain white folk. In the era that saw the invention of a dominant regional tradition, blacks were sometimes altogether invisible and omitted from the public presentation of the Southern Way of Life. This was the time of what historians have called "Negrophobia," represented by legal segregation, lynching, and disfranchisement. But more typical than exclusion was the inclusion of African Americans as figures in the tradition. Sometimes whites represented them as symbols of the region itself, as in the minstrel tradition; another example is Uncle Remus, the familiar figure of a southern white effort to combine folklore with a sense of history in a backward-looking tribute to Old South plantation blacks. They were "placed," in general, as secondary, inferior figures in the southern tradition, their presence in menial roles symbolically reaffirming their inferior role in the social order. In 1923, the Pageant of Progress parade in High Point, North Carolina, included a float with a slave cabin – this was the image of black life in southern history to be remembered. The frequent invisibility of African Americans within the dominant southern tradition was apparent: the people riding on the float, representing slaves, were actually whites in blackface, members of the United Daughters of the Confederacy, the Children of the Confederacy, and the Rotary Club.[32]

African Americans responded to their social marginalization in several ways in the late nineteenth and early twentieth centuries. Leaders like Frederick Douglass criticized the emerging white supremacist ideology after the Civil War, seeing the glorification of the Lost Cause as legitimating an unequal society. The South "has been selling agony, trading in blood and in the souls of men," he wrote in 1870. From Reconstruction until the end of the century, blacks contested public spaces in the South. Lincoln Day festivities, Emancipation Day events, fraternal society gatherings, church anniversary celebrations, and other activities asserted a black memory of the Civil War differing from the white Lost Cause memory and claiming southern space. After the imposition of legal segregation and disfranchisement, a black middle class uplift philosophy enabled African Americans to build a parallel society to whites and at times advance their interests. As historian William Blair writes, respectability "served as a form of political agency through which they intended to earn greater rights."[33]

For some African Americans, accommodation was the most realistic alternative, a viewpoint that Booker T. Washington understood. Culture became an important part of the overall hegemony exercised by the southern white ruling class, incorporating blacks tacitly into a slot, the familiar place, in the southern tradition that became rigidly defined near the turn of the twentieth century. African Americans did not embrace the Lost Cause ideologically, but they sometimes participated in its rituals because they were the rituals of the community to which they belonged, even if marginally. In fact, of course, many blacks of the middle class and the professions did have a stake in the system and participated in community life. One saw this sort of participation especially on occasions when the southern community faced the outside world. Sociologists Allison Davis, Burleigh Gardner, and Mary Gardner, in their study of Natchez in the 1930s, concluded, for example, that black resentment at the elite at least momentarily "tended to dissolve" when the elite functioned "as symbols of the total community on such occasions as the annual Historical Week, when visitors from the entire nation came to Old City." The economic welfare of the black community was at stake here sufficiently in this community ritualization to bring momentary release from daily grievances.[34]

The limits of the inclusion of blacks into the southern tradition were seen in the failure to incorporate black rituals as part of the southern tradition. American culture often included the rituals of ethnic groups as part of the reciprocal act of making immigrants Americans. Immigrants participated in melting-pot homogenization, but the American Way of

Life affirmed ritual occasions such as Columbus Day, St. Patrick's Day, and others. Authentic black rituals rooted in regional history, such as the celebration of Emancipation Day, Juneteenth, or the John Canoe festival, were a part of neither the official nor the unofficial agenda of the inventors of the southern tradition.[35]

As Hobsbawn has noted, World War I was a dividing line in the invention of tradition in the Western world, separating those traditions that endured from those that faded away or were incorporated elsewhere. In the South, one sees the notable decline of the ritualized activities associated with the public celebration of the southern tradition, as the separate ritual occasions devoted to the Lost Cause became less significant in the South after 1920. Confederate Memorial Day was still celebrated, but with less community participation. It was given over to the custody of southern women in groups like the United Daughters of the Confederacy, and they kept the day alive, but fewer southerners joined them. The individual symbols associated with the Lost Cause and, more broadly, "the southern tradition" continued, nonetheless, to be displayed. The playing of "Dixie," for example, easily touched southern regional patriotism. The ritual scene for the singing of the tune after 1920 became sporting events. High schools and colleges throughout the South in the mid-twentieth century sang the song and waved the Confederate battle flag to get the athletic juices flowing, including those of spectators. The setting of organized sports was representative of modern social organization and norms, and white southerners easily adapted their regional sense of tradition to this new order. By then they did indeed regard the traditions of the South as being of ancient heritage. Did the vague memory of the folk mind somehow, without quite having it figured out, imagine that John Smith and the others at Jamestown had sung "Dixie" and waved the flag? Would Smith have made a good quarterback?[36]

Ritualization of history entered another forum as well. As with other Americans, white southerners celebrated history itself in local pageants. The southern pageant, however, always included invocation of the specifically regional dimension of the heritage as well as celebration of the "American" dimension of the local community. These pageants asserted the progressive New South but at the same time fostered a renewed appreciation for the distinctive Old South and Confederate past. The connection between such pageants of the post-1920 era and the sense of regional tradition that had developed earlier was seen in the words of the chair of a pageant committee in Greenville, South Carolina, who noted in 1921: "It has often been said that history has been made in the South and written in the North. The purpose of our pageant is to create interest among the people of our section in our own history, thus increasing their pride in their own towns, communities, and in their section." Southern pageants recreated local Civil War battle scenes and honored local Confederate heroes. Montgomery recreated Jefferson Davis's inauguration. Mass spectacle invoked the Reconstruction myth as well. During a scene in a Morgantown, North Carolina, pageant in 1925, the audience broke into enthusiastic applause when the Ku Klux Klan rode on stage. These pageants, the new ritual locales for the celebration of the southern tradition through the presentation of regional history, combined sectional pride with the theme of national reconciliation. Southern historical pageants after 1920 included both tributes to the Lost Cause past and celebrations of the local community's economic development. The future was always healthy in such presentations, but the past was healthy too.[37]

The idea of a dominant southern tradition, resting on symbols and images from the regional past and celebrated on ritual occasions, continued as part of southern culture into the recent age. Southern intellectuals after 1920, to be sure, experienced an identity crisis based in their questioning of the inherited southern tradition. Allen Tate, one of the Vanderbilt Agrarians, became disenchanted with the sentimentalized idea of southern tradition. His poem "Ode to the Confederate Dead" shows his distance from those earlier southerners. But Tate did not abandon the effort to define a "southern tradition," and the subtitle of *I'll Take My Stand: The South and the Agrarian Tradition* (1930) expressed this effort. Although contributors to that symposium disagreed among themselves, what they apparently could agree on was that you should be able to define the southern tradition. Born in 1900, W. J. Cash grew up in the period that had seen the invention of southern tradition, and it became easy for him to imagine a unified, continuous southern mind.[38] When southern blacks launched the civil rights movement, which culturally was a challenge to the tradition, defenders of the Southern Way of Life trotted out "Dixie" and the Confederate battle flag and other symbols of the southern tradition. They asserted that the Southern Way of Life, the southern tradition, was so ancient that it was impossible to imagine a southern society without such symbols and the countless other historically rooted rituals. In fact, the idea of southern tradition can be placed historically in more recent times than white southerners of that era thought, and its origins explained in terms of a people asserting the tenacity of their group identity in a fifty-year period in which that very identity seemed on the verge of dissolution.

"Tradition" was a common word in Western culture in this era. The southern experience perhaps most closely resembles that of Wales. As Prys Morgan has written in a study entitled "The Hunt for the Welsh Past in the Romantic Period": "The Wales we have been describing was not a political state, and for want of such a state the people were driven to give a disproportionate amount of their energies to cultural matters, to the recovery of the past and, where the past was found wanting, to its invention. The old way of life decayed and disappeared, the past was very often tattered and threadbare, and so a great deal of invention was needed. The romantic mythologists had succeeded so well, in some ways, that they made things Welsh appear charmingly and appealingly quaint."[39] White southerners, too, devoted considerable energy and indeed material resources to cultural matters. Unlike the case of the Welsh, one event, the Civil War, provided a central focus for defining the importance of the past in the twentieth-century South. Southern whites in the years from 1880 to 1930 adapted the idea of tradition to their own experience to make it seem their own device.

2   The Burden of Southern Culture

The South Carolina legislature voted in May 2000 to remove the Confederate battle flag from the state's capitol, an event of enormous symbolic significance in the redefinition of southern culture. The flag had once flown over several state capitols in the South. One of the last states to remove it, Alabama, did so in 1993, after a lawsuit from African Americans, but the battle was fully fought in the state that had been secession's birthplace. The National Association for the Advancement of Colored People (NAACP) initiated a boycott in 1999 that had a dramatic economic effect on South Carolina, forging an effective alliance among political moderates across party and racial lines. The symbolism of the flag coming down was dramatic, but some black leaders saw only a partial victory in an ongoing struggle, because the compromise that removed the flag from the capitol stipulated that it would be moved elsewhere on the capitol grounds, near an existing Confederate monument. The NAACP opposed the arrangement, to the chagrin of black legislators who worked for the compromise, and some whites remained emotionally upset about the removal. One white man interviewed at the Sportsman's drinking establishment along the Catawba River observed: "That's one thing people do around here. They get attached to things, they may not be worth anything, but they want to keep them." The reaction of the defenders and critics of the Confederate flag suggested, nonetheless, that it was worth much to them, indeed.[1]

South Carolina, like the rest of the South, assumes the burden of its traditional culture at those moments when African Americans challenge its historic symbolism, rooted as it is in the Old South and Confederate experiences that have resonated for whites since the Civil War as the defining time of southern culture. Southern whites defined such mid-nineteenth century symbols as the Confederate battle flag and the song "Dixie" as regional icons at a time when blacks in the region did not have cultural authority to influence that symbolism. With the end of Jim Crow segregation laws and disenfranchisement practices in the 1960s, African Americans launched a movement in the following decade to desegregate southern cultural symbols. It often was on the back burner, as economic and political issues predominated in public policy concerns; by the 1990s, however, blacks had achieved important victories in their efforts. L. Douglas Wilder, who would later be elected governor of Virginia, had scarcely been elected to the Virginia Senate in the 1970s when he called for the repeal of the law designating "Carry Me Back to Ole Virginny" as the state's official song; twenty-seven years later, the legislature finally removed the official sanction of the song. Another example was the University of Mississippi, which is always a bellwether of southern race relations given its historic role in educational integration in the 1960s. In the fall of 1982, the first black cheerleader at the university, John Hawkins, refused to carry the Confederate battle flag in that once bastion of Old South custom; his efforts began a long struggle that led in the late 1990s to the university's alumni association and student government officially calling for the end of the flag's display and the noticeable decline in its use. Reflecting dramatic symbolic change, the university's student body president and student newspaper editor soon were African American, and the university recently dedicated a memorial honoring its first black student, James Meredith.[2]

Having desegregated its restaurants and theaters, having made great strides in desegregating its schools, the South is in the middle of the process of desegregating its public symbols. With each struggle over these symbols, though, the region confronts once again the burden of its past. *Merriam-Webster's Ninth New Collegiate Dictionary* (1984) defines *burden* as "that which is borne or carried; a load," suggesting that duty and responsibility are parts of this meaning. A second definition, however, says that a burden is "that which is grievous, wearisome, or oppressive." One might look at southern history and conclude that everyone who has studied it, or lived it, has seen it as a burden. The South has never lacked for outside critics who have seen the region as burdened in this latter definition. Southern blacks have, in turn, seen themselves burdened with whites, while southern whites have seen themselves burdened with blacks and northerners.[3]

The most famous attempt to explore the idea of the burden of the South was C. Vann Woodward's collection of essays *The Burden of Southern History* (1960). At a time of fundamental changes in the region's politics, economics, and race relations, the volume attempted to define the distinctiveness of the South through its history. One essay, "The Search for Southern Identity," proposed historical experience as the enduring feature of southern identity; the South's legacy of poverty, defeat and failure, moral guilt, and sense of place gave the region a different perspective on life than the rest of the nation. Woodward's concerns were historical, but he clearly drew from cultural materials in a way that betrayed his appreciation of cultural history. The essay, to be sure, offered no theoretical framework on, nor conscious discussion of, southern culture, yet his use of such terms as "myth," "identity," "character," "collective experience," "heritage," and "tradition" suggested an understanding of cultural processes. He used the term "cultural landscape" in noting the changes in his era, and he talked about symbolism in passing, putting forward the image of the bulldozer at a construction site as a new symbol of the South. Woodward talked at length, however, about only one cultural form other than the awareness of history: he praised "the magnificent body of literature" created in the previous decades by the South's writers, and he pointed out in particular the "peculiar historical consciousness of the Southern writer."[4]

Although Woodward's book itself was a part of that "magnificent body of literature" produced during the Southern Literary Renaissance, advances in scholarship and new concerns inevitably make it seem dated now. Where is the South's music in its identity? The quality and quantity of the South's musicians surely rival those of its writers. The

South's musical renaissance, moreover, must offer some perspective on the question of the southern identity. Where is the folk culture, which David Potter would later argue was the key to southern distinctiveness? Woodward mentioned religion in the book, though mainly through a theological discussion of Reinhold Niebuhr in the final essay. He made no effort to gain insight on southern identity from the region's distinctive religious tradition, dominated for so long by evangelical Protestantism. Indeed, Woodward showed little interest through his career in exploring religion's role in the South, despite a wide-ranging appreciation for the significance of other forces shaping the region.

To fault Woodward for failing to deal with some of these matters is unfair, of course, because much of the literature on cultural concerns was simply not available to him as an essayist until a decade or so after he wrote. The point is simply to emphasize the rise of interdisciplinary studies of southern culture in the last quarter century and its contributions to understanding, and redefining, the region. Actually, such studies go back even farther than that. Sociologist Howard W. Odum, for example, produced some two hundred articles and twenty books in regional sociology, and sociologists such as Rupert Vance and Guy Johnson played a prominent role during the 1930s and 1940s in sketching the "Problem South," the southern burdens stemming from socioeconomic deficiencies. Scholars such as John Dollard, Hortense Powdermaker, Allison Davis, Burleigh Gardner, and Mary Gardner investigated the complex structure of race and class relationships in these decades as well. Social scientists in general were most comfortable with the research and writing of studies addressing cultural concerns before Woodward wrote. But regional sociology declined in the 1950s, while cultural study of the South took a back seat in the 1960s to social activism and social conflict.[5]

Since then, however, southern studies has become even more interdisciplinary, and concentration on cultural issues has risen. The title of Clifford Geertz's 1980 article, "Blurred Genres," suggests that what was happening in the study of the South was, of course, part of a broader intellectual development. Louis Rubin, Lewis Simpson, and Hugh Holman were among the leading advocates of studying southern literature by placing it in its social context, thus abandoning the New Critics' stress on the text. In the 1970s, Odum's successor at Chapel Hill, John Shelton Reed, rediscovered the sociology of the South (as distinct from sociological studies set in the region but not addressing particularly southern issues). Folklorists such as Henry Glassie produced sophisticated studies of folk housing, combining fieldwork and historical research to cast new light on old questions, and Michael Ann Williams produced a classic in the field, using oral history to enhance the study of material culture. Cultural geography emerged as the liveliest field in that hoary discipline, and many geographers charted the South. Religious studies offered perhaps the clearest picture of the new intellectual approaches. The key figure in the increasingly complex study of southern religious history has been Samuel Hill. In *Southern Churches in Crisis* (1966) and later works, Hill drew on his training in history, theology, and sociology, and his institutional involvement in both church life and university religion departments, to offer a cross-cultural and interdisciplinary perspective on the South's religion. His argument that the central theme of southern religion has been the dominance of evangelical Protestantism has since influenced other scholars who have, in turn, extended his insights to other disciplines.[6]

The unifying thread in this interdisciplinary study is the desire to understand the culture of the South – including both its internal relationships and its role within the broader national culture. In the 1950s, Alfred Kroeber and Clyde Kluckholn catalogued 164 definitions of "culture," suggesting the problems then and now of a precise definition. According to Raymond Williams, the term is "one of the two or three most complicated words in the English language," and few would dispute that, especially after seeing the various ways writers have used it. One could say the same for "South" or "region," both similarly problematic terms. But in our postmodern world, even Woodward's "history" is difficult to grasp, lacking any agreed-upon foundation that scholars across disciplines can embrace. What has surely become clear about all such terms is their lack of precision, the tentativeness with which we must speak of them. Nonetheless, that awareness should not blind us to their continued usefulness in scholarly work. Culture is neither static nor essential, and it is surely ideologically contested, but all of those traits suggest a continued function for the term in illuminating the particularities of differing social groups and nationalities. Southern studies is increasingly informed by the theories and approaches of cultural studies, which privileges texts and discourses, broadly understood. Fieldwork-based ethnography by anthropologists, folklorists, and documentary studies practitioners has also recently enriched the interdisciplinary study of the South, resting as it does on different theoretical models and methodological practices than cultural studies.[7]

Clifford Geertz's definition of "culture" has been usefully applied to the South and has the virtue of clarity. He sees culture as "an historically transmitted pattern of meanings embodied in symbols, a system of inherited conceptions expressed in symbolic forms by means of which men communicate, perpetuate, and develop their knowledge about and attitudes toward life." Although this definition may imply more unity to cultures than exists, it does reflect current approaches in stressing symbol systems and their role in giving human beings a framework for understanding each other, themselves, and the wider world. Furthermore, it makes particularly relevant both Woodward's 1960 discussion of symbols such as bulldozers and the black cheerleader's protest against carrying the Confederate flag.[8]

Two points are central in exploring this relationship and should form at least part of the agenda for redefining southern culture. One aspect is the complex pattern of institutions, rituals, myths, material artifacts, and other aspects of a functioning culture that creates the "webs" that Geertz suggests make symbol systems coherent despite all the complexity in them. Geertz used the method of "thick description" to understand a simple ritual of everyday life in Bali, the cockfight, and Ted Ownby and Rhys Isaac have shown that southerners, black and white, staged cockfights, the analysis of which can help unravel dimensions of southern life. The second broad point to explore is the connection between history and the sense of identity among southerners as a distinct social group. Have people in the South had characteristic assumptions, values, and attitudes apart from other Americans? When did that identity arise and how did they transmit it to future generations? How did historical events and forces create a sense of common purpose among people in the South – or did a common purpose exist at all? What have been the varieties of cultures in the region and their accompanying identities?

What is the relationship between a public South, based in power and authority and official pronouncements, and a private South of everyday life? What have been the cultural centers, borders, and margins in the South and with other parts of the nation? What have been the contingent cultural similarities between the South and the nation, and what have been the differences?[9]

One aspect of the burden of southern culture, then, involves the work of the scholar. I am suggesting that interdisciplinary cultural studies of the South can help address these questions and clarify understanding of region. There may indeed be many burdens of southern culture. I want to suggest one of them. Woodward said the burden of southern history was defeat, guilt, poverty, and place. Hence, the burden of southern culture may well be the persistent belief through the region's history that the South has some special role to play. It is a belief rooted in the symbolic. At the heart of both southern identity and the burden of southern culture is a distinctive sense of regional mission. This is a variation on ideas of national mission, but the assertion has been that the region, not just the nation, has a special destiny. The beginnings of a sense of southern mission could perhaps be traced back to the colonial era. To be sure, the Puritans who settled in New England set up colonies with an explicit sense of mission rooted in religion, but that was not true of the South. Although its colonies might not have been religiously driven, the first signs of an emerging southern self-consciousness in the colonial period did appear couched in religious imagery – the South as a new Garden of Eden. This image implied a beneficent climate and overall environment and also an innocence the New Englanders with their Calvinist theology would not have asserted. Historian John Alden argued that the first South – that is, the first time one can really talk about an identifiable regional consciousness – was in the Revolutionary era. Thomas Jefferson clearly asserted a sense of southern destiny as part of the new nation. His chosen people were agrarians, farmers toiling on the land, and this Virginian seemed to see southerners as the quintessential chosen people. Jefferson's – and the South's – early vision of destiny was American and also Arcadian: a timeless vision of human beings living and working on the land. It was a vision that grew out of the Enlightenment and also reflected Hebraic and classical influences.[10]

This vision of the South's "pastoral permanence," as Lewis Simpson terms it, did not, however, provide an enduring sense of mythic purpose for the region. Two developments in the early nineteenth century changed the orientation of southern thought to a distinctively regional sense of purpose. One was the development of the solid slave South. With the spread of the cotton kingdom into new lands in the Southwest came an accompanying greater reliance on slave labor and an intellectual and cultural defense of slavery as the basis of a good society. The myth of the Old South and its plantation culture was a romantic-era artifact that summed up the southern self-image of superiority. Southerners were cavaliers to be admired by the world, while Yankees were, well, Yankees, and the less said the better. The chief problem with Yankees was their greedy materialism in an age of northern commercial and industrial expansion, and, by contrast, the best thing about southerners was their supposed lack of this very materialism. Ever since the antebellum years, then, the southern self-image has often involved the idea of spiritual superiority to northerners.[11]

The second development that caused a retreat from the Jeffersonian vision of timeless agrarian civilization was in religion. After the Great Revival of 1800–1801, evangelical religion conquered the South. Groups such as the Baptists and Methodists, which had been dissenting sects in the eighteenth century, rose to dominate the region. Accompanying the new evangelical orientation was a triumph of orthodoxy. The religious rationalism that had existed in the Jeffersonian South and that became a major religious force in New England Unitarianism was in retreat by the 1840s in the South. The separation of southern Baptists, Methodists, and Presbyterians from their northern brethren in the 1840s and after made these popular southern denominations the carriers of southern nationalism – and the idea of southern destiny – even before the conflict of the 1860s. They injected new passions into southern identity that carried it far beyond Jefferson's vision, rooting it in vernacular fears, resentments, and aspirations truly emerging out of the frontier.[12]

These developments reached a new stage in the Civil War and Reconstruction. The Civil War brought a full-fledged sense of southern mission into existence. The Revolution of 1776 had inspired Americans to see their history in transcendent terms, and the experience of fighting a war for Confederate independence led white southerners to a new awareness of their role in history. Those who reflected on the region's experience came to see that the results of the Civil War had given them a history distinct from that of the rest of the nation. At the end of the war, they tried to come to terms with defeat, giving rise to the idea of the Lost Cause, which became the foundation of a southern sense of mission in the post-bellum era. It suggested that white southerners had been destined to crusade for principle, as they saw it, and even though they lost, the battle had not been in vain. Southerners would emerge with what they saw as a degree of spiritual discipline and understanding that the Gilded Age, money-hungry North did not have. The basis of the sense of mission underlying the Lost Cause was no longer Jefferson's vision of a time-less Arcadia, an agrarian civilization of sturdy farmers; the new model of the South's destiny was the memory of wartime suffering and defeat and the hope of Christian resurrection. In order to be prepared when destiny called, the South, white southerners felt, had to preserve its moral and religious values, its peculiar spiritual outlook within the American nation. The South represented a redemptive community in this new vision of a regional spiritual destiny. The precise mission of the region was not always clear in the rhetoric of the Lost Cause, but the emphasis was on white southerners remembering the past ("lest ye forget," as observers saw on so many Confederate monuments) and knowing it had spiritual meaning. The defense of white superiority was, of course, allied with the Confederate memory from the beginning, and it became a primary buttress for tenacious southern white racial obsessions.[13]

The Confederate and postwar Lost Cause explanation of southern destiny had waned by the 1920s. Allen Tate's poem "Ode to the Confederate Dead" expressed the frustration of a modern young white southerner standing at the gate of a Confederate cemetery. He thinks of the "inscrutable infantry rising" and of the battles fought. He envies the Confederates their convictions, their knowledge of why they fought and what they believed. The modern southerner of the 1920s knew too much, in effect, for simple convictions. He doubts and questions, making it impossible to regain the faith of the past. The writers of the Southern Literary Renaissance, such as Tate, themselves extended the belief in a southern destiny. They converted the southern experience into high art, into parables of the human condition. But Tate and his literary colleagues were largely without influence with the masses of the southern people themselves. In the modern South, most southerners preferred to forget the tragic lessons of defeat in the Civil War and to think in more upbeat ways. Tate attended a Confederate memorial service in Clarksville, Tennessee, where a Baptist preacher told him that God had ordained Confederate defeat in order to position the South for later industrial development – not exactly the mission the high-minded Tate had foreseen for his South.[14]

Regional writers kept alive, nonetheless, the image of the South as a redemptive community. Critic Lewis Simpson has argued that "the Southern writer has tended to be a kind of priest and prophet of a metaphysical nation," one who has tried to "represent it as a quest for revelation of man's moral community in history." Writers increasingly placed the South's experience in the broadest possible perspective, making their profoundest achievements when, as Simpson says, "they became sufficiently aware that the South is a part of the apocalypse of modern civilization." As among the most sensitive chroniclers of the South's spiritual destiny, the literary community would play a crucial role in refocusing southern cultural concerns beyond the Lost Cause.[15]

The 1950s and 1960s represented a watershed in symbolic southern culture. On the one hand, the older Lost Cause symbolism and explanation of southern destiny reemerged in a harsh new movement that emphasized their racial meaning. Segregationists used the symbols of the Lost Cause, and they became explicitly, almost exclusively even, tied in with white supremacy. On the other hand, a fresh vision of southern destiny appeared – the ideal of a biracial South. This was a southern liberal dream, which Leslie W. Dunbar, director of the Southern Regional Council, invoked in 1961: "I believe that the South will, out of its travail and sadness and requited passion, give the world its first grand example of two races of men living together in equality and with mutual respect. The South's heroic age is with us now." This dream might have seemed a white man's fantasy in 1961, but the terms "travail and sadness and requited passion" reveal its essentially spiritual foundation, suggesting that spiritual suffering could promote ethical rebirth, within a specifically southern setting.[16]

This was not just a white dream, though. Martin Luther King Jr. spoke of the civil rights movement's national and international significance for black liberation, but he also understood its specifically southern context. Achieving racial justice would nurture "our cultural health as a region," as well as our individual well-being and national political health. He recoiled from the South's "tragic attempt to live in monologue rather than dialogue," and yet he also spoke overtly of "our beloved Southland." Applying heroic language to describe black southerners in his era, language that had once been used in the South to describe the mythic figures of the Lost Cause, he told of suffering, tragedy, honor, virtuous conduct, and the achievement of dignity by a defeated people – his southern black folk. He became even more direct in seizing the southern white legacy, noting of African American freedom protestors in 1963 that "the virtues so long regarded as the exclusive property of the white South – gallantry, loyalty, and pride – had passed to the Negro demonstrators in the heat of the summer's battles." Much like white southerners before him, King hoped that "spiritual power" and "soul force" would transform the South and, from there, the nation and the world. In 1963, his "I Have a Dream" speech prophesied national salvation in a specifically redemptive South. Likewise, King evoked the traditional southern appreciation for place in suggesting that the nation's transformation would be at a specific site – his South – not in some disembodied location. To be sure, the region had been the scene of black suffering and of flawed humanity, but ultimately the virtue of blacks and decent whites would produce reconciliation on the "red hills of Georgia," where blacks and whites would "sit down together at the table of brotherhood." Even Mississippi, "a state sweltering with the heat of injustice, sweltering with the heat of oppression," would become transformed into "an oasis of freedom and justice."[17]

The southern dream of King and other black freedom fighters became a central metaphor that still evokes the belief in a distinctive regional destiny. One cultural meaning of the civil rights movement within the southern context was the public acknowledgement that blacks were southerners too. Earlier generations of people living in the South often used the term "southerner" to mean white southerner. The ideas of southern destiny were white visions of the region's mission. In the past, whites created the symbols of southern public culture, and the burden of southern culture in the contemporary era is partly this symbolism. Hence, the region is searching for new symbols that express its changed circumstances – the new reality that blacks will assert their peculiar claims on southern identity and use their authority to help shape a new southern destiny.[18]

The issue is the southern community itself. The concern for community and sense of place are often mentioned as giving a distinctive character to the South; the question for the scholar of southern culture is what was, and is, the southern community. Cultural history promises a way to gain greater understanding of that fundamental issue. By studying the way of life of southerners – the rituals, myths, material artifacts, institutions, and values of southerners, both black and white – scholars can gain deeper understanding of the southern community that comprises diverse social groups. Benedict Anderson writes of the "imagined community," which suggests the crucial role of the symbolic imagination in defining communities. Scholars use other terms, such as "invented traditions" and "social constructions," that also indicate that communities have no essence outside of what people invest in them. But that investment can be considerable, with tangible manifestations.[19]

Scholars increasingly read "southernness" as a construction. However, they often fail to grasp the moral meanings that individuals from many ideologies in the past invested in the term. Woodward's *The Burden of Southern History* pointed out that blacks should look at their southern heritage, but his "burden" mostly dealt with the white southern identity, coming especially out of the experiences of the guilt of slavery and defeat in the Civil War. Blacks had no reason for guilt over slavery, and the Civil War was not a defeat for them but a victory. The burden of southern culture has taken on new dimensions, though, since the civil rights movement allowed African Americans to claim a South that is their homeland, a new South that is redefined based on their experiences as well as those of whites. As whites and blacks work through these changes, they continue to see this redefined South as one with moral meaning. During the South Carolina debate over the Confederate battle flag, John S. Rainey, a prominent white Republican and businessman, used the language of a southern mission, rooted in moral values and the possibility of redemption, to urge the state to bring the flag down from its symbolic center, the state capitol. "It's about doing the right thing, the honorable thing," he said. "There is a sea change going on in South Carolina, an awakening to what we can be if we really start tackling the old, hard issues."[20] It is still a South struggling with its heritage of tragedy and suffering, a place still invested with the hope that suffering can lead to salvation.

3 Saturated Southerners
The South's Poor Whites and Southern Regional Consciousness

James Agee spent much of the summer of 1936 in rural Alabama, observing the hard life of white sharecroppers. "These children," he wrote, after visiting pupils at a local school, "both of town and country, are saturated southerners, speaking dialects not very different from the negroes. *Brother* Rabbit! *Old Southern Tale!*" The families that Agee and photographer Walker Evans documented – named Ricketts, Woods, and Gudger – seemed the poorest, most isolated of southerners, and yet they were indeed saturated with southern culture. People like them became national symbols during the Great Depression, when southern poor folk took on a new ideological meaning for a nation itself facing hard times. Traditionally in American culture, the southern plain folk were invisible, seen only as stereotypically "poor white trash," but during the Depression, the suffering of the southern poor had a disturbing national relevance, and they were even, at times, ennobled.[1]

The 1930s saw a heightened southern regional awareness as well, among such intellectuals as the Vanderbilt Agrarians of *I'll Take My Stand* (1930) and the North Carolina sociologists associated with Howard Odum. They and others explored the meanings of southern culture in an increasingly modern society. What was the relationship of southern poor whites to regional consciousness in this era? How did they relate to the southern identity, that sense of self-conscious difference from other Americans that has been a standard characteristic of "southernness," a sometimes vaguely defined but nonetheless powerful motivator of white regional behavior? Poor whites have been used as disreputable symbols of southerners beyond the pale since Virginia aristocrat William Byrd first had a glance at them during his visit to North Carolina in the early 1700s. He was not impressed, describing them as "indolent wretches" who "loiter away their lives, like Solomon's sluggard." While nonsoutherners have stereotyped southern poor whites and had much fun with the image of the region as Lubberland, the typology really first appeared and has always flourished among better-off white southerners like Byrd and, later, William Alexander Percy. To them, the comic laughter hid a profound uneasiness that the South *was* Lubberland, or at least it would be if poor whites ever crawled out of the muck and took over. This was William Alexander Percy's fear in describing the political rise of the southern common people – poor whites were seizing control of his version of the South: "They were the sort of people that lynch Negroes, that mistake hoodlumism for wit, and cunning for intelligence."[2]

A cultural elite of planters such as Percy's ancestors and middle-class intellectuals and professionals developed the dominant tradition of southern regional self-consciousness in the mid-nineteenth century, focused around the issue of political sectionalism and expressed through the conventions of romantic cultural nationalism. It would tenaciously survive, symbolized by columned plantation houses, the mythology of the Old South and the Lost Cause, and legally codified racial segregation. This was the South's civic culture, celebrated in officially sanctioned public events and enforced with the rule of law. We know this public culture worked to the advantage of people like the Percys, who had good reasons to embrace this version of southern identity and the cultural status it bestowed upon them.[3]

If the poor whites of stereotype seemed the antithesis of the cavalier of mythology, a more viable countertradition to the elite planter and middle-class intellectual version of the Southern Way of Life long existed. Sometimes it rested in isolated hill country and piney woods enclaves, where small farmers and their poor white kin wanted to be left alone, and sometimes these same people expressed their discontent through such political struggles as agrarian populism and, later, the efforts of the Southern Tenant Farmers' Union. The attitudes of the South's majority population of small white farmers toward the mythology of the traditional public South were surely complicated. Small yeoman farmers marched off to war to fight for the Confederacy and honored the memory of the Lost Cause afterward. Their status, though, both economically and culturally, declined dramatically in the years from the Civil War to the Great Depression. The heyday of small farming had been in the pre–Civil War era, when many more white southerners lived on subsistence farms than on plantations, but after the war they were increasingly drawn into the market economy. Cotton occupied more and more acreage, even though European markets that had driven the South's growing agricultural commitment to the crop leveled off after the war. As the South grew more cotton, prices kept falling, impoverishing white farmers as well as the freed African Americans who fell into a common tenant farming system. In 1880, tenants worked 36 percent of southern farms; by 1930, the figure had risen to over 55 percent. Two out of three tenant farmers were white in 1935, the year before Agee and Evans went to Alabama.[4]

This economic decline matched a loss of cultural authority that had once been invested in the rural South, as in rural America. Around the turn of the twentieth century, new terms appeared, such as "hillbillies," "rednecks," and "hicks," to describe the people Thomas Jefferson had once said were "God's chosen people." Ever more marginalized, such people had tenuous connections to an old regional identity centered around plantations and memories of the increasingly distant Civil War. A thin social boundary separated the landowning yeoman farmer from the near-destitute rural tenant, especially in the Depression era. Moreover, southern working people in the twentieth century filled industrial as well as rural occupations. Textile workers could be employed one moment and poor the next; it often took a "family wage" of parents and children working long hours in the mill to prevent poverty from overtaking people. Even town, city, and industrial workers often had been culturally formed by the rural life of their upbringing, again blurring the lines between categories bearing on whether one was "poor white" or not.[5]

James Agee, by contrast, grew up in a middle-class east Tennessee family, a southern background that still resonated for him when he returned to the South in the 1930s to document Alabama's undeniably poor tenant families. Agee's paternal ancestors had lived in isolated rural communities for nearly two centuries and epitomized the Tennessee saying that only three generations separate the plow handle from the silk hat. As Walker Evans notes, "Backcountry poor life wasn't really far from him, actually. He had some of it in his blood, through relatives in Tennessee." Agee spent time as a child at his grandfather's farm, which he later noted was in "deep mountain country" and from which he took an enduring pastoral sensibility. The farm figures explicitly in his reflections on southern housing in *Let Us Now Praise Famous Men*. His father, Jay, embodied a country male style for the young Agee, who recalled his father singing him to sleep with traditional mountain melodies after nightmares. One needs surely to be cautious here. As Alan Spiegel notes, "People who subscribe to the myth of Country Jim are happy to avoid awareness . . . of the hillbilly hero enrolled in Yankee institutions." Agee indeed spent most of his life "not in deep southern loam," but in and around such places as Exeter, Cambridge, Brooklyn, Greenwich Village, and Hillsdale, New York. Still, his sophistication sometimes fostered in counterpoint an idealization of the simplicities of southern country life that embodied an appealing primitivism. His earlier writing in *Fortune* had often shown this sentiment, and his time in Alabama brought out his latent southern identification. As Walker Evans recalled, "He was in flight from New York magazine editorial offices, from Greenwich Village social-intellectual evenings, and especially from the whole world of high-minded, well-bred, money-hued culture, whether authoritarian or libertarian. In Alabama he sweated and scratched with submerged glee."[6]

Agee spoke often in *Let Us Now Praise Famous Men* of human consciousness, but where did a regional consciousness fit? He notes early on that "the governing instrument – which is also one of the centers of the subject – is individual, anti-authoritative human consciousness." Later he observes that "there opens before consciousness, and within it, a universe luminous, spacious, incalculably rich and wonderful in each detail," and his attempt to render accurately the details of his sharecroppers' universe brings him closest to capturing their "southernness."

"How am I to speak of you as 'tenant' 'farmers,' as 'representatives' of your 'class,' as social integers in a criminal economy, or as individuals, fathers, wives, sons, daughters, and as my friends as I 'know' you?" He concludes, "That it is in all these particularities that each of you is that which he is." Regional particularities figure prominently in this portrait. In reflecting on how his account "might be constructed," Agee positions the tenant lives within a broader "globular" structure, "of eighteen or twenty intersected spheres." A tenant life must be seen with its "ancient, then more recent, its spreaded and more local, history and situation." The broader human background, in other words, must yield to a "convergence in local place of time." In this case, the tenant "is of the depth of the working class" but, just as important, "of southern alabamian farmers." Moreover, the tenant and his family "are living in a certain house, it is not quite like other houses," and "they are farming certain shapes and strength of land, in a certain exact vicinity."[7]

In identifying these particularities, Agee evokes little of the public South and its mythic identity. He mentions the Civil War only once and that in passing. Likewise, he mentions mansions only to note that most southern housing was different from them. He is painfully aware of the South's racial caste system, even portraying his own involvement in it as he relates his encounter with a young black couple frightened of this strange white man. Race receives surprisingly little attention here, though, perhaps bearing out criticism that Agee did not portray the suffering tenants in all their own meanness, preferring to dwell instead on their "innocence" as wounded creatures.[8]

In any event, race is clearly not a key factor in Agee's reflections on the tenants' relationship to regional consciousness. He dwells instead, to begin, on the environment in which they live. Agee uses the term *mediation* to suggest his role in entering the tenants' consciousness, and in so doing he repeatedly returns to their place as part of nature, living on Alabama hills. It is a sensuous southern consciousness. He sits with one of the families on the porch after supper, amid "the loudening frogs, and the locusts, the crickets, and the birds of night, tentative, tuning, in that great realm and drowned dew, who shall so royally embroider the giant night's fragrant cloud of earthshade." He repeatedly evokes the sound of the whippoorwills, with "their tireless whipping of the pastoral night," always "pleading; deploring." In discussing the Ricketts' house, he places not only human family members there but also "the dogs, and the cats, and the hens, and the mules, and the hogs, and the cow, and the bull calf." Describing the Gudger household, he identifies "George, and his wife, and her sister, and their children, and their animals, and the hung wasps, lancing mosquitoes, numbed flies, and browsing rats: All, spreaded in high quietude on the hill." Perhaps his best comment on animals and their ties to these people and this place is his observation of the Gudgers' dog Rowdy, who, Agee deliciously notes, "though he is most strictly suggestible in his resemblance to Andre Gide, is nevertheless as intensely of his nation, region, and class as Gudger himself."[9] That combination of "nation, region, and class," moreover, spells out Agee's belief that place consciousness is central to understanding these tenant farmers as part of a particular way of life.

Even though Agee sometimes sees lyricism in the southern countryside, he also has no illusions about it, identifying the climate as a dark force that debilitates the tenant southerners and others in the region. Near the end of the book, when Agee has gone to Birmingham after his time with the tenant families, he is overwhelmed with the heat on a summer Sunday. As he goes out into the street, he notes, "The sweat sprang out and ran on me," and he is overcome by the terror of "a summer Sunday . . . in a southern small town." The torpor was palpable, and he broods upon his awareness "that for miles and hundreds of hundreds of miles all around [him] in any direction [he] cared to think, not one human being or animal in five hundred was stirring." This climate-induced paralysis took its toll on the South's "victims and their civilization."[10]

Nonetheless, whether inspired to ruminations on the region's lyrical qualities or thoughts about the overbearing climate, Agee sees the consciousness of his tenant southerners anchored in the physical place. His fascination with their language reveals another key marker of regional consciousness for him. Agee repeatedly describes his tenants as speaking with a drawl, one of the most enduring ways in which southerners have been identified in the national culture. On the porch one night, for example, the sentences "spilled out in a cool flat drawl"; he overhears two of the tenant women in bed speaking in "flat, secure, drawled, reedy voices." When Mrs. Gudger uses the word "nest-es," instead of "nests," Agee contextualizes it as a common pluralization in the South, tying this poor white behavior to the broader regional identity. While the middle-class literati assume tenant southerners are being "cute" in using diminutives, Agee suggests it might be a remnant of Scottish dialect, implying their culture has preserved the practice through its provincial isolation. He also sees a revealing masculine language of southern violence – namely "that slow, keen, special, almost weeping yearning terror toward brutality, in the eyes, the speech, which is peculiar to the men of the south and is in their speech." This speech equivalent of W. J. Cash's proto-Dorian bond reflects how even human sounds express for Agee the sensuous, physical South.[11]

Agee himself grew up with a southern accent, one apparently resembling his mountain-bred father. By the time he was an adult, he no longer spoke, though, with an accent that would identify him with his southern origins. "His accent," observed Evans, "was more or less unplaceable and it was somewhat variable." Evans claimed that "in Alabama it veered towards country-southern," and "he got away with this to the farm families and to himself." Years later, though, one of the family members, Elizabeth Tingle, as she was called in the book, recalled that "at the start it was a little hard for [the family] to understand [Agee and Evans], but I'll tell you, there wasn't any harm said to one, or anybody made fun of them or anything." Her statement also reveals that they were aware that Agee and Evans were the alien ones, outsiders coming into their culture. "You could understand them, but they just sounded funny," she further remembered. "I asked Mr. Jimmy, I said, 'What kind of sound does your voice got?' He said, 'That is the northern kind of talk. All of them up there's like that.'" She added that by the time Agee and Evans left, "they got to where they was talking our kind of talk." Agee's use of his reborn southern accent was a way for him to further enter their regional consciousness.[12]

Agee also identifies the regional consciousness of his tenants through their houses, beginning, again, with sensual awareness. In the Gudger house, he smelled "a certain odor [he had] never found in other such houses," and yet the more important point was that it had "the odor or odors which are classical in every thoroughly poor white southern country house, and by which such a house could be identified blind-fold in any part of the world." One of his most explicitly regional dis-cussions finds Agee comparing tenant houses to other southern houses and placing them in terms of their distinctiveness from other American houses. He writes that "almost no one in the rural and small-town south lives 'well' or 'handsomely.'" Economics is the key factor in creating a regional house norm: "the houses aren't even 'kept up' as they are, for instance, in Ohio or in New England; and by general it would be said that everyone lives in homes equivalent to the homes of those a full cate-gory worse off in the economic-social scale than in the North."[13]

In spite of these seemingly critical observations, the tenant houses, for Agee, exemplified "an extraordinary 'beauty,'" and his reflections on the aesthetics of the houses suggest a key point about the relation-ship between the tenants' culture and their regional consciousness. Their houses represent "a classicism of sorts, created of economic need, of local availability, and of local-primitive tradition: and in their purity they are the exclusive property and privilege of the people at the bottom of the world." Here he links class and regional culture: their awareness of local materials and the inheritance of "local-primitive tradition," com-bined with their lack of alternatives because of economic need, have nurtured a distinctive way of building. "To those who own and create it this 'beauty' is, however, irrelevant and undiscernible," Agee observes. "It is best discernible to those who by economic advantages of train-ing have only a shameful and thief's right to it." Mrs. Gudger certainly embodies Agee's sense that the tenants are unaware of the aesthetics of their houses. "The only direct opinion I got on the houses as such," Agee says, "was from Mrs. Gudger, and it was, with the tears coming to her eyes, 'Oh, I do *hate* this house so bad! Seems like they ain't nothing in the whole world I can do to make it pretty." Just as the tenants are unaware of the beauty of their houses, so too they seem unaware of the broader meaning of their local consciousness – embodied in awareness of local materials and the inheritance of local tradition – in relation to other times and places. Indeed, awareness of the meaning of local ways in relation to other cultures provides a different regional identity, which they have not experienced because of their provincial isolation.[14]

The local culture of these "saturated southerners" nonetheless expresses their regional consciousness, albeit one far removed from the moonlight and magnolias of plantation tradition and the public civic culture of white supremacy and the enshrinement of the Lost Cause. It is a rural tradition, one that represents layers of country life, working-class life, and local life. Agee shows these overlapping meanings in a simple piece of clothing, men's overalls, which are a feature of Alabama country life. Although a mass-produced product of national consumer culture, they also reflect a regional culture. "They are pronounced overhauls," Agee writes, pointing again to the importance of language in expressing local consciousness. They are not for everyone but instead are a class marker "so that a new suit of overalls has among its beauties those of a blueprint: and they are a map of a working man."[15]

In mediating the consciousness of Depression-era Alabama tenant farmers, Agee sees them, then, as representing a regional consciousness rooted in a particular physical environment and a peculiar culture that intermingled localistic and social class features. Agee himself makes the explicit link between this localistic class consciousness and a broader southern regional consciousness at the beginning of *Let Us Now Praise Famous Men.* Addressing the question of "why we make this book," Agee writes that it is partly for "the whole memory of the South in its six-thousands-mile parade and flowering outlay of the facades of cities, and of the eyes in the streets of towns, and of hotels, and of the trembling heat, and of the wide wild opening of the tragic land, wearing the trapped frail flowers of its garden of faces."[16] In this passage, Agee sees the tenant story as bearing on the memory of the entire South, whether in cities or towns, all trapped by "the trembling heat" and "the wide wild opening of the tragic land." His ultimate judgment on the broader South may be seen in his term "the trapped frail flowers of its garden of faces," faces on the tragic land that has produced these suffering but dignified tenant farmers.

Hank Williams, who would later become the legendary star of country music, was thirteen years old in 1936 when Agee and Evans came to Hale County, Alabama. While he was no son of the tenant system, he could have been a character from a documentary study of poor whites.

Growing up in Butler County, about one hundred miles southeast of Hale County, Williams was then one of those young "saturated Southerners" that Agee saw in the Alabama schools he visited. Hale County is in the Black Belt, one of the South's richest cotton-growing lands, but Butler County is located along the northern edge of the piney woods of south-central Alabama. Williams grew up the descendant of farmers and part of a common poor white culture that linked many whites in the South's Black Belt cotton lands and the scrub piney woods country from North Carolina to east Texas. Even when he became rich and celebrated, he retained the outlook of his raising, and his songs are a repository of the culture and consciousness of southern white country people, whether they were still tenant farmers or had moved to town and city to become industrial workers. His family also illustrated the thin dividing line between the status of "poor white" and that of small farmer. Despite popular lore, his family was not destitute, though they were never far from it. To a large degree, families like that of Hank Williams shared a distinctive version of southern culture with poor whites and small farmers throughout the South.[17]

Known as the Hillbilly Shakespeare, Williams's song lyrics offer a direct, articulate voice from his people. Agee mediated the voices of the tenant farmers he documented, trying as he did to understand their culture and consciousness, but ultimately he denied them a direct voice, allowing few of them to speak for themselves in his text. He talked much about music in *Let Us Now Praise Famous Men*, including a famous passage where he advised readers on how to listen to Beethoven's Seventh Symphony or Schubert's C-major Symphony, and yet he never even commented on how significant music was to the people he studied. We do not see them in church or singing in their homes, as most southern country families would have done, and the book omitted an Evans photograph that showed them singing. Williams's song lyrics, then, provide a necessary supplementary text to Agee's, emanating from Williams's own grassroots origins.[18]

I want to consider several Hank Williams songs in order to explore his regional southern consciousness. The first is "Countrified," which establishes without dispute his understanding of the rural culture that had produced him. Williams's father, Elonzo H. "Lon" Williams, was born in 1891 on a farm in Lowndes County, Alabama, but he worked from age twelve at logging camps in south-central Alabama. Like many southern working men, he consciously moved between farming and wage employment in his early life, trying to preserve his opportunities in a sometimes limited world. "A company gets to feel it owns a man," he once told an interviewer. "I always felt I was a free man and could go off and work somewhere else." Like rural white southerners before him, Lon Williams prized his individual freedom and devised ways to retain it even in an economically changing world. When Hank Williams was born, his father and his mother, Lillybelle, were running a country store and a three-acre strawberry farm. Young Hank came of age immersed in country ways that had taken root in the small towns in which he grew up, towns which were so close to the countryside and its people that the lines between country and courthouse square were often culturally blurred, despite frequently existing in tension.[19]

"Countrified" is a classic expression of his rural, local consciousness. He sings that he "learned to walk behind a mule" and to read "by a kerosene light." People "make fun of our ways," he says, because his people "hang gourds on fence posts to keep up with the days." He praises the southern diet of country ham and turnip greens as "somethin' fit to eat" and admits he does not "feel comfortable / 'less [he's] ridin' on a wagon seat." His people's ways include working during the week, but "when Saturday rolls around / There ain't no keepin' [them] on the farm / that's when country goes to town." Williams uses one of his recurring themes, religion, to indicate the ultimate meaning of life. If he treats "[his] neighbor right / and to [his] God [he's] true," then he is assured to "get to Heaven just as quick as you."[20]

The song makes clear that "countrified" is a loaded term. Reflecting the decline in status for rural life in the twentieth century, Williams suggests that it is sometimes used as a derogatory term. As with other marginalized minority groups, rural southern whites like Williams embrace what others use as a demeaning term and celebrate it. "Go on and call me countrified," he sings, "you sure ain't sland'rin me." "I'm proud," he says, "to be called countrified."[21]

Williams's worldview links rural life with a working-class sense of grievance. Historian George Lipsitz has concluded that "even when he

later attained wealth and fame as a performer, Hank Williams continued to look at the world from the standpoint of a worker." Lipsitz identifies the themes of loneliness, alienation, instability, and class resentment
as the most pervasive ones in Williams's work, while historian Kent Blaser sees "sadness, lonesomeness, unhappiness and . . . a strong sense of
fatalism" as the most revealing. Surely, these sentiments express Williams's human reactions coming from a relatively powerless position in
the southern – and national – social system.

"I'll Never Get Out of This World Alive" is a graphic, if humorous,
depiction of his status. The song recounts specific examples of how
badly life is going for him, much of it related to his inability to have what
he needs. His shabby shoes are "full of holes and nails / And brother,
if [he] stepped on a worn-out dime, / [he] bet a nickel [he] could tell
you'f it was heads or tails." And another example: "If it was rainin' gold
I wouldn't stand a chance / I wouldn't have a pocket in my patched up
pants." My favorite example of his hard luck involves an attorney. His
"distant uncle passed away" and left him "quite a batch." Williams continues, "I was livin' high until the fatal day / a lawyer proved I wasn't
born, I was only hatched." His anger is in fact evident from the song's
outset: "Now you're lookin' at a man that's gettin' kind of mad / I had
lots of luck but it's all been bad." Williams does have a sense of grievance but not a well-articulated sense of class consciousness that identifies
the source of his agonies, his "bad luck." His anger is tempered by his
fatalism, as seen in the title of the song and its recurring chorus: "No matter how I struggle and strive / I'll never get out of this world alive." The
point remains, however, that Williams's reading of his people's experiences combines class grievance with a countrified outlook.[22]

Hank Williams's song "I Saw the Light" reveals a different facet of
regional consciousness, exemplifying the powerful religious sentiment
that permeates his culture. Scholars such as Lipsitz and Blaser, who stress
his class consciousness, fail to grasp the centrality of religion to Williams's worldview. His first memory was as a six-year-old boy sitting on
his mother's lap in church, singing hymns while she played the organ.
She sent him to a special school to learn about shape-note singing, a form
of music reading that began in New England but took deep root in the
rural South. As Williams's biographer Colin Escott concludes, "From the

holy songs, Hank learned how to express profound sentiments in words that an unlettered farmer could understand, and he came to appreciate intuitively the spiritual component of music."[23]

"I Saw the Light" is Williams's most famous religious song, one that expresses the essence of the evangelical Protestant faith that has dominated the South since the early nineteenth century. This tradition, represented by the Baptists and Methodists, is a religion of sin and salvation, stressing the possibility of conversion and redemption, the latter expressed by the hope of heaven. The singer relates his aimless wandering and his "life filled with sin" because he "wouldn't let [his] dear Savior in." Jesus came "like a stranger in the night / Praise the Lord, I saw the light." The pronounced biblicism of this faith is stressed through his paraphrasing of biblical references, such as "then like the blind man that God gave back his sight" and "straight is the gate and narrow the way," while its moralism is seen in his announcing he has "traded the wrong for the right." The conversion he relates is sudden, and the song is an emotionally charged one, befitting the evangelical model of the drama of conversion. Although Williams never explicitly says this song is a "southern song," it speaks to his understanding of the consciousness of working class and poor southerners who for generations have lived in a faith that has permeated south Alabama and elsewhere throughout the American South, shaping their consciousness of life and death.[24]

"Pan American" is the Williams song that most overtly *does* use the terms "southern" or "South," reflecting a highly self-conscious understanding that his Alabama is part of a broader region. The train is a pervasive symbol in country music, representing the freedom of travel but also the force of industrialism – the machine in the southern garden. "Pan American" is an almost patriotic song about a particularly southern train. The singer says he has heard about fast trains, "but now [he]'ll tell you 'bout one all the southern folks have seen / She's the beauty of the southland, listen to that whistle scream / It's that Pan American on her way to New Orleans." This train is "southern" because it traverses the region: "Ohio and Kentucky, Tennessee and Alabam' / The delta state of Mississippi, she's Louisiana bound." It is a train that "southern folks have seen." The mood is "wistful nostalgia," according to scholars David Anderson and Patrick Huber, punctuated by the sound of a screaming train whistle, a sound not of the natural southern countryside but of the New South.[25]

Hank Williams's presentation of southern consciousness was rarely addressed so specifically as in this song to the idea of the "southland," as he called it. He only used the terms "southland" and "southern" seven times in all the songs he wrote, with five of the references occurring in "Pan American." By contrast, he used the term "heaven" twenty-four times – a good relative guide to his personal imaginative geography. "The Log Train," which scholars believe is likely the last song he wrote and has only recently been released, perhaps best encapsulates Williams's version of a regional consciousness of the southern working class and poor. A narrative ballad of a working man and his family, the song begins with a reference to his father, "Daddy, who ran a log train," and then establishes the regional context in which his work took place: "Way down in the southland, in ole Alabam' / We lived in a place that they called Chapman Town." This narrative structure establishes Williams's understanding of the regional layering from local community to the state to the broader South, and he gives it authenticity because it corresponds to his father's work running a log train in south Alabama, in a real town called Chapman. Williams sings this song in a somber tone, with only a spare guitar accompaniment, establishing a timeless folktale atmosphere. His story is of a man who rose "every mornin' at the break of day," who would "grab his lunch bucket and be on his way" to "run that ole log train." It was hard work, "a-sweatin' and swearin' all day long," whether in "winter or summer, sunshine or rain." Williams ends the tale saying "this story happened a long time ago" and now the "log train is silent." As with so many of his songs, Williams strikes a religious chord: "God called Dad to go / But when I get to Heaven to always remain / I'll listen for the whistle on the old log train." A song that began with a reference to the southland thus winds up in heaven, linking primary places in the regional cultural imagination.[26]

In late 1952, shortly before Williams's death at age twenty-nine, an erstwhile reporter for, of all things, *Nation's Business* magazine interviewed the country singer. Williams said country music had become successful because of the sincerity of its singers:

He sings more sincere than most entertainers because the hillbilly was raised rougher than most entertainers. You got to know a lot about hard work. You got to have smelt a lot of mule manure before you can sing like a hillbilly. The people who has been raised something like the way the hillbilly has knows what he is singing about and appreciates it.

For what he is singing is the hopes and prayers and dreams and experiences of what some call the "common people." I call them the "best people," because they are the ones that the world is made up most of. They're really the ones who make things tick, wherever they are in this country or in any country.[27]

Williams here aggressively claims the term "hillbilly," another of those derogatory labels designed to demean the southern poor whites. The first use of the word that scholars have found was in a New York newspaper in 1900: "A Hill-Billie is a free and untrammelled white citizen of Alabama who lives in the hills, has no means to speak of, talks as he pleases, drinks whiskey when he gets it, and fires off his revolver as the fancy takes him." Williams, the Alabamian, invests the term with emotional depth and a certain dignity, based in the hard work and rough living demanded of his people. The term itself is a southern descriptor as well as class opprobrium, but he gives it a further regional anchoring by mentioning the southern beast of burden, the mule. Williams overtly renames his group not hillbillies but "the best people." Furthermore, he broadens the awareness of his regional social group to place it in a wider perspective – "the ones who make things tick, wherever they are in this country or in any country."[28]

Historian Clyde Milner has studied regional identity in the American West. "The regional identity of a people is not monolithic," he concludes; "it is expressed in a complex multiplicity of memories shared by communities and individuals." Sometimes these collective memories suggest broad regionwide experiences, but at other times, they represent a localized version of region. This latter seems to best characterize the poor white regional consciousness that James Agee understood from his mediation of Alabama sharecroppers and that Hank Williams better expressed from inside the culture of the southern working class, whether labeled "poor" or not. Kentuckian Wendell Berry insists that "the regional motive is false when the myths and abstractions of a place are valued apart from the place itself; that is regionalism as nationalism." The regionalism that Berry affirms is "*local life aware of itself.*" Instead of "the myths and stereotypes of a region," it substitutes "a particular knowledge of the life of the *place* one lives in."[29] James Agee attempted to understand that particular knowledge of a place; Hank Williams surely did know it. Together they contribute to our understanding of the regional consciousness of the South's poor but proud people.

4 Our Land, Our Country

Faulkner, the South, and the American Way of Life

In his essay "On Privacy (The American Dream: What Happened to It?)" William Faulkner complained of the invasion of his privacy by a writer who penned a story on him despite his wishes. He blamed corporate America: the magazine company, not the writer, was really at fault. This experience led Faulkner to speculate on the decline of individual liberty in a world increasingly dominated by "powerful federations and organizations and amalgamations like publishing corporations and religious sects and political parties and legislative committees" that use "such catch-phrases as 'Freedom' and 'Salvation' and 'Security' and 'Democracy'" to delude the public. The ultimate danger, for Faulkner, was mass conformity and the intimidation that went with it. He feared that someday anyone who was individual enough to want privacy "even to change his shirt or bathe in, will be cursed by one universal American voice as subversive to the American way of life and the American flag." He had a wonderful description of the voice of public conformity – "that furious blast, that force, that power rearing like a thunder-clap into the American zenith, multiple-faced yet mutually conjunctived, bellowing the words and phrases which we have long since emasculated of any significance or meaning other than as tools, implements, for the further harassment of the private individual human spirit, by their furious and immunised high priests: 'Security.' 'Subversion.' 'Anti-Communism.' 'Christianity.' 'Prosperity.' 'The American Way of Life.' 'The Flag.'"[1]

Faulkner's 1955 essay is a telling commentary on American culture of the 1950s – a time of the organizational society, the man in the gray flannel suit, McCarthyism, and pietistic patriotism. His overt use of the term "American Way of Life" is also most appropriate, as Americans used the term often in the decade to reify an ideology of the United States that would define what this country represented in the cultural front of the cold war with the Soviet Union. If the Soviets had communism, we had the American Way. Faulkner wrote as a southerner, but one at a particular moment in time. Like most southern intellectuals of his era, he is far removed from the concerns of "southern tradition" as outlined in chapter 1. By the 1950s, Faulkner had won the Nobel Prize for Literature and become an international figure. Yet he was keenly aware of the South's heritage and the fact that he was living through a time of enormous social change. He could see a turbulent future for the region's system of racial segregation.[2]

The term "American Way of Life" is a useful one in providing a structured way to investigate an aspect of Faulkner's understanding of the South and the nation. Public interest in an "American Way" rose simultaneously with the beginning of Faulkner's most creative years in the 1930s and lasted into the 1950s, when he was reflecting most explicitly in public statements about contemporary issues in American culture. I want to place Faulkner's attitude toward America in the context of the history of the term "American Way of Life" and a variant of it, the "Southern Way of Life." Faulkner, of course, inherited this latter term as well, and understanding its meanings can also help us appreciate Faulkner's efforts to relate his "little postage stamp of native soil" to broader regional and national issues. I want to position him, then, in terms of these concepts and also in relation to the term the "American Dream," which he used in two key essays in the 1950s. This chapter is a study of Faulkner the intellectual and his views at a particular moment in time; his use of the ideological term "way of life" evokes national and regional traditions in particular and revealing terms.

Mitford M. Mathews, in the *Dictionary of Americanisms on Historical Principles* (1951), identified the earliest use of the term "American Way" in 1885, when a magazine writer observed: "To use an expression made popular, we believe, by General Hawley some years ago in regard to a very different question, dynamiting is 'not the American way!'" It is good to know that blowing up things was not seen as peculiarly American in 1885, but Mathews's other references suggest that the term did not come into popular use until the 1930s and 1940s, when it appeared in at least four titles. It served as the title, for example, of a Kaufman and Hart theatrical play about an immigrant family, and the play ended with a patriotic flourish. The phrase "American Dream," which Faulkner used in the subtitle of his aforementioned 1955 essay, also came into widespread use during the Depression. The American Way and the American Dream, it would seem, suggested something during this period in the nation's history about the collective nature of the people of the United States, something abiding in their culture.[3]

These terms surely grew out of a related term, "Americanism," which was in vogue in the early twentieth century. The new order that emerged from modernization in the Progressive Era and the pressures toward conformity and idealism during World War I was sacrilized by the ideology of Americanism, which, according to historian Warren Susman, "replaced the older Protestant ethic as an ideological foundation of corporate capitalism." In one sense, Americanism of the early twentieth century stood for industrialism – it might even be called *Fordimus*, to honor Henry Ford, the saint of mass production. Rationality, order, science, respect for productivity, efficiency, discipline, work, planning, organization, and bureaucracy – these values of Americanism represented the modern way that the United States embodied by the 1920s. But Americanism was more than that. It also represented an embrace of mass culture, another form of modernity in this period. The manipulation of public opinion through advertising, together with the measuring of public opinion through polling, brought attention to the outlook of the masses more than ever before, at a time when consumer culture was emerging as a new stage of capitalism; technological developments such as the photograph, the radio, and the motion picture all created the potential to influence and shape a conformist society in unprecedented ways. Americanism was an idealistic statement of the American version of modernity, expressed with a moralistic tone that traced back to the Puritans.[4]

By the Great Depression, then, the ideal of Americanism – meaning values of the industrial order, mass culture, consumer capitalism, and moralistic idealism – was well established. As Susman has noted, the 1930s saw an "effort to find, characterize, and adapt to an American way of life as distinguished from the material achievements (and the failures) of an American industrial civilization." The economic catastrophe of the decade prompted a stress on cultural homogeneity among middle-class Americans. "Amid the psychic ravages of the Great Depression," writes historian Jackson Lears, "widespread longings for a secure sense of identity led to a quest for a sense of belonging in some comforting collective whole," and belief in the American Way fulfilled this aspiration. In the 1930s, Americans were less inclined than in the Progressive Era to identify their way simply with industrialism. Instead, democracy emerged as the central concept. At a 1939 forum entitled "Can We Depend Upon Youth to Follow the American Way," for example, moderator George V. Denny Jr. commented on the term: "I take it that by that phrase we mean the democratic way – the idea of 'giving everybody a chance to share in making the rules.'" During the Depression, Americans rediscovered a country rooted in democracy and in the nation's history, symbolized by filiopietistic biographies such as Carl Sandberg's *Lincoln* and Douglas Southall Freeman's *Lee*; the New Deal's cultural programs that documented the lives of the poor and brought American culture to communities of all sorts; and the enormous popularity of historical sagas of the past, such as Margaret Mitchell's novel *Gone with the Wind* (1936) and the 1939 film based on her book. The key term in describing the American Way in the 1930s, democracy, often implied a call to social action, as the nation rallied to fight the chaos of economic disaster but also reasserted the need to reform the country's democracy in a world where Americans faced competition with fascists, socialists, and communists.[5]

World War II reinforced this idea of an American Way, a peculiarly American national culture that all could affirm. In this new time of challenge and trial for American society, the American Way validated a belief in the homogeneity of the national population and in the social ideals of conformity and consensus. Commentators on the American Way emphasized cultural issues, such as lifestyles, patterns of belief and behavior, and the distinctive values and attitudes that represented the traits of a special people. The cold war further reinforced the belief in a unitary American culture that could serve as a counterweight to communism. The era's ideologists adapted the traditional belief system associated with middle-class Americans – including a commitment to individualism, democratic rights, and private enterprise – while faith emerged as an even more central concept than before. Since materialism was the distinctive philosophical component of the Soviet enemy, Americans elevated respect for religion to a new authoritative position, even in a seemingly secularized society. But, in 1950s America, religion itself was soon a part of the capitalist economy, through the commodification of religious practice. In 1954, the Ideal Toy Company marketed a doll with flexible knees that could be made to "kneel in a praying position," the company's response, it said, to "the resurgence of religious feeling and practice in America today."[6]

Frances FitzGerald's study of American school textbooks of this era found that "democracy," the central term of the American Way construction that had developed in the 1930s, had become simply a synonym by the 1950s for the status quo, in opposition to fascism and communism, rather than a call for social justice, as commentators in the 1930s used the term. The American Way appeared now as fixed and static, so entrenched, as historian Stephen Whitfield notes, that "it could not have been changed with a lug wrench."[7]

A leading student, and advocate, of the American Way of Life in the 1950s was religious sociologist Will Herberg. He wrote of it in 1955:

> The American Way of Life is, at bottom a spiritual structure, a structure of ideas and ideals, of aspirations and values, of beliefs and standards; it synthesizes all that commends itself to the American as the right, the good, and the true in actual life. It embraces such seemingly incongruous elements as sanitary plumbing and freedom of opportunity, Coca-Cola and an intense faith in education – all felt as moral questions relating to the proper way of life. The very expression "way of life" points to its religious essence, for one's ultimate, over-all way of life is one's religion.[8]

Herberg argued for a civil religion that grew out of a shared folk culture and projected an idealism that provided unity amidst the conflicts of American life. His American Way was especially significant in reconciling religion and democracy. As he noted, the American Way, with its stress on a generalized acceptance of religious faith, rather than validating any one particular religious tradition, had enabled Catholics and Jews, as well as Protestants, to be accepted in American culture.

One more meaning of the term "way of life" was relevant in Faulkner's cultural background. Southerners of his generation appreciated the ideological meanings of the American Way; in the decades from 1930 to 1960, the South was surely moving closer to embracing its tenets. The challenges and turbulence of the Depression, World War II, and the cold war did work to nurture a sense of American unity that affected the South as well as other places in the nation, and economic development and changes in transportation and communication surely contributed to the Americanization of Dixie. But the South had its own sense of regional identity, created by the cultural elite in the early nineteenth century during the sectional crisis and perpetuated for generations thereafter. Southerners and Americans in general used the term "southern civilization" in that era to represent the South with images of a hierarchical, paternalistic, racially conscious society, a familiar mythic place of cavaliers and their ladies.[9]

Although the idea of a regionally distinctive southern life goes back into the nineteenth century, writers did not generally use the term "Southern Way of Life" until *I'll Take My Stand* (1930), or at least that is the earliest usage I have found after sustained searching. In the introductory "Statement of Principles," the Twelve Agrarians noted that all the essays in their symposium tended "to support a Southern way of life against what may be called the American or prevailing way," and they insisted "that the best terms in which to represent the distinction are contained in the phrase, Agrarian *versus* Industrial." I have found over a dozen uses of the term "way of life" in the book, reflecting its pervasiveness in their discourse, which saw a distinction between industrial civilization and agrarian culture. Genuine humanism, they insisted, "was deeply founded in the way of life itself – in its tables, chairs, portraits, festivals, laws, marriage customs." The unreconstructed southerner, according to John Crowe Ransom, was the only American with a real sense of the past, persisting, he wrote, "in his regard for a certain terrain, a certain history, and a certain inherited way of living."[10] The Agrarians were passionate in dismissing the mass culture and industrialism of the American Way, especially for its effect on art. Donald Davidson had much fun in sketching the evil scene: "The industrialists in art . . . will naturally make their appeal to the lowest common denominator. They know the technique of mass-production, which, if applied to the arts, must invariably sacrifice quality to quantity." Thus, "the shop-girl does not recite Shakespeare before breakfast." Rather, "the shop-girl reads the comic strip with her bowl of patent cereal and puts on a jazz record while she rouges her lips. She reads the confession magazines and goes to the movies." Issues of humanism and the arts were driving forces in the Agrarians' manifesto, which posited a Southern Way as nurturing those qualities of civilization far better than the American Way.[11]

If the Vanderbilt Twelve created an enduring argument for agrarianism as the Southern Way, the 1950s saw a furious defense of racial segregation as the Southern Way. W. J. Cash's classic *The Mind of the South* (1941) had assessed the centrality of segregation to the southern life he had grown up with. The South, he wrote, lived "under the sway of a single plexus of ideas of which the center was an ever growing concern with white superiority and an ever growing will to mastery of the Negro. And of which the circumference was a scarcely less intense and a scarcely less conscious concern with the maintenance of all that was felt to be southern, a scarcely less militant will to yield nothing of its essential identity." By the 1950s and 1960s, the term "Southern Way of Life" was virtually synonymous for most Americans with racial segregation, an identification reinforced in white public opinion by black challenges to Jim Crow. An August 1964 editorial in the *Meridian (Miss.) Star*, for example, vowed to fight integration, to "keep up the sacred obligation to . . . fight for our precious Southern way of life." The term "sacred obligation" reflected that this was a regional civil religion equivalent to Herberg's American civil religion of the postwar years.[12]

After winning the Nobel Prize, William Faulkner began to speak out more openly than before on public issues, and many of his comments reveal his awareness of the tensions between the constructed cultural configurations called the "American Way of Life" and the "Southern Way of Life." As we have seen, the American Way evoked industrialism, nationalism, civil religion, mass culture, consumerism, and materialism yet also paradoxically idealism, and above all, democracy; the Southern Way, by contrast, had acquired meanings of agrarianism and racial segregation. How did Faulkner construct a public ideology related to these issues in the 1950s? What was the Faulkner Way?

Faulkner would have thunderously dismissed, of course, the very idea of a Faulkner Way, or any other "Way" in capital letters – namely, a unitary cultural idea that supposedly represented a group identity. Faulkner lampooned, ridiculed, and otherwise demolished terms that he believed had become shibboleths associated with troubling features of the human psyche en masse. "In fact," he wrote, "we must break ourselves of thinking in the terms foisted on us by the split-offs of that old dark spirit's ambition and ruthlessness: the empty clanging terms of 'nation,' and 'fatherland' or 'race' or 'color' or 'creed.'" As I noted at the beginning of this paper, Faulkner indicted the "furious and immunized high priests" of America, the theocratic celebrants of the civil religion, for "bellowing the words and phrases" which had been emptied of meaning: "'Security.' 'Subversion.' 'Anti-Communism.' 'Christianity.' 'Prosperity.' 'The American Way.' 'The Flag.'" One could hardly imagine a more incisive, rigorous, thorough critique of the American Way of Life in the 1950s than in that brief litany. The terms show Faulkner's dismissal of the nation's mindless anticommunism, soulless materialism, superficial religion, and bogus patriotism, and they suggest Faulkner would not have been a likely sunny spokesman for the well-scrubbed and cheerful *Father Knows Best* America of that decade.[13]

If Faulkner derided the idea of an American Way, he did claim the related concept of the American Dream, as seen in his usage of that term as the subtitle for two essays in the mid-1950s, which were part of an uncompleted series he had planned. He defines the term for us: "This was the American Dream: a sanctuary on the earth for individual man." The term "American Dream" did have a specific meaning to Faulkner that he could embrace, that of individual liberty. Faulkner put the American Dream in historical perspective, seeing it emerging as "a condition in which the individual human being could be free not only of the old established closed-corporation hierarchies of arbitrary power which had oppressed him as a mass, but free of that mass into which the hierarchies of church and state had compressed and held him individually thralled and individually impotent." He thus contrasts American liberty with Old World hierarchies of power from above, but he also emphasizes that American liberty enables individuals to escape entrapment as part of an anonymous mass, a condition to which hierarchies of power reduced human beings. He imagines "the individual men and women who said as with one simultaneous voice: 'We will establish a new land where man can assume that every individual man – not the mass of men but individual men – has inalienable right to individual dignity and freedom within a fabric of individual courage and honorable work and mutual responsibility.'" In Faulkner's ideological imagination, the American Dream of individual liberty is inalienable and offers dignity and freedom as part of a system that in turn demands from the individual courage, work, and responsibility.[14]

But Faulkner strikes a pessimistic tone and says in the mid-1950s that the American Dream has been lost – "it is gone now. We dozed, slept, and it abandoned us." He sets up, in effect, a dichotomy between the American Dream of individual liberty and a collective American Way of Life, even a democratic one, which he sees based in fear: "Because now what we hear is a cacophony of terror and conciliation and compromise babbling only the mouthsounds; the loud and empty words which we have emasculated of all meaning whatever – freedom, democracy, patriotism – with which, awakened at last, we try in desperation to hide from ourselves that loss."[15]

In discussions of the term by other observers from the 1930s to the 1950s, individual liberty was surely seen as a part of the American Way, albeit one aspect of a broader assemblage. Yet Faulkner argued that tendencies in American life associated with an American Way had eroded individual liberty. He identified two interactive forces in American life of the 1950s that had claimed and distorted the idea of America – "the giants of industry and commerce," on the one hand, and, on the other, "the manipulators for profit or power of the mass emotions called government, who carry the tremendous load of geopolitical solvency, the two of which conjoined are America." Like Eisenhower's warning about the military-industrial complex a few years later, Faulkner's critique of the American Way zeroed in on its underlying danger to the basis of political authority. Despite the centrality of democracy to it, the American Way represented to Faulkner a dramatic undermining of the democratic principles upon which the nation was founded. Instead of meaningful individual self-determination, Americans had to live with "what might be called almost a universal will to regimentation, a universal will to obliterate the humanity from man even to the extent of relieving him not only of moral responsibility but even of physical pain and mortality by effacing him individually into any, it does not matter which as long as he has vanished into one of them, nationally-recognized economic group by profession or trade or occupation or income-tax bracket or, if nothing else offers, finance-company list." These identities offered only "the anonymity of a group where he will have surrendered his individual soul for a number."[16]

While these giant institutions exercised their power, the mass of Americans were bought off with the commodities of consumerism. Gavin Stevens insists in *Intruder in the Dust* that "we in America have debased" the idea of the divinity of the individual soul "into a national religion of the entrails in which man owes no duty to his soul because he has been absolved of soul to owe duty to and instead is static heir at birth to an inevictible quit-claim on a wife a car a radio and an old-age pension." As Faulkner noted in his "On Privacy" essay, a "sickness" in American culture went "back to that moment in our history when we decided that the old simple moral verities . . . were obsolete and to be discarded," replaced by meaningless group identities and actions that represented the impulses of an eroding mass culture, consumer capitalism, and centralized government.[17]

Faulkner's critique of American corporate industrialism, materialism, and mass culture could have come from the pages of *I'll Take My Stand*, expressing as it did a southern conservative view of modernity. He is not asserting, though, an agrarian solution; little of agrarianism is found in Faulkner's public rhetoric of the 1950s. In *Intruder in the Dust* he does have Gavin Stevens admiringly lift up the simplicity of the black man's aspirations: "Not an automobile nor flashy clothes nor his picture in the paper but a little of music (his own), a hearth, not his child but any child, a God a heaven which a man may avail himself a little of at any time without having to wait to die, a little earth for his own sweat to fall on among his own green shoots and plants." This passage does not really reflect Faulkner's public voice of the 1950s, though, and we do not want to enter into the well-worn debate of whether Stevens speaks for Faulkner or not. Traditional agrarian culture in the South, in any event, even by the early 1950s was a vanishing form, and Faulkner did not seem inclined to use it as a metaphor to critique the dominant American Way.[18]

He, nonetheless, does present a meditation on the Southern Way of Life in his 1950s public rhetoric. Writing after the Brown decision of 1954, Faulkner saw the coming conflict between the Southern Way that whites were embracing in defending Jim Crow and the American Way as symbolized by the national government's new resolve to end it; or as he put it, "The impasse of the two apparently irreconcilable facts which we are faced with in the South: the one being the decrees of our national government that there be absolute equality in education among all citizens, the other being the white people in the South who say that white and Negro pupils shall never sit in the same classroom." This formula left out the group who would in fact bring about the change — namely, African Americans who worked to put an end to Jim Crow through their community organizing and direct action in the South, but few whites, even moderates and liberals, saw that on the horizon in the mid-1950s.[19]

Faulkner tried to carve out a position as a moderate. In a letter to the *Memphis Commercial Appeal*, he criticized the dual school system of the South, necessitated by the regional commitment to Jim Crow, earning in the process irate letters and phone calls in the middle of the night from other white southerners who were, as he said, grasping "at such straws for weapons as contumely and threat and insult to change the views or anyway the voice which dares to suggest that betterment of the Negro's condition does not necessarily presage the doom of the white race." Yet Faulkner also, of course, criticized black leaders and northern liberals for going too fast on integration. He predicted in 1956 that blacks would indeed gain their civil rights, but he urged civil rights leaders to allow southern whites to adjust to changes to prevent bloodshed against their people. He was convinced, like many other white moderates and liberals, that a racial war would result if blacks continued pressing for their rights, although white moderates, in their gradualism, never fixed a date when civil rights would indeed be delivered with black agitation in abeyance. Faulkner believed that the southern white identity in the 1950s was "an emotional condition of such fierce unanimity as to scorn the fact that it is a minority within the country and which will go to any length and against any odds at this moment to justify and, if necessary, to defend that condition and its right to it."[20]

The economics of the Southern Way, Faulkner insisted, was the underlying basis of the South's racial obsessions. The southern white fear was "not of the Negro as an individual Negro nor even as a race, but as an economic class or stratum or factor, since what the Negro threatens is not the Southern white man's social system but the Southern white man's economic system," which Faulkner pointed out was "established on an obsolescence – the artificial inequality of man." He acknowledged the "southern white man's shame" of denying blacks economic opportunity and the "double shame" of fearing that social equality would lead to economic advance. The "bugaboo of miscegenation" was a "triple shame" because whites raised the issue only to obfuscate the underlying economic basis of the Southern Way of Life.[21]

Faulkner also sketched, though, a vision of the Southern Way beyond economics and racism, a bicultural dream that later became common among liberal southern whites. He was no segregationist, yet he could affirm southern culture as a lived experience inherited from the past, a shared experience of the region's blacks and whites. "In fact, there are people in the South, Southerners born," he wrote, and would have included himself in this group, "who . . . Love our land – not love white people specifically nor love Negroes specifically, but our land, our country: our climate and geography, the qualities in our people, white and Negro too, for honesty and fairness, the splendors in our traditions, the glories in our past." Those people, including himself, he wrote, loved the South enough to work, in effect, to save the South by changing it, even if they earn along the way "the contempt of Northern radicals who believe we dont do enough" and the "contumely and threats of our own Southern reactionaries who are convinced that anything we do is already too much."[22] His phrases "our land, our country" reveal his ownership of the South as a part of America.

Along with Faulkner, other white southerners claimed a biracial southern identity, explored its burdens, and saw significance in it related to the South's — and the nation's — tragic saga of race relations. South Carolina farmer, Presbyterian layman, and social activist James McBride Dabbs was a liberal southerner who worked more actively than Faulkner for social change, but he and Faulkner represented a similar effort to reconcile, in effect, an American Way and a Southern Way in the 1950s and 1960s. "They say we are defending our way of life," Dabbs wrote in 1958. "What is our way of life? They say segregation," but he would have none of it. He insisted there was "the Southern way of life which men have longed for when absent and fought for when challenged." It was not the separation of segregation, and, he added, "it's more than hot biscuits" — although I have a feeling Dabbs loved hot biscuits, too. Like the Vanderbilt Agrarians and Faulkner, Dabbs rejected industrialism as a source of values and urged southerners not to accept "the straight American religion" and forget their past: "It seems to me sheer waste to throw away so much only to gain — more shares in General Motors!" The South should look at its own people and their experiences to understand the meaning of any Southern Way. The "entity called the South was hammered out by black man and white man working together." The land was the setting for building a biracial community, which was at the heart of any talk of a Southern Way. "Through the processes of history and the grace of God we have been made one people," he wrote, adding that now "there is no telling what great age might develop in the South." The South would show the way to the rest of the world.[23]

Dabbs and Faulkner thus saw the southern story of race relations as abiding in its human significance, having something to offer the nation and, indeed, the world. One of the most revealing aspects of Faulkner's thoughts concerning the American Way of Life, the Southern Way, and the American Dream was his consideration of the international context, as well as a regional one, in exploring the meaning of America in the 1950s. The resonance of these related ideas abroad is the final aspect of decoding Faulkner's attitude toward an American Way. Faulkner traveled overseas after winning the Nobel Prize, and his observations reflected his understanding of America. He went to Japan, the Middle East, North Africa, and Europe. Communism was on his mind. Given the economic blight he often saw, he was surprised that the people of many of the nations he visited were not more inclined toward communism. "Then suddenly I said to myself with a kind of amazement: It's because of America. These people still believe in the American dream," Faulkner concluded. They followed the American lead, "not because of our material power: Russia has that: but because of the idea of individual human freedom and liberty and equality on which our nation was founded, which our founding fathers postulated the word 'America' to mean." Faulkner's explicit definition of the American Dream identified "individual liberty" as the goal, but in considering the international ramifications in his own age, he broadens the American Dream to include equality as well as liberty. He noted, writing in 1956, that the countries he had visited were still free of communism because of "that belief in individual liberty and equality and freedom which is the one idea powerful enough to stalemate the idea of communism."[24]

Faulkner used his peculiar position as an internationally celebrated American writer from the South to see the connection in the 1950s between his region, nation, and world. And at the center of this connection were race relations. The fundamental issue was liberty. "And if we who are still free want to continue so," Faulkner wrote, "all of us who are still free had better confederate and confederate fast with all others who still have a choice to be free – confederate not as black people nor white people nor blue or pink or green people, but as people who still are free, with all other people who are still free: confederate together and stick together too, if we want a world or even a part of a world in which individual man can be free, to continue to endure." Faulkner understood the force of history, which in the post–World War II era meant the rise of nonwhite peoples expelling imperialists from their colonial empires; into this vacuum of departing imperialists communism rushed "that other and inimical power which people who believe in freedom are at war with," as Faulkner put it. Communism was an ideology that offered to nonwhite peoples not freedom "because there is no such thing as freedom," Faulkner explained, "your white overlords whom you have just thrown out have already proved that to you. But we offer you equality, at least equality in slavedom; if you are to be slaves, at least you can be slaves to your own color and race and religion."[25]

If the American Dream was to be believed abroad, it must be practiced at home, in his country, in his South. Faulkner fell back on racist imagery in lauding the progress of African Americans under the idea of America, writing of "the people who only three hundred years ago were eating the carrion in the tropical jungles," but he did laud "the Phi Beta Kappas and the Doctor Bunches and the Carvers and the Booker Washingtons and the poets and musicians." He praised their ability to embody what was an important part of Faulkner's own ideology, "that to gain equality, one must deserve it, and to deserve equality, one must understand what it is: that there is no such thing as equality *per se*, but only equality *to*: equal right and opportunity to make the best one can of one's life within one's capacity and capability, without fear of injustice or oppression or violence." In international competition between communism and freedom, Faulkner was confident that if America lived up to its ideals with its own nonwhite people, then we could educate the world's nonwhite peoples about the American Dream. "We don't need to sell the Negro on America and freedom," Faulkner wrote, "because he is already sold." Faulkner understood the centrality to American liberty of what was happening to African Americans. Consideration of African Americans thus led him to broaden his understanding of the American Dream from liberty to include equality as well. This shift in thinking was part of his broader reflection on the relationship between Western culture and the third world, on the necessity of free people practicing freedom in their own countries if they wanted to extend its sway.[26]

Inadvertently, then, Faulkner became a spokesman of sorts for the American Way of Life. His travels overseas for the U.S. government, his work with the People-to-People program, his reflections on incorporating nonwhite peoples into free society, his anticommunist stance – all these factors made him a figure of the American Way as the *Saturday Evening Post* so often wrote about it, an ironic development given his impassioned strictures against so many of its manifestations. Remember his litany of shibboleths: Security. Subversion. Anti-Communism. Christianity. Prosperity. The Flag. To the degree that Faulkner perceived the American Way of Life as an expression of McCarthyesque fear, mindless anticommunist hysteria, consumer materialism, and pious Christian patriotism, he could dismiss it. He saw the American Dream as a category of the American Way, and he could endorse its ideals of liberty and equality, even if he was pessimistic about their survival in American culture.

Faulkner consistently wrote against the regimentation he identified as a characteristic feature of 1950s America, which the term "American Way" evoked for him, with its overtones of a strangling orthodoxy. His recurrent reference to being not of "the mass of men but individual men" suggests the crucial point. The term "American Way of Life" implied to Faulkner the collective orthodoxy of a fearful 1950s American culture. It reflected democracy but a democracy that combined the worst instincts of the right-wing conspiratorial populist rage of a Senator Joseph McCarthy and the soulless materialism of a Flem Snopes. That was a democracy he did not care for. But Faulkner discovered in his world travels that American democracy still represented the ideals of individual freedom and equality. Reform of the Southern Way to extend these principles to African Americans would be essential for the promise of America to continue to resonate. Faulkner thus linked his region and nation with the world in defining an ideology of 1950s America.

5 The Myth of the Biracial South

Charles L. Black, a born-and-bred white southerner, was teaching at the Yale Law School in 1957 when he wrote an article for *The New Republic* in which he outlined the legal and moral appeals that might be made to sympathetic whites to promote desegregation of the South. At the end of the essay, he revealed a dream he had long had, formed from pondering "[his] relations with the many Negroes of Southern origin that [he had] known, both in the North and at home." He continued: "Again and again how often we laugh at the same things, how often we pronounce the same words the same way to the amusement of our hearers, judge character in the same frame of reference, mist up at the same kinds of music. I have exchanged 'good evening' with a Negro stranger on a New Haven street, and then realized (from the way he said the words) that he and I derived this universal small-town custom from the same culture." Despite such cultural affinities, whites and blacks in the South, though, had failed to acknowledge them, these common traits that reflected a kinship. "My dream is simply that sight will one day clear and that each of the participants will recognize the other," Black hoped. If this happened, "if the two [races] could join and look toward the future together – something would have happened uniquely beautiful in history. The South, which has always felt itself reserved for a high destiny, would have found it, and would come to flower at last."[1]

Black's words in 1957, when the black freedom movement was well underway, expressed a mythic view of southern culture that would become in the 1970s a major ideological underpinning of the contemporary American South. The myth of the biracial South embodies the idea that the region has the potential to achieve a truly integrated society characterized by harmonious race relations with meaning for American culture and beyond. Like a good evangelist, Leslie W. Dunbar, executive director of the Southern Regional Council, expressed this faith even more directly in 1961, testifying to his belief "that the South will, out of its travail and sadness and requited passion, give the world its first grand example of two races of men living together in equality and with mutual respect."[2] This chapter examines the historical origins of this myth of the biracial South, explores its full emergence in the 1970s, suggests its meanings for various southerners, and briefly assesses its development since the 1970s.

The South, of course, has long been the focus for mythmaking, both by southerners themselves and by outsiders. Since George Tindall's seminal article "Mythology: A New Frontier in Southern History" (1964), scholars collectively have developed a framework for interpreting southern history in terms of myth. The mythic perspective on southern history would begin with the idea of a colonial Eden, then portray the romantic Old South and the crusading Lost Cause followed by the materialistic New South, and proceed into the twentieth century, replete with repeated expressions of a savage South, and yet the myth would culminate seemingly in the idea of the Sunbelt, which mysteriously fused the South with the heart of darkness, Southern California, in a prosperous world anchored by Disneyland and Disney World. Racial myths have been prominent in this frame of mind, especially the myth of white supremacy, which became institutionally embodied in the Jim Crow laws from the 1890s to the 1960s. The South's distinctiveness in such myths was within a national context. Winthrop Jordan properly points out that "racial attitudes in the South have been peculiar not for their existence or their content but for their virulence, saliency, pervasiveness, and the predisposition of white people to overt action and of black people to fear, accommodation, resistance, and retaliation."[3]

One of the most enduring southern myths has been that of the savage South, the opposite of the myth of the biracial South. It traces back to the colonial era and flowered in full expression in the antebellum era of North-South conflict. The South appeared in the national culture as backward, sexually licentious, irreligious, alcohol drenched, and morally suspect. In an ironic reversal, the Menckenesque version of the savage South in the 1920s saw the region as benighted for the exact opposite reasons – it now seemed the prisoner of a Puritan worldview that made it too religious, too sexually inhibited, and too morally uptight. In either event, though, race was central to the image of the savage South – brutal public lynchings of African Americans, the sinister Ku Klux Klan, legal outrages like the Scottsboro case, and the violent white resistance to desegregation in the 1960s at places like Birmingham, Oxford, Neshoba County, and Selma. All of these actual events take their place in a broader ideological view of the South as irredeemably evil. Fred Hobson, the historian of the myth of the savage South, has traced its decline, noting that in the 1960s "the white South was taking its last racial stand." Since then, the nation's and the region's writers have continued to portray savagery in southern places, but it "appears, if not contrived, at least removed from the social base which gives rise to the fiction."[4]

Hobson speculated that "a powerful positive myth" of the racial interaction of blacks and whites, an example to the world of racial harmony, would succeed the myth of the savage South. In 1989, George Tindall, writing several years after Hobson, pointed out that scholars had not studied "that newer version of the old religious myths that reserved the South for a high destiny – the Integrated South, purged by suffering and prepared to redeem the nation from bias and injustice."[5] For Tindall and Hobson, the issue is not whether the South actually is savage or integrated; they are interested in the cultural constructions that project these representations. The myth of the biracial South is thus one of the most recent representations of the South. What were the origins of this myth of the biracial South? When did it appear as an identifiable construct? How widespread has it become since the 1960s?

If the myth of the biracial South expressed the belief that the South had the nation's most harmonious race relations, then one might trace its origins back to the region's traditionally conservative ideology. The paternalism of the slave system embodied the ways a social structure of owner and slave functioned in a biracial context – with owner wielding power but the slave influencing the working relationship and the broader culture as well. The biracial myth could trace back to the conservative idea of the South as having a hierarchical social structure, with society working smoothly when everyone understood and accepted his or her place. Although the racial radicals, whose frenzied rhetoric and wild violence periodically came to the fore, typically questioned blacks having a place at all in southern society, conservatives understood the region's economic need for African Americans, if nothing else. Besides, the popular traditionalist metaphor of southern society as a family writ large would suggest an ideological awareness of the need to keep a place at the supper table for blacks, even if their table was separate and in the kitchen.[6]

A variant of this outlook was the New South creed of the 1880s, which promoted the ideal of racial harmony as essential to the good business climate necessary to lure northern investment south after the Civil War. This view has surely remained an enduring justification for seeing southern society as embodying harmonious race relations. Proponents of the New South praised the end of slavery but looked back fondly on the prewar plantation and its interracial relationships. As Henry W. Grady wrote, "The Northern man, dealing with casual servants, can hardly comprehend the friendliness that existed between the master and slave." Thomas Nelson Page sketched more fully this sentimental view of harmonious race relations in a biracial society. In his essay "Social Life in Old Virginia before the War," he portrayed an unpretentious plantation life, with honorable planters, joyous children, happy darkies, and devoted ladies. Grady went further as a booster of his society, insisting that the friendly relations between the races had "survived the war, and strife, and political campaigns." He concluded, "it is the glory of our past in the South. It is the answer to abuse and slander. It is the hope of our future." White southerners in the twentieth century became a cliché in the national culture, claiming that the South's race relations were better than elsewhere, that racial harmony had been achieved, as long as outside agitators remained outside.[7]

The deeper source of the myth of the biracial South that emerged in the 1970s, though, was not in the conservative ideology but in the

South's liberal reform ethos. Antecedents could be found in the nine-teenth century among advocates of biracial coalitions in Reconstruc-tion and in the era of agrarian reform in the 1890s. Unfortunately, these attempts at interracial cooperation had been limited by racial assump-tions of white reformers, economic rivalries, and the chicanery of their opponents. In the twentieth century, organizations emerged that were more direct influences on the biracial ideology that flowered after the 1960s. Women's groups like the Association of Southern Women for the Prevention of Lynching and the YWCA worked toward modera-tion on racial issues in the early twentieth century, fostering contacts between the races and promoting interracial ideals. More intentionally, organizers formed the Commission on Interracial Cooperation in 1919 and the Southern Conference for Human Welfare in 1938, both dealing with southern regional problems through an interracial lens. The South-ern Regional Council (SRC) succeeded the Commission on Interracial Cooperation in 1944 and thereafter served as the most effective agency for exchange of information and advocacy of interracial goals. While the SRC in its early years did not call for the overthrow of Jim Crow segre-gation but worked for African American betterment within the separate-but-equal system, the organization was surely in the forefront of biracial efforts in the middle decades of the twentieth century. Small numbers of southerners, meanwhile, lived out their interracial ideals in places like Clarence Jordan's Christian community, Koinonia, in south Georgia, and the Providence Cooperative Farm in Tchula, Mississippi.[8]

Liberal reformers drew from democratic ideals in justifying racial moderation and eventually the end of Jim Crow, but they also relied on the South's religious culture – its evangelical character and aspirations toward salvation in a sinful world. This source was especially significant for the minority of southern liberals in the period from 1930 to 1950 who championed not just racial moderation but the end of Jim Crow segrega-tion altogether. Such reformers came to believe that the caste system vio-lated basic Christian ideals of brotherhood. As historian Morton Sosna has observed, "The importance of evangelicalism to Southern liberal-ism can hardly be overemphasized." Howard Kester, for example, who was a union organizer and antilynching crusader in the 1920s and 1930s, confessed his motivation was simply Christian love. "The kind of healing the region and the nation needed wouldn't come through politics or economic organization," he said; "there had to be an ethical orientation, a moral confrontation based on the teachings of Jesus." Another liberal reformer, Will Alexander, confessed in 1951, "I have never lost faith by what I seemed to glimpse in the New Testament. I have been influenced more by this than by anything I have ever known." Atlanta newspaper editor Ralph McGill revealed in his autobiography that his "Calvinist conscience was stirred by some of the race prejudice [he] saw." McGill, like other southern liberals, used the language of evangelicalism, speaking of "shame" and "guilt" in particular, to describe how his feelings were led to change on racial issues. The southern faith is one that knows of the wickedness of human nature and yet believes in the possibility of conversion and ultimate redemption. In this religious context, the southern liberals working most actively before the Brown decision for the end of Jim Crow knew of the South's sins but thought redemption possible. Racial healing could follow, resulting in the dream of racial harmony – the South then redeeming the nation.[9]

Southern blacks also advanced the idea of a redemptive South, especially the ministers of the civil rights movement. In a 1961 interview, Dr. Martin Luther King Jr. spoke of "an intimacy of life" in the South that could become "beautiful if it is transformed in race relations from a sort of lord-servant relationship to a person-to-person relationship." He argued that the nature of life in the region would "make it one of the finest sections of [the] country once . . . this problem of segregation" was solved. King noted in 1963 that "when [he finds] a white southerner who has been emancipated on the issue, the Negro can't find a better friend." While King used the words "transformed" and "emancipated," he might have substituted "converted" to catch the evangelical flavor of the personality change required in white southerners to embrace the integrated society in his age. But it was possible. Even the state of Mississippi, he said in his "I Have a Dream" speech, "a state sweltering with the heat of injustice, sweltering with the heat of oppression, will be transformed into an oasis of freedom and justice."[10] The liberal dream, then, even in the 1950s and 1960s, was one of the racially converted South, washed in the blood of the civil rights martyrs, redeeming the nation.

The nation saw the 1960s South, though, as the savage South. Southern whites surely rejected King's lyrical vision as they defended, or acquiesced to the defense of, segregation. With the end of Jim Crow legal segregation in 1964 and of voting disfranchisement of African Americans in 1965, the southern cultural context had new realities. As a public ideology, white supremacy had been vanquished. The Ku Klux Klan and the Citizens' Councils had been defeated, and rabble-rousing, old-time politicians had lost the battles and ultimately the massive resistance war they had proclaimed in the 1950s. The hearts of southern whites were not transformed overnight on racial issues simply because of the changes the federal government mandated as a result of the pressures from their fellow black southerners; white southerners would, however, have to adapt their public culture. Beginning in the early 1970s, new ideologies came to the fore as emerging justifications for southern public life and values.

The myth of the biracial South was a formative ideology in the post-segregation era. The L. Q. C. Lamar Society, which was organized in 1969, near Durham, North Carolina, was a good example of an organization that actively promoted the new mythology. Named for a Mississippi secessionist who became a post–Civil War advocate of regional reconciliation, the Lamar Society attracted a constituency of middle-class and upper middle-class professionals who advocated a vision of a still regionally distinctive South dedicated to transcending endemic problems of racial conflict, poverty, and environmental abuse. Like the Vanderbilt Agrarians four decades earlier, who had championed a conservative vision of southern traditionalism in the face of modernity, members of the Lamar Society worried about the survival of a distinctive regional culture in an industrialized modern world. Unlike the Agrarians, though, these southern intellectuals and policy makers were reformers pushing for a new racial vision in the South. As writer Willie Morris said of the South in the introduction to the society's defining symposium volume *You Can't Eat Magnolias* (1972), "Racism was the primeval obsession. No longer is this so. It will hold out in places, but it will never again shape the white Southern consciousness." For generations, Morris wrote, racism had "misdirected the South from its other elemental problems of poverty and exploitation." The changes in the 1960s he foresaw having "a profoundly liberating effect" on the region.[11]

Alabama newspaperman H. Brandt Ayers, a founder of the Lamar Society, openly dismissed the continued attachment of the South to its old Lost Cause symbols, writing of the "viral weed of mythology" that "has been allowed to grow like kudzu over the South." Ayers urged southerners to embrace a different heritage, symbolized not by the White House of the Confederacy but by reverence for "the symbols of Monticello or the Hermitage – houses built by white southerners who led the nation" and represented egalitarian ideals. Ayers saw contemporary southerners within the long perspective of southern history and within the framework of evangelical culture that saw the possibility for redemption: "Southerners, black and white, locked together in yet another uniquely Southern experience, should be addressed with the humanity that teaches wise and just men to hate the sin, but love the sinner." Ayers also saw history overcoming the separation of the regions. "North and South," he wrote, "we have now been reduced to the same historical dimension." The frustrations of the Vietnam War and the nation's recognition of racial problems extending beyond the South had "shattered the Yankees' innocent illusions that they have been ordained by God to trample out immorality and that His truth marches with them into every war."[12]

Just as the older racial myths of white supremacy were institutionally supported in a weblike structure of the Democratic Party, the Ku Klux Klan, Protestant churches, state laws, and racial etiquette that virtually all whites enforced against all people of color, so now the myth of the biracial South was reinforced by institutions like the Lamar Society and its periodical *Southern Journal*, the Institute for Southern Studies in Durham and its *Southern Exposure*, the Southern Growth Policies Board, and academic regional studies centers such as the University of Mississippi's Center for the Study of Southern Culture. Like other such institutes in the South, the Center for the Study of Southern Culture, which the university established in 1977, had a pronounced interracial theme. African American artist Romare Bearden's painting of black musicians adorned the cover of its first publication, *Southern Journal*, a glossy annual report issued in 1980. Inside, photographs of black blues singers and basketmakers were interwoven with illustrations of white quilting ladies and people enjoying a dinner on the grounds after church. The center, located in the once-benighted state of Mississippi, symbolically embraced the new recognition of biracialism by picturing Alex Haley and Eudora Welty side by side in its first annual report.[13]

Southern politics also reflected the impact of the myth of the biracial South in the early 1970s, at a time when African Americans were becoming a major force in southern politics. The most racially obsessed states, those of the Deep South, dramatically changed from supporting proseg-regation candidates in the pre-1970 era to supporting those who did not use racial rhetoric or campaign on the segregation issue. In 1976, African Americans represented between 17 and 26 percent of the electorate in the Deep South states, and by then politicians were openly courting black votes. This was not a sentimental gesture on the part of white politicians. The growing power of African American political strength led southern white politicians to increasingly acknowledge black aspirations. As Congressman Andrew Young noted in 1976: "It used to be Southern politics was just 'nigger' politics – a question of which candidate could 'outnigger' the other. Then you registered 10% to 15% in the community, and folks would start saying 'Nigra.' Later you got 35% to 40% registered, and it was amazing how quick they learned how to say 'Nee-grow.' And now that we've got 50%, 60%, 70% of the black votes registered in the South, everybody's proud to be associated with their black brothers and sisters."[14]

Progressive young governors symbolized the change in southern politics that would make political discourse a prime carrier of the new racial mythology in the early 1970s. Dale Bumpers in Arkansas, Jimmy Carter in Georgia, John West in South Carolina, Reuben Askew in Florida, William Waller in Mississippi, and Edwin Edwards in Louisiana, followed by politicians like William Winter in Mississippi and Bill Clinton in Arkansas, all promoted new interest-group politics that resulted in biracial coalitions and a new rhetoric of the South as the chosen place. They did not appeal to traditional southern defensiveness about the federal government or fears about outside agitators, nor did they throw around racial code words. They overtly repudiated traditional southern mythology, distancing themselves from the past and expressing hope and optimism for the future. George Busbee, elected governor of

Georgia in 1974 with black support, stated in his inaugural address that "the politics of race has gone with the wind," using an especially evocative term in Margaret Mitchell's home state to dismiss past racial ideology. Edwin Edwards spoke directly to blacks in his 1972 inaugural address, pledging, "The old imaginary barriers no longer exist. My election has destroyed the old myths, and a new spirit is with us."[15]

Dramatic new images came along with the rhetoric. Eugene "Bull" Connor could be seen singing "We Shall Overcome" in a black church while campaigning unsuccessfully. George Wallace crowned a black homecoming queen at the University of Alabama. The governor of Georgia, Jimmy Carter, dedicated a portrait of Martin Luther King Jr. in a prominent spot in the state capitol building. When Forrest "Fob" James was inaugurated governor of Alabama in 1979, he boldly linked two central symbols of a newly emerging rhetoric of biracialism: "I believe if Robert E. Lee and Martin Luther King Jr., were here today, their cry to us – their prayer to God – would call for 'The Politics of Unselfishness' – a people together – determined to climb the highest plateau of greatness."[16] The imagery of Lee and King praying to God together projected an explicit image of civil religion – both southern heroes blessing the region. Their photos would soon be linked in a new iconography within southern public institutions.

The revealing gestures of even segregationist politicians like Connor and Wallace to seek black support reflected the political aspects of a broader redefinition of the symbolic southern community in the 1970s. Whites had shaped the imagery and meaning of previous outcroppings of the southern instinct for mythology, and white-dominated organizations had institutionalized and promoted traditional myths. Just as blacks in the older South had been politically disfranchised, racially segregated, and economically exploited, so too had they been virtually powerless in influencing the South's public culture. They did not have a vote on the symbols the South's culture projected nor on the civic rituals its people acted out. The process underway in the 1970s represented the beginnings of a redefinition of a new southern community, one that reflected black influence. While the changed political rhetoric of a George Wallace could be attributable simply to his craven instinct for success, he was part of a broader society grappling with the need for a new ideological foundation that could buttress a sense of purpose and direction. Myths only last if they unify and can evoke feelings from a broad range of citizens, who may identify with them for differing reasons. The myth of the biracial South filled the void represented by the decline of older southern myths at a time when the racial basis of southern society had shifted dramatically.[17]

At the heart of the myth of the biracial South stood a moral earnestness that enabled southerners to make claims upon national idealism that were far removed from the region's civil rights disgraces of the 1960s. Reuben Askew stated the idea of southern moral superiority in 1972: "For many years now, the rest of the nation has been saying to the South that it is morally wrong to deprive any citizen of an equal opportunity in life because of his color. I think most of us have come to agree with that. But now the time has come for the rest of the nation to live up to its own stated principles. Only now are the other regions themselves beginning to feel the effects of the movement to eliminate segregation." He insisted that "the rest of the nation should not abandon its principles when the going gets tough." Just as the nation had "sought to bring justice to the South by mandate and court order," so now "perhaps it is time for the South to teach the same thing to other regions in a more effective way – by example."[18]

New England, the moral center of antebellum abolitionism and other reform movements, became the counterpoint of the new southern racial mythology, lending weight to the South's new moral claims in the 1970s. Violence and disorder accompanied efforts to desegregate Boston schools from 1973 to 1975, bringing national condemnation. At the same time, schools desegregated with far less turmoil in Charlotte and countless smaller southern communities. Of course, this desegregation was not voluntary but the result of federal court orders. Southern schools, nonetheless, became the nation's most desegregated schools in the 1970–71 academic year. In any event, these developments led Texas writer Larry L. King to chastise northerners for their hypocrisies: "Do you good Boston folk – who once sold slaves on Boston Common – wanna step over here in the pea patch and talk to me about Louise Day Hicks and the violence heaped on your kids while they were being bussed to school? Naw, I expect you'd rather talk about George Wallace or busing violence in South Carolina a decade ago."[19] King linked New England woes to its past sins, thus reversing the usual Yankee saint–southern sinner expectation.

Southerners were, nonetheless, not the only Americans proclaiming the myth of the biracial South. The national culture rediscovered the South during the Jimmy Carter presidential campaign in 1976, and one of the country's fascinations was with race relations in what seemed a new South indeed, compared to the national news media's last barometric reading of the region, taken in the South of massive resistance to desegregation in the 1960s. The nation no longer saw the region as the savage South but in favorable terms as a storehouse of valuable qualities seemingly threatened in the rest of the nation at that time. *Time* magazine's special edition on Carter in September 1976 was typical in its representation of the South in the post–civil rights era. "The Spirit of the South" was the lead article, portraying the South as "a place apart," "the last American arena with a special, nurtured identity, its own sometimes unfashionable regard for the soil, for family ties, for the authority of God and country." The South was a place apart, not the cloud cuckoo land of W. J. Cash but rather "a redoubt of old American tenets, enshrined for centuries by the citizenry." Indeed, the use of the term "spirit of the South" as the title of the article tied it to old ideas about the South's role in the nation.[20]

The *Time* magazine article portrayed a progressive South, a place vitalized by the coming of industry, thanks to air conditioning. "Tyrannical heat," the article surmised, "delirious summers, dog days that breed flies and sloth, squabbles and morbid introspection are gone with the vent." The writer of the piece stressed, though, the continuities between this New South and the older one – in religion, patriotism, attachment to family, and respect for the law. "Could it be that in many ways it can now teach the nation something about how to live?" the article asked, reflecting appreciation now of a superior South. Recognizing that "the idea can easily be exaggerated," it saw hope in a redemptive South because of race relations, reflecting that "the harshly segregated South showed the rest of the nation that it was possible to change despite deeply held prejudices – and to achieve at least the beginnings of racial amity." A national culture that had discovered its own racism now began looking hopefully to the South as embodying perhaps a way out. The myth of the biracial South is here anchored in broader southern virtues: "Other parts of the U.S., without consciously turning to the South, began to long for some of its values: family, community, roots."[21]

By the middle 1970s, the South had not only rejoined the nation, it was beginning to dominate it. A generation after Confederates lost their crusade against the nation – a century before Carter's election – the nation's culture enthusiastically embraced the Lost Cause, as southern writers became popular in American magazines, theatrical plays with southern heroes and heroines dominated American theater, and American popular music projected appealing romantic lyrics of the lazy, hazy South. Similarly, having lost their massive resistance movement, southern whites now found themselves influencing the national culture more profoundly than at any time since the late nineteenth century. Country music, evangelical Protestantism, films and television shows about southerners, southern literature – all were in vogue. Even in politics, the nation turned south, electing the first Deep South politician since the Civil War, Jimmy Carter, as president.[22]

If southern politicians endorsed the myth of the biracial South and the national culture became fascinated with it, black southerners were, if anything, even more enthusiastic promoters of the myth in the 1970s. The new ideology reflected real, dramatic changes in the region that began in the aftermath of the civil rights movement, the epochal event in the new mythology equivalent to the Civil War in the myth of the Lost Cause a century before. In 1975, the Reverend Frederick Reese, a veteran black leader, concluded that "we've come a long way." His evidence was largely changes in white behavior toward blacks: "Whites who wouldn't tip their hats have learned to do it. People who wouldn't say 'Mister' or 'Miss' to a black have learned to say it mighty fine. We've got black policemen, black secretaries, and we can use the public restrooms. The word 'nigger' is almost out of existence." His words evoked the older South of racial etiquette that the region's public culture had indeed finally rejected. Jessie Campbell, a black store manager on the Mississippi Gulf Coast, insisted that race was "almost nonexistent now." He saw a "new generation of people, black and white, here," again suggesting behavioral changes associated with the end of old racial ways as well as new beginnings. Campbell also pointed to economic developments, noting "there's been a pretty big rise in the standard of living of the black people." Andrew Young told a meeting of southern black mayors that "we can't help but be people who believe in doing the impossible, because we've already done so much of it." Young, in 1974, overtly summoned the image of the redemptive South: "I strangely think we're going to be able to deliver in the South. . . . I think the direction of this nation is going to be determined by the direction that comes from the southern part of the United States."[23]

Migration patterns suggested the demographic basis for this rhetoric. In the 1970s, for the first time, more blacks moved from the North to the South than were leaving the South for other parts of the United States. In the first three years of the 1970s, eighty thousand more blacks came to the South than left it, and in the last five years of the decade five hundred thousand African Americans moved to the region, reversing the historic outward migration. Writing in 1972, North Carolinian Mary E. Mebane remembered that "the names Alabama and Mississippi aroused something akin to terror." She had always viewed blacks from there "with awe" and wondered "how they could possibly have survived." The North, by contrast, "seemed the Promised Land." When blacks from New York City came home to visit, Mebane wrote that "the men drove big cars and the women dressed in fine clothes and wore false eyelashes." New York was "where everybody wanted to go." But in the previous few years, she had begun noting that "blacks in the Northern cities were coming home, down South." Mebane admitted that "disenchantment caused by the disorder in Northern cities" was one reason that some African Americans left the North for the South, as were new job opportunities, but she concluded that "the primary reason for the influx of blacks into the South [was] the Civil Rights Acts of 1964–65." The key to the North losing "much of its allure" was the South's removal of "the overt signs of racial discrimination" and the discontinuance of "some of the most vicious racist practices."[24] To Mebane, blacks seemed to be waiting for the South to welcome them home.

The South in the 1970s and 1980s became home to more black elected officials than any other part of the United States, further contributing to the ability of southern blacks to affirm the ideology of the biracial South because of their increased potential to exercise power in the region they shared with southern whites. The South represented about 50 percent of the nation's African Americans in 1987, but it had 62 percent of elected black officeholders, as compared to the next largest region, the North-Central census states, which had 19.2 percent. Mississippi led all states with 548 officials in 1987, and four of the five states with the largest number of black officeholders were in the South. Curtis M. Graves, a black representative in the Texas legislature and a vice president of the Lamar Society, pointed out that many of these electoral successes were because of black numerical strength, not attraction of white votes. But he looked to the biracial South for the future of black political success in the South. "Our real strength lies in coalition politics," he wrote. He himself had been elected as a result of such a coalition. "For the first time, whites and blacks in the South are working together in mutual trust. Realizing that things in the South are not as they should be for either blacks or whites, the two groups are beginning to talk over their common problems; they are joining forces to see that a better South is created." He suggested in his optimistic scenario that the South's "biggest problem today, our mutual problem" was replacing "the centuries of hatred and suspicion with a new era of respect and trust." Graves went beyond the then-present realities of southern coalition politics in the early 1970s to project a hopeful scenario for the future.[25]

Black endorsement of the myth of the biracial South became part of a process of African Americans redefining what "the South" means, as they wielded not only their political power but new cultural influence as well. As Thadious M. Davis has argued, the recent return of African Americans to the South, both physically and spiritually, represents "a laying of a claim to a culture and to a region that, though fraught with pain and difficulty, provides a major grounding for identity." She goes further, speculating "that this return to the South is a new form of subversion – a preconscious political activity or a subconscious counteraction to the racially and culturally homogeneous 'sunbelt.'" Rather than a "nostalgic turning back to a time when there were 'good old days,'" this embrace of the South "is gut-wrenching revisioning of specifics long obscured by synoptic cultural patterning." As part of the redefinition of "the South," black writers tried to evoke the texture of black culture and to understand the nature of black history in the South – its distinct character apart from issues of white supremacy. Alex Haley, Ernest Gaines, Margaret Walker Alexander, Clifton Taulbert, and Alice Walker are only a few of the best-known figures exploring the southern black community from within. "No one could wish for a more advantageous heritage," writes Alice Walker, "than that bequeathed to the black writer in the South: a compassion for the earth, a trust in humanity beyond our knowledge of evil, and an abiding love of justice." Walker evoked the spirit of the biracial South in insisting that black southerners had to "give voice to centuries not only of silent bitterness and hate but also of neighborly kindness and sustaining love." Davis also brought to mind the nurturing spirit of the myth of the biracial South in arguing that African American contemporary literary and intellectual works illustrate "the creative power of telling about the South and the healing power of uniting with another story in order to weave a necessary future."[26]

Out of this effort to understand the black community came an insistence that whites acknowledge the black role in the region as part of formal public culture in the South. This imperative among black southerners to reenvision the South has figured in the recent conflict over southern public symbols. The traditional symbols and images that public institutions projected often had associations with the Old South and the Lost Cause of the Confederacy. Beginning in the 1970s, black southerners pressured officials to remove symbols they regarded as offensive. "To appreciate the differences in feelings about the South by white southerners and black southerners," wrote Paul Delaney, the deputy national editor of the *New York Times*, in 1983, "one need only play 'Dixie' or wave a Confederate flag. Whites, many of them, respond with rebel yells; blacks, almost unanimously, flinch, finding the old symbols detestable." Black protests in the 1970s did lead to the removal of Confederate battle flags from many southern universities and public schools, institutions which had once flown them as symbols of school spirit that tied contemporary sporting events to white regional tradition. "Dixie" is no longer the pervasive public anthem it once was. Likewise, the commemoration of Confederate Memorial Day, a once-vibrant ritual that brought out white celebrants each spring, has continued its decline, which began well before the civil rights movement, to where it is a marginal activity in most southern communities, if it is held at all.[27]

As the commemoration of the Old South and the Lost Cause declined, southerners have deepened their collective memories of the civil rights movement. Maya Lin's dramatic memorial to the martyrs of the movement is at the Southern Poverty Law Center in Montgomery. Jackson, Mississippi, has its monument to Medgar Evers; the University of Mississippi honors its first African American student, James Meredith, with a statue; and Arthur Ashe now stands in statue on Richmond's resonant Monument Avenue, near the images of Lee, Jackson, and Davis. The celebration of the Martin Luther King Jr. federal holiday is the most obvious example, though, of the commemoration of the people and events of the civil rights movement, which is no longer recognized simply in the black community but by the broader southern public as well, making these occasions into rituals of the myth of the biracial South. King is often honored in the South, for example, in schools, universities, and community centers, and in church memorial services for blacks and whites; yet the commemoration of his memory is often held at the same time as state holidays for Robert E. Lee, whose birth date is close to King's.[28]

This joint celebration of a King-Lee holiday is surely a ritual triumph of the myth of the biracial South – one holiday that blacks and whites can celebrate for differing reasons. Arkansas newspaper editor Paul Greenberg argues that the South will never achieve racial peace until "southerners, black and white, accept the same symbols." He rejects the idea of "hauling down the Confederate battle flag at Montgomery," when the better solution is to "erect a statue of Martin Luther King Jr. on the Capitol grounds, and celebrate both." Writing in 1988, Greenburg showed the continuing power of the biracial ideal. "The South will rise again," he said, "when it rises as one – when we rise together, not against each other." Looking into the future, he predicted that "the South will be one when a march celebrating King's birthday is led by some brave and discerning soul carrying the Confederate battle flag."[29]

African Americans might admire the grandness of Greenburg's millennial vision, but their skepticism about its plausibility deepened, given the worsening of American race relations in the 1980s, which suggested the millennium was not at hand and challengers were questioning the myth of the biracial South. The economic and civil rights policies of the Ronald Reagan administration worsened race relations. "I am not the optimist I was twenty years ago as a young reporter in Atlanta," wrote black editor Paul Delaney in 1983. "I see the future of race relations in the South, and the nation, as bleak," with Reagan's policies suggesting that "white racism still lies just beneath a thin veneer of racial civility." Despite this pessimistic view, even Delaney allowed himself to grasp the hope of the redemptive South at the heart of the biracial ideology: "If the South can counter that psychology, it will have made an everlasting contribution to racial understanding. Perhaps the South can solve the problem, for its heritage of person-to-person relationships, its aversion to abstractions, and its commitment to good manners suggest that people should be respected as individuals." In 1984, the year after Delaney's words, Republican candidates in several southern states earned the condemnation of black leaders for their use of racial code words in campaigning, and by the late 1980s, David Duke's prominence as a southern politician drawing on a white racial constituency symbolized the opposition to the biracial myth from at least a sizeable number of southern whites.[30]

The assertion of black identity was met in the 1990s with a resurgence of an older southern myth among contemporary whites – the myth of the Lost Cause. White working-class culture likely never affirmed the myth of the biracial South, but that culture lost much of its influence on southern public culture as a result of the changes of the 1960s, leading to the white populist rage that politicians from George Wallace to David Duke have exploited. However, not working-class whites but intellectuals and middle-class southerners were responsible for reasserting the Lost Cause, which they began to do at the end of the decade that gave birth to the biracial myth. In 1979, *Southern Partisan* magazine appeared, steadily expanding its circulation. Peter Applebome pointed out that "even most Southerners are not familiar with its somewhat schizoid mix of Old South gun-and-musket lore, scholarly Burkean-Calhounian political philosophy, and contemporary hard-right politics." Articles explored many facets of southern white culture, yet cohered in stressing the centrality of the Confederacy to the southern identity. As one cover story concluded, "This storm-cradled nation has much to teach us – as does the terrible war by which it lived and died." Southerners interested in the neo-Confederate identity could also subscribe to *Southern Heritage,*

Confederate Underground, The Journal of Confederate History, The Confederate Sentry, and *Counterattack*. They could join organizations such as the Confederate Society of America, the Culture of the South Association, the Southern Heritage Association, and the Sons of Confederate Veterans, one of whose chapters published *The Rebel Yell*, a newsletter with the motto "If at first you don't secede, try, try again." The neo-Confederacy received a boost in June 1994 when organizers formed the Southern League as "an activist organization of unreconstructed Southerners pursuing cultural, social, economic and political independence for Dixie." None of these organizations was large in itself, and none of these publications had an impressive subscription list, but together they represented a new organizational structure pushing for an older ideological perspective on the South. Their significance came from their active role in Republican politics in the South and their tapping into the frustrations of white southerners who did not see a need to redefine southern identity as something other than its historic meanings associated with a white-dominated South.[31]

The southern psyche was thus deeply divided, again, judging by its mythological outcroppings as the millennium neared. As long as the South's population, though, remained biracial, as long as the South's people had to struggle to live together and to make a common culture and society that both blacks and whites could acknowledge, rooted in the bitter realities and soaring hopes of the past, the myth of the biracial South would likely remain a relevant one – especially for a world that in the twenty-first century faces increasing interaction between differing ethnic and cultural traditions, as the Western world faces the third world. This particular southern myth tells about what happened in one isolated area of the world when such people met and continued to struggle with each other for centuries. As Charles Joyner, Mechal Sobel, and others have shown, southerners do indeed have a biracial cultural heritage, one seen in the music, language, foodways, religion, and many other cultural practices of the traditional South.[32] The ideology of the biracial South says this should be acknowledged, the kinship between blacks and whites – as Charles Black long ago dreamed – should be embraced.

The religious aspect of the contemporary myth of the biracial South is crucial because it suggests that the southern story still has moral meanings to share, that the struggle in the end will signify more than just sound and fury. The moral meanings projected in this contemporary myth are not the same ones that the antebellum proslavery advocates saw in southern mythology, believing the South was the last noncapitalist hope against a materialistic and egalitarian wave that had conquered Europe and the northern United States. The myth of the biracial South does not embody the same moral meaning that the Lost Cause did for its true believers, nurturing as it did its supposed wisdom from wartime defeat and purification. It does not embody the same redemptive meanings that southern evangelicals have long cherished – the South as the last enclave of spirit-filled religion, which must send forth missionaries to the world to convert it. Common to all of these expressions of what Lewis Simpson calls the southern spiritual community is the belief that the southern experience has spiritual-moral meaning. The myth of the biracial South embodies the same aspiration, although no longer with conservative content. Oscar Carr Jr., a white Mississippian who headed the national Office of Development for the Episcopal Church in New York City in the 1970s, argued that "once Southerners can jump into the economic mainstream they will be more liberal than people in Connecticut," but in doing that "the greatest thing the South can offer the nation is its religious and moral sense."[33] It was the same contribution that earlier generations of southerners had claimed as a potential one for the region's people within the nation.

Despite challenges, the myth of the biracial South abided through the 1990s. *Washington Post* columnist William Raspberry, a native of Okolona, Mississippi, wrote in 1991 of his home state, once the epitome of the savage South, as now the embodiment of the biracial South. He praised "the infectious friendliness of the bigger towns" in Mississippi, whose racial practices had earlier driven him out as a young man. He gloried now, though, over the friendly folk of his hometown and the "laid back sophistication" of the Mississippi Gulf Coast, marveling "at how seldom this pervasive graciousness is spoiled by racial rudeness." Raspberry was clear-eyed about Mississippi's failures, noting the segregation academies that were white racial islands, the "places where a black stranger in town walks with care," and the state's governor, Kirk Fordice, "who had shown a willingness to play the race game." Still, he lauded the "easiness to relationships, a mutual respect and a willingness to move beyond race that," as he concluded, "quite frankly didn't exist during [his] years in the state."[34] His words indeed reflected real changes that fifty years earlier represented a revolution in the Southern Way of Life. The danger of Raspberry's viewpoint, though, is for southerners to conclude that the myth has been achieved. We may indeed be at the same crossroads as New South advocates after the 1880s – having proclaimed their ideology, they soon came to believe it had become reality, though the South remained provincial, economically underdeveloped, and racially divided. The myth of the biracial South in the 1970s had especially rested, nonetheless, on the idea of behavioral changes in the aftermath of the epochal civil rights movement, and Raspberry framed his vision of his reformed home state in that same image, suggesting that this behavioral change was the myth's compelling insight: if human behavior could be so dramatically changed in what had seemed a morally evil society, in Mississippi, the most savage state of the South, perhaps the myth's redeeming hopes still could be achieved. Today the state of Mississippi has an active racial reconciliation community, including the William Winter Institute for Racial Reconciliation at the University of Mississippi and Mission Mississippi, a faith-based nonprofit that brings white and black people of faith together to nurture cross-racial friendships and sponsor projects for social improvement. The latter's motto is "grace not race," a fitting recent expression of hope for the biracial South.

The best judgment about what will happen with the myth of the biracial South in the future may be found in the tentative words of one of the wisest of southerners, black critic Albert Murray. Back in 1976, at the peak of the Carteresque embodiment of the biracial South, Murray wrote, "I hope the changes are permanent," but he foresaw that "there could be a counterthrust." He added, "As a Southerner, my main response is through the blues. The nature of the blues is improvisation . . . you must be ready for all eventualities."[35]

Visualizing the Spirit

David Wharton's photographs show visual flashes of a southern spirit in the contemporary era. "I believe the social and physical fabric of any given place to be all of one piece, and that each continually shapes the other," Wharton has written. His photographs demonstrate how matters of the spirit are central features of that "social and physical fabric" of the South. Director of documentary projects and assistant professor of southern studies at the University of Mississippi's Center for the Study of Southern Culture, Wharton has been in Mississippi since 1999, photographing the mid-South region of north Mississippi, west Tennessee, Arkansas, and Louisiana, but he has also roamed over the entire South in a period of notable transition for the region. His images often juxtapose tradition and change in ways appropriate to a region long rooted in traditional practices but now carving out a new global role.

For many white southerners, the idea of tradition evokes memories of the Confederate States of America and a melancholy spirit of loss in the Civil War. The Lost Cause narrative dominated southern public culture for a century after the war, justifying the fight for southern ways, including white supremacy, and Confederate monuments still tower over town squares, cemeteries, and hilltops, as in Wharton's photograph of Sylva, North Carolina. The monument dominates the physical landscape, despite decades of social change. Likewise, Civil War reenactors perform the Lost Cause narrative, evoking heritage in the twenty-first-century South. Nostalgia for antiquity comes through as well, appealing to a particular regional spirit of family honor. The nostalgia in the photographs here suggests differing moods of this expression of regional tradition. A solo, somewhat lonely reenactor sits by himself in front of a Civil War replica tent, as though surrealistically existing out of time, while in another photo, a father and son enthusiastically participate in firing an artillery piece.

Women were central in the creation of the Lost Cause narrative that celebrated the glories of the Old South and the romantic crusading spirit of the Confederates, and the image of the southern lady became a key prop for the white-dominated public culture of the twentieth-century South. Women in the contemporary South play many roles and can escape the earlier confines of "the lady" mythology. The photo from the annual Holly Springs, Mississippi, Pilgrimage, though, includes white women performing traditional roles as embodiments of the regional patriotic spirit rooted in the nineteenth century. The image is ironic in its portrayal of generations of southern women.

Tradition includes more than the historical resonance of Civil War images in the contemporary South. The photo here of participants in a watermelon festival shows a celebration of small-town life with a sense of community and wholesomeness that many southerners—and others as well—associate with the older South. The celebratory spirit of such a scene harks back to memories of a nostalgic past and a sense of place invested with considerable meaning.

Wharton's images convey the blending of patriotic and religious spirits. Patriotic and religious signs in close proximity to one other in one photo blur the line between religiosity and national identity. JESUS IS LORD OVER VARDAMAN is a civil-religious blending that sacralizes a place. The southern landscape is indeed marked by the predominant religion of the South, evangelical Protestantism, in many of Wharton's images. The GOD sign proclaims a divine presence in the countryside, away from the church, and is an example of the outcroppings of popular religion I discuss throughout latter portions of this book. Evangelical Protestant churches believe in witnessing for their faith, and the recreational vehicle with religious sayings on it becomes a traveling testimonial—it is a contemporary expression of the New Testament's Great Commission to convert the world gone mobile on wheels. The spirit remains alive in the outdoor South, and the photograph of men at a river baptism in Mississippi shows the continuing performance of a central cleansing ritual still held in flowing water in such places.

The South's modernization has been a prolonged one, and the contemporary South bears marks of its role in transforming the region. The abandoned church in a photograph from South Carolina marks the landscape with a sacred presence, but the railroad tracks in front of the church suggest the passage of time. Once, speedy trains could make or break communities by running through them or bypassing them; now, the train itself evokes nostalgia, and the photo has a rough beauty yet also a mournful quality.

Some of these photographs show the religious spirit of the South in its most compelling way. Elder Tatum has long preached in Primitive Baptist churches in the mid-South, and the photograph here shows the spirit working through him to his congregation. Casey Dixon sang religious music in Mississippi until his death in 2009; this photograph captures how music can be a conduit for the spirit in African American religion. The spirit and the body may be analytically distinct categories (as discussed in the introduction to this book), but the women praising the Lord in Toccopola, Mississippi, demonstrate how the two can be related, and both moved, through spiritual experience. The religious spirit among southerners can be dramatic and energizing; it can also be more reflective, as in the scene of men in a prayer room. Another image shows a man with a Bible, at the site of a baptism, representing icons of evangelical faith. The wild workings of the spirit are suggested by the sign for Holy Ghost Disturbed Church.

Chapter 10 explores Elvis Presley's spirituality, and Wharton's image of the tattooed Elvis devotee suggests Elvis himself may take on powerful spiritual meanings for some of his followers. Most of this book—like these photographs—explores the predominant evangelical Protestant spirituality of the South; the photo that juxtaposes the OKRA sign and the Virgin Mary, however, reveals a south Louisiana landscape that represents a distinctive sensibility within the larger South. Finally, the last image is particularly suggestive in providing a contemporary take on traditional southern spirituality—a young woman photographs a river baptism on her cell phone camera, showing the intersection of modern technology and the workings of the spirit in the South.

Confederate monument
Sylva, North Carolina, 2002

Civil War reenactor
Shiloh National Battlefield, Tennessee, 2003

Belles at pilgrimage
Holly Springs, Mississippi, 1999

Photographing prize melons
Water Valley, Mississippi, 2009

JESUS IS LORD OVER VARDAMAN
Chickasaw City, Mississippi, 2001

GOD sign
Thomasville, Georgia, 2005

Two men before baptism
Rocky Mount Primitive Baptist Church
Panola City, Mississippi, 2002

Abandoned church by railroad tracks
Brunson, South Carolina, 2005

Elder Tatum preaching
Rocky Mount Primitive Baptist Church
Panola City, Mississippi, 2000

Casey Dixon singing
St. Peter's Missionary Baptist Church
Lafayette City, Mississippi, 2002

Women praising
Toccopola, Mississippi, date unknown

Sign for Holy Ghost Disturbed Church
Louisiana, 2003

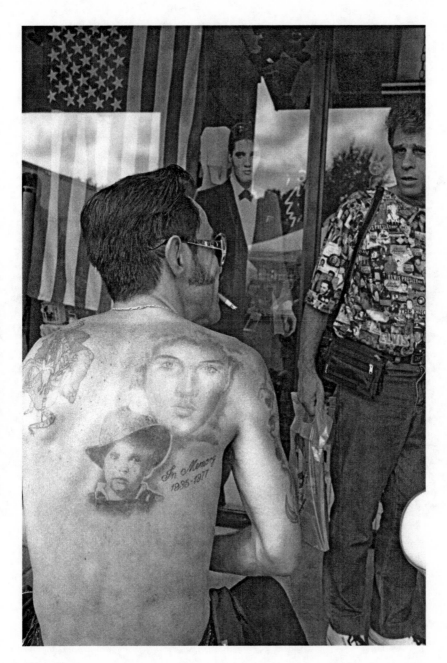

Elvis devotee
Memphis, Tennessee, 2002

Madonna and OKRA
St. Charles Parish, Louisiana, 2001

Cell phone baptism
Rocky Mount Primitive Baptist Church
Panola City, Mississippi, 2008

PART TWO

Creativity

6 Beyond the Sahara of the Bozart

Creativity and Southern Culture

In *One Writer's Beginnings*, Eudora Welty gives a superb portrait of the creativity nurtured in her by her family and community in Mississippi. Her parents embodied a creative dialogue. The inspiration from her father came in the form of technology – the telescopes around the house to look at the moon and stars, the clocks that taught her the importance of time, the Kodak camera that gave her a visceral sense of imagery. His creativity with such things looked toward the future, toward the progress to which creative inventions could lead. Welty's mother's creative gifts were different ones. She loved books, reading, and artistic beauty. Every room in her home was one in which young Eudora could hear stories read from books, books for which her parents scrimped and saved. Her mother sang to her, resulting in Welty developing an inner voice, so that when she read, she heard a voice. Her mother sent her to preschool art classes, where she learned to associate the smell of flowers with the pictures she drew.

Fannie, the black sewing lady, came around weekly, and young Welty heard from her stories, stories of black people and white people, of good people and bad people, of gossip, rumor, wild exaggeration, and truth. Conversation was a simple daily art but an important one. A friend of

Welty's mother would go with them on Sunday afternoons for a ride. "My mother sat in the back with her friend," Welty writes, "and I'm told that as a small child I would ask to sit in the middle, and say as we started off, 'Now *talk.*'"[1]

Eudora Welty, of course, is one of the premier embodiments of creativity in the American South, and her reflections suggest some of the forces promoting the different kinds of creativity that existed there – the role of parents, the creativity often associated with men and women, the folk culture of storytelling and conversation, the role of community institutions that present opportunities like preschool art classes, the importance of books, the centrality of individuals who serve as teachers. Welty is certainly not typical, but she is prime evidence of the South as fertile ground for the creative spirit.

One might gain a different picture of creativity in wondering about the origin of the blues. After all, it was working-class music. Delta blues performer Bukka White once noted that the blues started "back across them fields . . . right behind one of them mules or one of them log houses, one of them log camps or the levee camp. That's where the blues sprung from." Mississippi bluesman Eddie "Son" House agreed: "People wonder a lot about where the blues came from. Well, when I was coming up, people did more singing in the fields than they did anywhere else." Folklorist David Evans concludes that near the end of the nineteenth century, the vocal expressions of traditional southern black field hollers "were set to instrumental accompaniment and given a musical structure, an expanded range of subject matter and a new social context" that gave birth to the blues. The field hollers had been vernacular group music among African Americans on farms and plantations, but the blues especially encouraged creativity among performers, who worked for individuality of expression and timeliness, while also drawing from oral tradition. The emergence of this new creativity in the blues in the 1890s was surely directly related to the social context, as the first generation of African Americans born under freedom came to maturity. Their extraordinary musical innovations would include not only the blues but the cakewalk, jazz, ragtime, barbershop quartet singing, and gospel music as well.[2]

What is creativity and how is it related to the broader culture in which creative people, whether writers or musicians or others, live? Creativity is bringing something new into existence. The most honored individuals make the big leaps – like Charley Patton, who came as close as anyone to defining a new art form, the blues, out of the folk ingredients of African American music in the Delta; or like William Faulkner, who took the stock characters of earlier southern literature and more deeply than anyone before explored their humanity. The modern world often sees creativity in terms of psychology, identifying such personal qualities as intelligence, spontaneity, originality, or sincerity. Some individuals are so wild and unorthodox in their creative expressions that we naturally think of "genius," and the South has surely produced those spirits. But the deeper question raised by the region's cultural history is how a place with so many historically apparent social problems has still nurtured a deep creativity in many of its people. How do we reconcile the social context with individual creativity? A social focus on the matter points toward the culture of the South, with creativity not just the result of individual genius but also emerging from a social context that encouraged certain kinds of ingenuity while perhaps discouraging other expressions. The cultural base set the parameters for individual achievements.

Looking at the twentieth-century South and considering what are generally regarded as the region's highest cultural achievements, I want to argue that this creativity resulted from the long dominance of a traditional culture and the stimulus the southern environment and social system have provided to individuals who have generated creative sparks. The modernization of the region itself became the final spark that galvanized the creative spirit of numerous artists; expressed in a commercial mass culture, creativity empowered many of the South's people to achieve a heretofore unimagined level of success.

If we had considered this issue in the early twentieth century, though, the South would have seemed an unlikely spot to even think about the possibility of high cultural achievement. H. L. Mencken, the liveliest critic of the region's culture, complained in the 1920s of the cultural barrenness he saw in the region, claiming that classical musicians, symphonies, ballets, and good poets were hard to find south of the Mason-Dixon line. He blamed this sorry state of affairs on the region's decline since antebellum times, the rural nature of the South, and the religious orthodoxy that stifled innovation. He saw no arts in the South except "the lower reaches of the gospel hymn."[3] Mencken was witty indeed, and he had a point. He might also have mentioned the poverty that blanketed the region after the Civil War; as late as the 1930s, the federal government proclaimed the South "the nation's No. 1 economic problem." The lack of funding available for formal cultural institutions meant that the region did have fewer symphonies and ballets – and also fewer libraries and good universities and schools – than were found in other parts of the nation. This weak infrastructure inadequately supported certain kinds of creative and intellectual life.

The predominantly rural nature of life in the South meant that the region lacked big cities, which have been associated with nurturing innovative cultural achievements since the classical age of Greece and Rome. London, Paris, and New York City have been the cultural capitals of the modern era, at least in most matters related to high culture. And then, of course, people still puzzle over how a region with such a high illiteracy rate produced all those writers: "there are more people who write novels down there than can read them" is a familiar saying that reflects the perspective of the national culture. In a predominantly rural, agrarian society, illiteracy did not prevent you from learning traditional practical skills, but it did hamper certain kinds of creativity because it meant a population less capable than otherwise of utilizing written knowledge and the innovations that come from that medium of communication.

Racial obsessions haunted the South of Mencken's day, providing another restriction on creative spirits. Richard Wright pondered how he became a writer living in the "southern darkness" of Jim Crow segregation. "The external world of whites and blacks," he wrote, "which was the only world that I had ever known, surely had not evoked in me any belief in myself." He realized that he existed "emotionally on the sheer, thin margin of southern culture," experiencing dreadfully the obstacle of racial categorization. Whites and blacks, too, told him he could not aspire to the highest cultural realms.[4]

These obstacles were mighty ones, tragic burdens for many of the South's people. And yet Wright went on to become a literary giant, part of the flowering of creativity in the Southern Literary Renaissance after 1920. Mississippi, which had earlier been the birthplace of the blues, became one center of the region's literary acclaim, as writers from that state alone received one Nobel Prize, eight Pulitzer Prizes for fiction, drama, and journalism, and four New York Drama Critics Awards. William Faulkner used the specifics of southern history to embody his dramas of "the human heart in conflict with itself." Thomas Wolfe, Robert Penn Warren, Katherine Anne Porter, Ralph Ellison, Carson McCullers, and Tennessee Williams are only a few examples of the accomplished literary culture of the modern South. They typically came out of middle-class backgrounds, often university educated and well traveled. They had grown up in the South that for two generations had lived with the dislocations and turbulence of Confederate defeat, which stimulated their ability to create new art that went beyond earlier examples of southern writing. Their themes of agrarian life, the memory of the Old South and the Civil War, religious values, the tensions of the biracial society, and the modernization of society were epitomized in *I'll Take My Stand* (1930), a polemical statement by the Vanderbilt Agrarians near the beginning of the Southern Literary Renaissance.[5]

When we think about the folk and popular musicians who emerged in the twentieth-century South, we need to broaden the idea of a Southern Literary Renaissance to a Southern Cultural Renaissance in the same midcentury years. Whether the blues music of Robert Johnson, Muddy Waters, and Blind Lemon Jefferson; the country music of Roy Acuff, Jimmie Rodgers, and Hank Williams; the jazz of Louis Armstrong, Lester Young, and Thelonious Monk; or the early rock of Elvis Presley, Little Richard, and Fats Domino – the South fostered a world-class musical culture. These entertainers were typically working class, often coming from very poor backgrounds and frequently African American. Family and church had taught them about the centrality of talking and singing to their lives, and their creativity now took them into profitable new venues. Their work displayed some but not all of the same concerns as southern writers in those years – the memory of agrarian life, the importance of religion, and a sense of changing times were surely strong, but the folk and early popular performers rarely sang of the Civil War, and only black performers spoke in an idiom of overt racial concerns.[6]

More recently still, the South is receiving recognition for its painting, sculptural, and photographic achievements. Two recent masters, William Christenberry and William Eggleston, for example, draw explicitly from the southern cultural context and yet achieve broad artistic acclaim. Christenberry photographs in Hale County, Alabama, where Walker Evans earlier documented the life of tenant farmers, while Eggleston has captured the visual wonders of Graceland, among other places. The Ogden Museum of Art in New Orleans and the Morris Museum in Augusta, with their focus on southern fine and folk art, are only the most notable examples of museums and cultural centers opening in the South that collect and exhibit southern art. Southern outsider artists since the 1960s, such as Howard Finster, R. A. Miller, and Lonny Holley, have come out of a rural southern aesthetic that represents the latest phase of regional creativity rooted in the South's culture. A century from now, this art may be seen as the equal of the region's earlier literary and musical flowering, which also rested in rural traditions undergoing social change. These examples do not exhaust the list of cultural achievements, yet the point should be made that these accomplishments are not just individual ones but represent a cultural phenomenon.[7]

Modern southern cultural creativity grew out of the region's folk traditions. In the early 1950s, Vanderbilt Agrarian writer Donald Davidson and North Carolina sociologist Howard Odum had a pointed exchange about whether the sociocultural context could explain why a William Faulkner could possibly have emerged from Mississippi and not from a state like Massachusetts or Wisconsin, states that typically led the nation in indices of social health. Davidson denied the value of looking to the social-cultural context, but Odum wrote the South of Faulkner's time was "rich soil for the growing of varied cultural crops" and suggested the need to look not for one causal factor but at the overall sociocultural milieu. Odum seems to have hit it right in emphasizing the South of the early twentieth century as notable for being in transition from a folk society to what he called a technological civilization. Southern cohesiveness had rested in an agrarian culture that had taken root in the early South, spread westward in the nineteenth century, and survived the Civil War. Southern rural and small-town people knew each other relatively well, living as they did in a face-to-face society. They gathered around the courthouse square or the country crossroads store. Crop cycles, community life, and church worship structured daily life. It was a deferential society, with a hierarchical class system rooted in differences in wealth, gender, and skin color. Orthodoxy ruled, yet it allowed for eccentricity as long as the foundations of the society were not challenged. Diversity, tensions, and conflicts existed, openly expressed, but these often fed creativity. The region's two predominant ethnic groups, whites from western Europe and blacks from West Africa, contributed folk aesthetic principles of symmetry and balance, in the former case, and improvisation, in the latter, that combined in the distinctive natural environment of the rural South to produce a new material and spiritual culture.[8]

The relationship to the land was the central context for southern life in the folk society that dominated the South until recently, resulting in a sense of place to which creative people responded, giving them a special vantage point from which to see the world. The idea of a southern sense of place has proven a contested but remarkably enduring concept. Commentators once argued for a unique sense of place in the South, differentiating southerners from other Americans who were supposedly too mobile to put down roots. Attachment to local places implied an organic society, a belief that now seems dated. Literary critic Patricia Yaeger has recently questioned the traditional grounding of a sense of place in the South, finding not a special rootedness and connectedness in works of southern women writers but rather images of fragmentation, decay, and melancholy. She concludes, however, that place was central to southern writers, but racial segregation always haunted their landscapes. Humanist geographer Yi-Fu Tuan points to the experiential importance of space and place to humans in general, and southerners are no exception. Affirming attachment to place in the South is certainly not unique to southerners; what is significant are the particular ingredients that southern observers identify with place. Writer Albert Murray claimed a specifically southern black sense of place in the 1970s, and a generation of black writing has further explored that claim. Martyn Bone has recently identified a "postsouthern sense of place" that finds writers responding to the ramifications of the extension of capitalist institutions and ways into the South, while a leading scholar of globalization, James Peacock, sees the region's embrace of localism, represented by its "sense of place," as a grounding factor for overarching global forces.[9]

Especially important to the southern sense of place was the environment. Southern artists have lived in a place that stimulated their senses.

"Let us begin by discussing the weather," wrote historian Ulrich B. Phillips in the early twentieth century in discussing southern distinctiveness, and artists have long used the supercharged heat and humidity of the Southeast – especially the Deep South – and its sometimes exotic flora and fauna for dramatic effect. The sensory South, the world of sight and smell and sound, the efflorescence of the landscape, has stimulated not only southerners but artists from other places who have come south to paint or photograph as well.[10]

Theorists talked of the importance of "place" to the social system, and indeed, it could seem almost medieval in its stress on individuals staying within their "place" in the social order. One could embrace the sense of place that came from the South's natural world, though, while rejecting its social meanings. Richard Wright noted that "[his] deepest instincts had always made [him] reject the 'place' to which the white South had assigned [him]," and yet this conviction did not prevent his appreciation of the sensory southern place, as seen in the following passage from his memoir *Black Boy*:

> There was the delight I caught in seeing long straight rows of red and green vegetables stretching away in the sun to the bright horizon.
>
> There was the faint, cool kiss of sensuality when dew came on my cheeks and shins as I ran down the wet green garden paths in the early mornings.
>
> There was the vague sense of the infinite as I looked down upon the yellow, dreaming waters of the Mississippi River from the verdant bluffs of Natchez.

African American memoirs written under the cloud of segregation are filled with appreciation of the southern environment as counterposed to the grim world of social segregation.[11]

The sense of place also rested, though, on the cultural memories of the past. Writers could look around and see customs, rituals, and ways that connected to generations of people who had lived agrarian-centered lives. Partly, this sense of place rested in a sense of history, a tangible awareness of the past's impact on the South. White southerners remembered Confederate defeat, and black southerners remembered slavery and segregation as seminal moments, past yet still alive. Partly, too, this sense of place rested in family, in the ties between generations and the place of honor the elderly occupied. Alice Walker has noted this sensibility in terms of African American creativity: "What the black Southern writer inherits as a natural right is a sense of *community.*" Her mother was "a walking history of [her] community," and "always, in one's memory, there remain all the rituals of one's growing up." The "daily dramas" that grew out of this agrarian-centered place "are pure gold."[12] Writers, musicians, painters, and photographers in the South lived within a stimulating physical and social environment that encouraged expressiveness.

The southern folk culture that produced an intense sense of place was an oral culture, and the facility with language that emerged from this storytelling- and conversation-oriented society was surely of central importance to nurturing creative expression. For instance, remember Welty's story of riding between her mother and her friend and telling them to talk. Bluesman Son House saw the oral culture working through the pervasiveness of song. He recalled that black workers in the fields would sing all the time: "They'd sing about their girl friend or about almost anything – mule – anything. They'd make a song of it just to be hollering." Blues singers themselves often came from churchgoing families, and the songs, stories, proverbs, and sermons they heard in religious settings were also part of a culture whose features – sacred and secular – were in close proximity, within "shouting distance" even. Zora Neale Hurston identified a specifically southern, biracial facility with language, observing that "an average Southern child, white or black, is raised on simile and invective. They know how to call names." Moreover, this language-based creativity came from what was still a predominantly rural southern society in her lifetime. "They take their comparisons right out of the barnyard and the woods," Hurston further explained.[13]

The South's folk culture thus bequeathed language gifts to the southern people, but that culture itself began to change under the impress of modernization – the economic development that produced cities, factories, and consumerism in the early twentieth-century South. One cultural change that resulted from modernization was the appearance of mass culture, beginning especially in the 1920s. Literary critics have debated the origins of the Southern Literary Renaissance, disagreeing over whether the South had modernized enough by the 1920s for literary creativity to have emerged from the awareness of social change.

Creativity in some forms, however, such as folk and popular music, did not depend on a general economic development. With a broadened focus beyond just the literary culture, evidence surely suggests that musicians and performers knew quite tangibly times had changed, and the changes contributed to new opportunities for expressions of southern creativity – the phonograph, commercial radio, and the public address system, which made possible the recording, marketing, and performance of southern folk music for profit by the 1920s and early 1930s.[14]

What was new about the cultural context of creativity in the South at that point was its movement beyond the localism of the folk culture to a broader regional and national context. This change did not at all destroy southern creativity musically, any more than new access to northern literary markets ended the creativity of southern writers. Indeed, these changes, including increasing commercialization, were a spur to creativity. The South became a prime source of performers and lyrical themes for the national culture, just as its writers soon came to occupy a central stage in the American literary world. These creative people drew from earlier southern traditions yet gave innovative interpretations of them appropriate to the modern world.

Southern creativity brought empowerment to resourceful and inventive spirits who had often grown up economically disadvantaged. Historian Pete Daniel writes of the region's "lowdown culture," which in the 1950s produced a flowering of creative music through early rock 'n' roll. Sam Phillips, the founder of Sun Records in Memphis, recognized the "untamed streak" in poor white and black youth who had recently moved from the rural South to Memphis. The middle class could not get beyond their "accent, dress, and decibel level," and these young people often violated their society's Jim Crow segregation strictures in their search for new opportunities to escape the limitations of the poverty with which they had grown up. In doing so, they seized the opportunities of a South that after World War II was rapidly modernizing. Having made their way to Memphis, they found a guiding force in Phillips, who nurtured the creative energy of this new southern generation. And with Elvis Presley, Phillips found what he wanted musically as a producer – "the blues with a mania," a phrase that suggests the creative energy that led to one of the South's major cultural achievements. Indeed, due to their combination of creativity and musical ability, early southern rock performers, including Presley, found the psychological and economic success that was sometimes beyond their dreams.[15]

In the twentieth century, southern creativity thus came out of the cohesive background of the region's folk culture, its sense of place that gave southerners a well-rooted point from which to observe the world, a stimulating physical environment, and facility with language, all brought into focus for creative spirits undergoing the uprooting traumas of modernization. Finally, though, one must reckon with another central factor – the biracial context of creativity in the South. Despite the desire of southern whites to maintain a segregated culture, blacks and whites from early in southern history engaged in cultural interaction. It is the story of cultural groups with distinctive ways, Europeans and Africans, who created a new culture in the South. In the course of living on southern soil for three centuries, blacks and whites developed two societies, two cultures. But they also exchanged cultural knowledge and blended their expressive traditions in creative ways. Structurally they were separated, but culturally they interacted to create something new. Jimmie Rodgers heard black singers on the railroad crews of Mississippi and then created the white blues as the father of country music. Hank Williams learned to play the guitar from a black Montgomery, Alabama, street singer. Ray Charles listened to country music growing up in Georgia, so it was not surprising when he chose to record a soulful country music album in the 1970s. Elvis Presley grew up poor, in a society that threw together blacks and whites who shared economic deprivation and also their music.[16]

Looking back on it, the southern biracial history that produced not only the musical geniuses of the 1950s but also other creative achievements has been a magnificent social drama, complicated in the twentieth century by southerners moving from a largely traditional society into modern life. As much as any American place, the South has wrestled with deep-seated human hopes, fears, and anxieties rooted in cultural interaction and social change. Its social system has been turbulent, given to vibrant emotional displays and clear, passionate expressions. It is no wonder that the South has nurtured its artistic people: the tensions of southern society have fed efforts to create new ways to shed light upon these human dramas.

7

Flashes of the Spirit
Creativity and Southern Religion

Long ago, while driving through rural North Carolina, I came across a hand-lettered sign on rough wood, fastened to a tree. A primitive drawing portrayed a hand with a nail through it and drops of blood, painted in bright red, flowing out of the hand. Beneath this drawing were the words HE LOVED YOU SO MUCH IT HURT. This graphic icon seemed to jump off the tree and confront the viewer, whether believer or skeptic, with a raw, religious sentiment, evoking the crucified Jesus on the cross and all that image suggests about death and resurrection. More recently, while driving in north Mississippi, I saw a billboard advertising a nearby Pentecostal church. In a bold design, it said, JESUS FORGIVES THINK ABOUT IT. "Forgives" appeared in dramatic, almost dripping letters, like the drooping clocks of Salvador Dali's surrealism, intended in this case to suggest flowing tears.

Writer Harry Crews has said that down South, "where [he comes] from," folks "have compressed and boiled down the religious experience to something that is hard and fast and simple in the best sense of the word," and these roadside messages illustrate his point. Both cases renewed my sense that I live in the Bible Belt, one of those "belts" and "lines" that have long set the South apart from other parts of the United

States. H. L. Mencken, the distinguished early twentieth-century editor, came up with the words "Bible Belt" to label orthodox Protestant
areas of the South and Midwest. He did not mean it as a compliment.
Mencken insisted that the Protestantism in these areas – and especially
the South – stifled creativity. The South, he said, was "a cesspool of Baptists" and "a miasma of Methodists," an inhospitable landscape indeed
for the flowering of fine literature, music, and painting. "When you come
to critics, musical composers, painters, sculptors, architects and the like,"
he complained, "you will have to give it up, for there is not even a bad
one between the Potomac mud-flats and the Gulf." The only arts that did
exist hardly deserved his approbation as arts. Sacred harp singing, for
example, combined, he said, the sound of a Ukrainian peasant melody
with that of a steam calliope.[1]

Mencken had much fun with such characterizations, and we must
acknowledge that the South of his day was indeed poor in certain kinds
of creativity – the region supported few distinguished art galleries and
museums and probably even fewer notable symphony orchestras and
dance companies. For generations after the Civil War, the South was
beset by widespread poverty, and the region had few resources to devote
to creating the infrastructure that is needed to nurture the achievements
of high culture. As seen in the last chapter, the region nonetheless experienced a stunning flowering of creative expression. The Southern Cultural Renaissance began in the 1920s and produced acclaimed writers and enormously gifted musicians. In music, the region arguably
gave birth to the blues, jazz, ragtime, country music, and rock 'n' roll.
Furthermore, while the South's painting and sculpture have not been as
acclaimed, its artists, nonetheless, also produced work in those areas that
reflected many of the same themes found in its literature and music, and
more recently, its folk art has flowered and earned the increasing recognition of the national artistic community.

Religion has been a central theme in the creativity that emerged from
many southern places and genres. Preachers, revivals, baptisms, church
services, and other aspects of religious life are abiding topics in southern writing. Gospel music is not just found in the American South, of
course, but southerners surely played a central role in its formation and
subsequent development. Gospel represented the introduction of modern forms into southern religious music, including lively new songs,

publishing companies, quartets, and well-organized singing schools, all of which reinvigorated the old-time evangelical message. Most recently of all, visionary folk artists have appeared, mainly in the southern countryside, as a vestige of traditional regional culture. "The paintings, carvings in stone and wood, and yard art displays of self-taught artists are," according to art historian Lisa Howorth, "like blues and gospel music, quintessentially Southern – a potent and vital blend of tradition, history, environment, individual expression, and religion."[2]

Religion offers an entryway into understanding how southern culture produced such a broad flowering of creative expression in the twentieth century. This creativity has reflected the peculiar admixtures of the spoken word and the visual image in southern culture. Often one sees cross-fertilization of different genres. For his pastoral landscape entitled *Peace in the Valley*, visionary artist O. W. "Pappy" Kitchens drew from the description of the peaceable kingdom found in the book of Isaiah, but the gospel song "Peace in the Valley" (by African American songwriter Thomas A. Dorsey) also influenced him. Black visionary artist Gertrude Morgan painted *Jesus Is My Airplane*, inspired by a gospel song of that title, first recorded by Mother McCollum in 1930. Morgan herself recorded the song on her 1970s album *Let's Make a Record: Sister Gertrude Morgan.* Another visionary artist, Eddie Kendrick, portrayed his own climb to heaven through modern transportation – again, inspired by a black gospel song. Another folk artist, Howard Finster, heard his mother sing old-time religious songs at home in Valley Head, Alabama, and himself learned shape-note singing as a boy at a singing school. One of the first tunes he remembers learning was "Some Have Fathers Over Yonder," which was not even in a songbook but was orally transmitted. Finster could play dozens of gospel songs and hymns by ear on the piano, guitar, and mouth harp. In addition, he improvised hundreds of songs that told of his visions of other worlds and his convictions about right and wrong moral behavior.[3]

Southern creativity has flourished partly because the region's writers, painters, and musicians have lived in a place that has taken seriously the images, symbols, and worldviews of a particular variety of religion that has long dominated the culture. Those creative people might be believers or skeptics, but religion was part of the landscape in which they lived. Writers, musicians, and artists use biblical stories and characters and also reveal an intimate familiarity with God's presence, through revelations, dreams, and visions. A complex southern spirituality, rooted in the region's culture, produced a tradition of creative expression that drew from church life and from individual inspiration.

Evangelicalism has profoundly influenced southern culture because of its long religious hegemony in the region. Its rise dates back to the frontier revivals of the early nineteenth century, which saw Baptists and Methodists come to dominate American religion in general. No other religious tradition has seriously challenged the dominance of evangelicalism in the South, whereas northern religion had changed considerably by the turn of the twentieth century because of the growth of the Roman Catholic Church and the cultural influence of Judaism (both stemming from European immigration, little of which went south compared to the Northeast and Midwest). Even Protestantism itself had changed in the North by the advent of twentieth century, responding much more than the South did to the liberal theological trends that led to the social gospel and an accommodation with Darwinian science.

The predominant churches were not just conservative theologically and mostly evangelical; they were also deeply southern. The largest southern Protestant groups had split off from their northern brethren during the sectional crisis leading up to the Civil War, and the Baptists, Methodists, and Presbyterians remained divided along regional lines long after the war ended. Those churches retained their separate ways from the northern faithful and dramatically rose in numbers after the Civil War, when open religiosity seemed an affirmation of one's southern identity. Hence, these separate religious traditions became the folk expressions of a distinctive southern culture.

Southern evangelicalism insists that religious experience is the essence of faith. With a Calvinist-inspired dim view of human nature, it is a religion of sin and salvation. The central theme is the search for conversion, which can then lead to a transformed life. One must be born again, cleansed in the "precious blood of the lamb," as one gospel song puts it, "washed white as snow." The sinner seeks God's grace and with conversion entertains the "blessed assurance" of redemption (to quote another gospel song). Holiness and Pentecostalism emerged at the turn of the twentieth century as sectarian groups outside the mainstream of Protestant culture and yet closely related to its message of sin and salvation. They injected a new infusion of the Holy Spirit into southern evangelicalism, one that added considerably to the vitality of the tradition among the poor and disfranchised – as well as evoking special disdain from intellectuals such as Mencken. Evangelical churches are not unique to the South at all, but the distinctiveness of southern religion is that this interdenominational evangelical tradition, centered in Baptists, Methodists, Pentecostals, and sectarians, has been the dominant one in the region for so long, profoundly shaping not just religion but social, economic, and political life, as well as cultural expression.[4]

Religious life in the South has been racially segregated. African Americans have worshipped in the African Methodist Episcopal Church and the National Baptist Convention, while whites attended the Southern Methodist Church (until the 1930s) and the Southern Baptist Convention. Still, the predominant style of religion in the South is a shared tradition, one that reflects black influence as much as white. Distinctive African American church practices reinforce southern evangelicalism. For instance, southern black worship is often expressive, and ministers inculcate individualistic moral virtues. Historians, moreover, have demonstrated that slaves who attended early camp meetings fundamentally shaped the developing evangelical tradition in style and substance. The Bible, of course, is the literal word of God for blacks as well as whites. Indeed, the interaction of the races around manifestations of religious practice predates Emancipation: in the antebellum South, blacks and whites sometimes worshipped together in the same church spaces, facilitating exchange of cultural ways. In contemporary times, blacks join evangelical Baptist and Methodist churches in even greater percentages than whites, while religious songs continue to represent a shared body of cultural expression. The biracial heritage of the southern religious tradition is reflected in the creative expressions of the region's artists. Old church fans from pre–air conditioning days showed similar scenes in black and white churches of Jesus with the lambs, peaceful pastoral landscapes, and smiling young children with such words as "Go to Church." Ron and Jesse Cooper's *Praising the King: Kerosene Heater* portrays the evangelical choice – sin or salvation, heaven or hell. "I put black and white people in heaven and hell," Ronald Cooper explains. "I feel like both races will be at both places."[5]

A religious culture has permeated the South, influencing the region's ways outside church doors as well as within. Sometimes creative people have been believers, other times not, but their culture has given them dramatic spiritual materials with which to work. William Faulkner recalled the workings of this religious culture on him as a child. In explaining his frequent use of religious references, he pointed to his "childhood, in a very small Mississippi town," where he grew up with religion all around him. "I assimilated that," he explained, "took that in without even knowing it. It's just there." He noted that "it had nothing to do with how much of it [he] might believe or disbelieve – it's just there."[6] More recently, Reynolds Price has written that southern culture "provided [him] with a daily world in which religion played an omnipresent role," which was "immensely important" to those who would later become writers. It embodied a concrete sense of "the relation of human creatures to the Creator," but that relationship grew out of the particularities of daily life. It "depends very intensely upon where we came from and when we came from and who was behind us, who was cooking the meals and who was taking us places on Friday nights or Saturdays and Sundays." Except for those "extraordinary moments when God breaks through to an individual creature," Price insists that "those things that make us most fully human largely occur, and are taught, in the way that table manners are taught. From mother to child. From father to son or father to daughter." He characterized the southern version of this as "that very complex, bittersweet marination in religion that was available right on down through the 50s and 60s to the standard southern child." For southerners, church "provided us with a direct possibility of serious encounter with the center of things – the Creator." As a result of growing up in this "bittersweet marination of religion," Price is convinced he is "naturally graced with being a believer."[7]

Another contemporary southern writer, Larry Brown, grew up in rural Lafayette County, Mississippi, the real county upon which Faulkner based his mythical Yoknapatawpha County. Brown was from a working-class family and moved to Memphis, attending a Methodist church there as a boy. He agreed that southern writers have been inspired artistically by the religious culture around them: "Well, I think in my case religion crops up so much because I heard it all my life. From the earliest times I can remember, I was in the church, raised in the church, went to Sunday school, vacation Bible school, church on Sunday night, church on Sunday morning, all that stuff." His "whole family was heavily involved in it," and he suspects the same was true for other southern writers. "Because they were exposed to so much of it at an early age," he suggests, "it makes an impression on them."[8]

Many southern writers reflect the tension between faith in and skepticism about southern evangelicalism, which shaped their lives and that of the region. William Faulkner, who grew up Methodist but became a nominal Episcopalian, once described being Southern Baptist as an "emotional condition" that emerged "from times of hardship" in the region, when people found "little or no food for the human spirit." Religion "was the escape they had." Reynolds Price sees southern evangelicalism as sometimes a danger to creativity. He dislikes its proselytizing tendencies: "The conflict usually arises when an author feels that his or her own spiritual convictions require him to evangelize, to proselytize to win fellow adherents to the faith. I am many quarts low on evangelism." He does not embrace the evangelical mission of "signing people up for a particular belief system." The limit of organized religion for him "is when institutional beliefs become inimical to the creating that . . . [artists and writers] are capable of doing." Herbert Singleton, a folk painter, also betrays an artist's skepticism of organized religion, albeit in a different idiom from Price: "No matter if you're going to a preacher, a priest, a psychiatrist, a witch doctor, or a voodoo queen, you're only getting confidence by proxy. Can't nobody solve the problem but the person hisself."[9]

Southern writers, artists, and musicians have drawn from the rich oral culture of the South, which has produced renowned politicians, lawyers, storytelling entertainers, and singers – people with special language gifts. The South is not famous for producing influential theologians but surely is well known for cultivating preachers. Martin Luther King Jr. and Billy Graham are among the most celebrated Americans around the world. Southern evangelicalism prizes religious experience, and its characteristic experiential orientation is toward sound. It is a religion of the word.

Church services, for example, take place in what congregants usually refer to as auditoriums, not sanctuaries. As anthropologist Miles Richardson has noted, "seeing and touching are the principal religious modalities" for Roman Catholics, represented in the sacraments and in the visual context of the mass, whereas speaking and hearing are paths to the sacred for southern evangelicals. Southern Baptists listen for God's voice during devotional moments, and Pentecostals wait for the Holy Spirit to descend upon them and inspire them to speak in tongues. Church services revolve around the word. Music directors occupy a spot just below the preacher and typically orchestrate much of the first part of worship services in Baptist, Methodist, Church of Christ, Pentecostal, and other congregations well represented in the South. "Sweetly echo the gospel call; offer pardon and peace to all" is the beginning of the classic Southern Baptist hymn "Wonderful Words of Life," which sets the tone for the service. Members of the congregation may testify to the saving power of grace on their wicked souls, and Jimmy Swaggart is only one celebrated example of the many preachers who have recounted their salacious life experiences in order to receive pardon from their congregations. Ministers themselves traditionally came to their profession not through theological education but simply by receiving "the call," as God communicated "His" will to them. Congregations then judged their ministers on their preaching effectiveness. How many souls have his words saved? A preacher needs the reassuring verbal response of "amen" to validate his point. In African American evangelical services, the call-and-response interaction of minister and audience is often especially prized as an expression of collective worship.[10]

Evangelicalism follows Christ's Great Commission to go into the world and convert the lost, placing a premium on open religiosity, witnessing to the world about one's faith. People ask you what church you attend when you move into a new community, easily assuming everyone does so. The general public is not surprised at street preaching. The oral is usually seen as the most direct route to the divine in southern religion, and the best way to proselytize is by witnessing verbally to others. But the culture outside of churches and official doctrine has devised its own way to combine the visual and the oral. Roadside signs, for example, have long witnessed, through such messages as JESUS SAVES,

GET RIGHT WITH GOD, and PREPARE TO MEET THY GOD. I recently saw a sign on a Mississippi highway that said, PREPARE TO MEET THY GOD: LAST CHANCE. Among visionary artists in the region, visual imagery spreads the word of God in similar ways. The words LORD LOVE YOU appear frequently on Georgia artist R. A. Miller's works, which he usually paints on cut tin, a contemporary version of a traditional southern roadside sign. Mary T. Smith's yard art in rural Mississippi often uses well-known religious sayings that could also have appeared on hand-lettered roadside boards. Her piece *The Lord Is Head of the World* portrays Christ.[11]

The creative expressions of southern visionary artists reflect this missionary-like outreach work, using sounds along with images to spread the good word. Many artists are preachers themselves; others are active in their churches. African American sculptor William Edmondson was a Primitive Baptist who saw his sculpture as his service to God: "Every time I try to read the Bible, or preach, the Lord takes my mind off it and tells me I got work to do." North Alabama's Benjamin Perkins, who is white, preached his first sermon in 1929 and was ordained in a Pentecostal denomination, the Church of God, in 1948. He began erecting his own chapel at age sixty-two, renaming it eventually the Heartline Assembly Church of God. Ronald and Jesse Cooper are also Pentecostals who insist their work teaches the Bible and attracts "sinner people who don't believe in much, don't go to church or worship." They hope it "might make them think about their own soul." Gertrude Morgan started the Everlasting Gospel Revelation Mission to anchor her street preaching in New Orleans. She said God had spoken to her: "My heavenly father called me in 1934. . . . Go ye into yonder's world and sing with a loud voice. . . . You are a chosen vessel to call men, women, girls, and boys." Her vision came in words reminiscent of Christ's commission to go into the world.[12]

Perhaps the best-known southern visionary artist is Howard Finster, who preached for years at the Berrytown Baptist Church in north Georgia and resolutely saw his art as a way to communicate God's message. God called to Finster. While painting a bicycle, he dipped his finger in white paint and saw a face on the tip of his finger. God said, "Paint sacred art, Howard." The voice and the image worked together, inspiring

Finster, and thereafter his work combined sacred words, often biblical, with visual images. In *Howard's First Painting*, one of his messages on the canvas is "Those He Calls He Qualifys for That He Shall Do." Each Finster painting or sculpture is a sermon expressing his faith. He also established a chapel, the Worlds Folk Art Church, Inc., a forty-foot-high wooden building. It is adjacent to his Paradise Garden, a landfill several acres large between his home and chapel, which includes signs, figures, broken TVs, flowers, hubcaps, gourds, bicycle parts, and other artifacts of his natural and man-made landscape.[13]

Nothing has been more influential in southern religious creativity than the Bible, which reflects the regional culture's orientation toward the word. Children begin to learn its significance when they sing, "Yes, Jesus, loves me. / The Bible tells me so." When walking into church, worshippers may first see a sign outside with the sermon title of the day, accompanied by a relevant biblical quote, such as "For God so loved the world" (John 3:16). The baptistery may say, "This is my beloved son" (Matthew 3:17), recalling in this place of new baptisms Christ's own in the river Jordan. Worshippers bring their own Bibles with them to church, and pews contain extra copies as well as songbooks. As for the service itself, brave is the evangelical minister who would not begin his sermon with a biblical verse. The Bible is regarded in most southern churches as authoritative in itself, containing sufficient knowledge for the faith. Southern Baptists are a contentious lot, but whether fundamentalists who believe the scriptures are inerrant (right in every detail) or moderates who believe they are infallible (in accomplishing God's revelation to humans), they share the belief that, through the Bible, God *speaks* to them. As Miles Richardson notes, the Bible "is not simply a source of information, but the very voice of God."[14]

The Bible is profoundly interwoven with regional life – it is the essence of the religious faith and a language for communication outside of churches. Creative people had a rich common cultural source – the King James translation of the Holy Bible. "We became as southerners in the evangelistic Protestant South," writes Susan Ketchin, "intimately familiar with the resounding beauty of the biblical language and the unmistakable rhetoric of sermons, the rhythm and meter, symbols, the metaphors, the cataloging of images, and the building up of tension in the narratives." Reynolds Price adds that while other American places read the King James translation, "[southerners] perhaps capitalized on that in ways that other regions of America didn't," because of "its marvelous reverberations in [their] lives."[15]

The South has been a storytelling place, a trait at the heart of southern creative expression, whether in literature, music, or painting. Doris Betts sees the source of her fiction as "Bible stories, beyond question." They are "wonderful stories," which "make the place where you live nontemporal; it is always possible that if an angel showed up on a threshing floor, appearances could happen anywhere. It makes you feel the ordinary is not ordinary." She recalled as a child having to memorize books of the Bible and to compete on teams with other children to find stories in the scriptures. The graphic illustrations in older editions (such as Dore's sometimes gory engravings), showing David holding Goliath's head by its hair or John the Baptist's head on a platter, piqued her imagination, as did the "presence of a lot of truly bad people in the Bible, what writers call 'round characters.'" All of that taught "[her] how to make characters in fiction."[16]

Southern musicians drew from this biblical knowledge in generations of hymns, spirituals, and camp meeting songs. When gospel music appeared as a new variety of southern religious music in the twentieth century, it rested still on a biblical idiom, even as it drew from new sounds. Consider, for example, the Golden Gate Quartet, one of the most influential African American gospel groups to emerge in the first half of the last century. They formed in a barbershop in Berkeley, Virginia, in 1930. One member of the quartet, Willie Johnson, added jazz syncopation and a beat to familiar plantation religious music and southern folk songs to create a lively new gospel sound, which was typical of the emergence of black gospel in the early twentieth century. Despite these innovations, the Golden Gate Quartet continued to retell biblical stories – "God Told Nicodemus," "Joshua Fit the Battle of Jericho," "Moses Smote the Water," and "Jezebel" were only a few of the old stories that they made famous in their new style. Like earlier preachers, the first gospel music singers conveyed the fallen nature of humanity through lively tunes about Jezebel's wickedness, David's weakness for Bathsheba, Peter's denial of Christ, and countless other biblical tales.[17]

Visionary artists also draw from the store of biblical knowledge. God's creation of the world, the Garden of Eden, and Adam and Eve's fall from grace are recurrent scenes, often fancifully so. Edgar Tolson's *Original Sin* is a carving that depicts Adam and Eve engaged in a ménage à trois with the wily serpent. Johnny Swearingen's *The Creation of the World* reflects traditional southern narrative technique, achieved through multiple sequential images showing human genesis up to Cain's killing of Abel. The New Testament has also provided themes for visionary artists, especially stories centered around the life of Christ, from the manger to the cross. Jesse Aaron's *Crucifixion*, for example, is a wooden sculpture – the figure of Jesus cut with a chain saw from a single piece of wood. George Williams portrays a black Jesus hanging on a white painted cross in his *Crucifixion*. The Bible provides folk artists with scenes of heaven and hell, the Devil, and the Apocalypse that passed from the scriptures themselves through generations of southern sermons, religious music, and oral folktales.[18]

This widespread familiarity with the Bible and artistic use of it mattered not only in providing a unifying subject matter and language but also in its influence on the worldview that dominated the region. Southern creative expression rooted in religion has rested on a dynamic tension between darkness and light, the sense of human limitation yet the possibility of divine illumination. Indeed, judging by their cultural expressions, southerners typically took from the Bible an understanding of the centrality of the fall from grace that tainted and limited human nature. Southern history reinforced biblical wisdom for the region's writers, singers, and painters. Confederate southerners discovered they were not David killing Goliath. Another attempt to draw a parallel with the Bible also failed to come to fruition when they declared their cause a holy war as it began; they lost and had to live with an abiding sense of defeat. For black southerners, the oppression of slavery and the brutalities of Jim Crow similarly inculcated a sense of powerlessness and human frailty. For so many southerners, white and black, cruel poverty left hopes unfulfilled and aspirations unsatisfied. It is no wonder that southerners could respond to the biblical tale of Job, who falls, suffers plagues, hears the voices of prophets, and still manages to be saved.

Walker Percy once commented that the South produced so many fine writers "because [it] lost the War." Flannery O'Connor interpreted his

comment to mean "[southerners] have had [their] Fall." Southern identity, she said, came from "those beliefs and qualities which [the South]
has absorbed from the Scriptures and from [its] own history of defeat
and violation: a distrust of the abstract, a sense of human dependence
on the grace of God, and acknowledgment that evil is not simply a problem to be solved, but a mystery to be endured." Southerners, she wrote
in the 1950s, "have gone into the modern world with an inburnt knowledge of human limitations and with a sense of mystery which could not
have developed in our first state of ignorance." Several core mythic stories from the Bible thus dramatized for creative people the sense of mystery, human limitation, and yet hope for redemption that southerners
prayed for. "Thus it was for many imaginative southerners," writes Doris
Betts, "that stories overlapped: the Bible story, the regional story of the
South, the personal story of oneself."[19]

If biblical knowledge and southern history reinforced interpretations
of regional experience regarding human limitations, southerners learned
the same lesson from their life as agrarians. Randall Kenan, who grew
up in Chinquapin, North Carolina, contrasts a Roman Catholic sense of
religious mystery, rooted in ritual, with the attitudes of "the hard-nosed
Southern Baptist." Southern farmers who work the fields every day are
anxious over "whether the crops are going to rise. It's a totally different
kind of mystery, based on the natural rhythms of the land and weather,
not dependent so much on the keeping of rites in an institution." Reynolds Price sees the southern land as crucial in his developing during
childhood "some special relationship in [his] own life with God." He
recalls that "this time coincided with [his family] having bought land in
the country outside of town," and he spent much time alone, "just wandering in the woods and playing in the creek."[20]

If the Bible, regional history, and personal experience have drawn
southern creative artists to a sense of mystery rooted in hard experiences, southern spirituality has also provided resources for nurturing a
sense of grace as well. The spirit is alive and well in southern religion.
The biblical text is 1 Corinthians 12:7: "But the manifestation of the
Spirit is given to every man to profit withal." There may be many gifts
to the southern faithful – visions, wisdom, healing, prophecy, speaking
in tongues (to some), "but all these worketh that one and the selfsame

Spirit, dividing to every man severally as he will." Visionary folk artists use the same language to describe their creative process. "That's a gift I got," says Louisiana artist Royal Robertson. "I was having a vision. . . . I call it spiritual travel." Another African American artist, Bessie Harvey, uses similar language: "I have a vision. I have a gift. I can close my eyes and see things other people can't." This intuitive creativity rests in the subconscious, but southern culture authenticates such mysterious religious experiences because they embody the centrality of individual religious experience. To be sure, mainstream church cultures would see the additional need for believers to submit to church discipline and moral rigor. Nonetheless, they share with sectarians the belief that Jesus can speak intimately to the devout and the Holy Spirit can infuse the individual.[21]

The spirit communicates through voices from on high in ways that suggest a relationship between the spirit world and words. The spirit is understood through visual images that contain words – the graphic embodiment of the spirit moving. J. B. Murray, like many southern folk artists, received a vision that told him to do "Spiritual Work." "When I started I prayed and I prayed, and the Lord sunk a vision from the sun." He began writing in an "unknown tongue," as art historian Judith McWillie has termed it. "It was then I began to write these letters," Murray explains. "Different writing represents different languages and folks. The Lord changes the instrument on me and that is why you see different writing. It's the language of the Holy Spirit, direct from God." The source of this is the spirit, but reflecting a Christian view, his inspiration comes also from another expression of the godhead and reflects the southern stress on talking and listening. "Jesus. He moves in mysterious ways and wonderful forms," notes Murray. "He tells me direct." Words and images are intertwined for visionary artists. "I draw, sketch, and paint what I see," says Pappy Kitchens, "or visualize from a reading."[22]

African American spiritual traditions rest easily alongside the evangelicalism of the South. "In African lore, where spirits and the living mingle freely, visions are accepted," Alice Rae Yellen notes. Bessie Harvey consciously expresses her African American heritage in her art: "Just about everything I touch is Africa. I think I'm of old African descent." Randall Kenan does not attribute his memories to an African heritage directly, but he does recall that ghosts occupied the old family homestead in North Carolina, which his great-great grandfather had built. "We would sit around and talk about the family," says Kenan, "and my mother would say, 'Well, in that room back there my mother died,' (and she'd tell you about the day her mother died); then she'd say, 'Then my brother, he died back in this room . . . and then up in this room Papa died,' and so on." Each room took on meaning not because of its ostensible function as a bedroom or pantry "but for who died there. So [Kenan] always had this palpable sense of these presences." More than with white southern spirituality, African American religious tradition in the South portrays death as a spirit that actively moves among the living: "Death comes creeping in the room," as one black gospel song puts it. Kenan remembers that his mother "would spin these yarns of being visited by departed relatives, particularly when she was ill." Her stories were "wonderful dovetailing blends of medical science, out-of-body experiences, and other unexplained phenomena – and these things would heal her, strangely enough." His childhood southern world thus "condoned a concrete spiritual world."[23]

The spirit has seemed to move among the South's economically deprived in particular. The South that generated the literature and gospel music of the twentieth century was a poor place, the "nation's No. 1 economic problem," as the federal government described it in the 1930s. Contemporary visionary art thrives in places outside the mainstream of American life, such as Appalachia, the Alabama Black Belt, and the Mississippi Delta. Visionary art comes out of this world, and southern writers, if not impoverished themselves, have been viscerally aware of their neighbors. Flannery O'Connor insisted that the fiction writer should be concerned with the poor, whose experiences have spiritual significance. According to O'Connor, the writer's "concern with poverty is with a poverty fundamental to man. . . . The basic experience of everyone is the experience of human limitation," which is the "bedrock of all human experience." She noted that the scriptures provided "that mythos which the poor held in common." "When the poor hold sacred history in common," O'Connor further observed, "they have ties to the universal and the holy, which allows the meaning of their every action to be heightened and seen under the aspect of eternity."[24]

Religion has offered empowerment through the spirit to suffering southerners such as these. Robert Coles documented the life of North Carolina tenant farmers. "Again and again I have heard from them a virtual cry for approval, for authorization of sorts," he recalled. As one tenant farmer told him about church: "I come out of there and I'm taller. I'm feeling bigger. I feel God has taken me to Him. He put His hand on my shoulder, and said, 'Brother John Wilson, the reason that I want you praying to Me is so you won't be looking at yourself and feeling so low.' . . . My daddy used to tell me when I was a boy that he didn't want my spirit to go and break, and if I prayed to God, He'd keep me strong, and I'd never lose my spirit, no matter how bad they treat you, and no matter what words they call you, the bad words." God imbues this farmer with the power of the Holy Spirit to keep his human spirit from breaking.[25] The connection between the Holy Spirit and the human spirit is thus revealed on southern ground, especially here among people lacking material possessions and acknowledged status yet open to accepting the spirit.

Randall Kenan sees a difference between the spirituality of the poor and the well-off among the African Americans of his rural youth, symbolized by music: "I honestly believe that there is a directly proportional relationship between the poor churches where the actual music is really horrible, but spiritual and powerful in a visceral way, and the rich ones where there is less spirit, where they sing this soul-entrancing music with perfect notes, but where there is a hollowness and lack of conviction behind the music." The music was never great at his Baptist church when he was growing up; what affected him was "the sense of everybody singing, everybody participating, the climbing that stair toward that particular form of ecstasy, that [people] can only get in a fellowship service in which [everybody is] rhythmically climbing and getting out of [themselves] in that fashion."[26]

The image of light is central to southern evangelicalism, and the region's creative expression suggests that the spirit works to inspire artistry in a flash, as with conversion. "Jesus Christ is the Light of the World and He is the Answer to the World's Problems" is a familiar saying in the interdenominational southern religious tradition, one that Benjamin Perkins of north Alabama places at the center of one of his paintings. This statement appears on a gold cross, painted to approximate neon's warm light. However, no creative piece better captures the centrality of religious light to southern creativity than Hank Williams's "I Saw the Light." Williams was a product of the southern religious culture. He grew up a poor boy in Alabama, one who absorbed the beliefs of southern evangelicalism, even if his later life was far from outwardly righteous. Along with singing of honky-tonk carousing, though, he also wrote religious songs, including his classic "I Saw the Light," which conveys the evangelical message of the centrality of conversion. Speaking after his conversion experience, he testifies that he had "wandered so aimless, life filled with sin." But then "Jesus came like a stranger in the night / Praise the Lord, [he] saw the light." Williams uses the image of himself as a blind man, wandering alone, beset by "worries and fears [he] claimed for [his] own." He draws from a New Testament miracle, seeing himself as "like the blind man that God gave back his sight." After his conversion, after he "saw the light," he looked forward to "no more darkness, no more night." The song ends with the suggestion that a changed heart will be expressed in terms of a moral transformation, as Williams sings, "I have traded the wrong for the right," employing the language of moral behavior.[27]

Southern spirituality is thus a complex mix, resting on tensions that often go unresolved. Creative expression, however, helps to resolve those tensions. Black North Carolina writer Randall Kenan sees his religious experience as a child and an adolescent shaping his imagination: "I took the whole thing very serious . . . all that hell-fire preaching." He sees the religion as "a very simple formulation" that represented "this profound spiritual tension between good and evil." The experiences of the southern poor embody a synthesis or resolution of the underlying southern spiritual dichotomy between the awareness of human limitation, rooted in hard lives, and the possibility of transcendence, which provides inspiration for the creative. Mississippi author Larry Brown spoke for southern creative culture in commenting that he wrote "about people surviving, about people proceeding out from calamity . . . about the lost." They may be lost, but they "are aware of their need for redemption."[28]

The revelation that guides the creative individuals who come out of this southern religious culture is indeed the possibility of grace, mercy, and redemption. It is a hard religion, with much rigor, taking root in a society of much suffering for many of its people, and yet God forgives and nurtures. An inscription in Herbert Singleton's portrayal of Adam and Eve says, "In the eyes of God true love covers all fault." Or as Reynolds Price says from within a different creative medium, "I think the end of fiction is mercy."[29] Southern culture has given its artists the gift of seeing the spirit working even within this hard world.

8 The Word and the Image

Self-Taught Art, the Bible, the Spirit, and Southern Creativity

Flannery O'Connor, the Georgia-born, Roman Catholic writer whose most acclaimed works appeared in the 1950s, saw the South through a lens of faith that would have enabled her to appreciate the region's self-taught artists. She was a storyteller and so too have been these creative visionaries. The storyteller, for O'Connor, "is concerned with what is," and for a storyteller of faith, "what [she] sees on the surface will be of interest to [her] only as [she] can go through it into an experience of mystery itself." The mystery she speaks of is "the mystery of [humankind's] position on earth," and she used an accompanying word, "manners," to describe the work of the creative person dealing with matters of faith: "The manners are those conventions which, in the hands of the artist, reveal that central mystery." She saw the fiction writer as "concerned with ultimate mystery as [found] embodied in the concrete world of sense experience." Sense perceptions are indeed the raw stuff of creative people everywhere, but O'Connor saw clearly that the senses should tie the creative imagination to place, to region. "The things we see, hear, smell, and touch affect us long before we believe anything at all, and the South impresses its image on us from the moment we are able to distinguish one's own from another," she wrote.

The southern writer discovers "being bound through the senses to a particular society and a particular history, to particular sounds and a particular idiom," and that discovery is the beginning of a realization that puts that writer's work "into real human perspective."[1]

O'Connor's observations about the southern writer are revealing about the creative context for the imagination and its use of religion in the American South. The region's writers, musicians, and folk artists operate within a cultural context in which a particular form of faith, evangelical Protestantism, has dominated for so long that it offers creative people an idiom of its own, with images, stories, symbols, rituals, institutions, and experiences they can explore. O'Connor notes further that "the writer whose themes are religious needs a region where these themes find a response in the life of the people" (200), and the creative imagination is surely spurred by a place known as the Bible Belt because of its fervent religiosity. Without question, the American South has become a place of significance on the world's spiritual map. V. S. Naipaul visited the region in the 1980s and concluded he had never been anywhere where people took right behavior and religious faith so seriously.

In recounting the importance of the senses to the budding writer, O'Connor mentioned first the "things we see," and the visual sense has indeed been a key one in southern creativity. Much more familiar, though, is the oral orientation of the South, its inclination toward experiences that are perceived through the aural sense. The word has been central to the South's culture, whether folk philosophers telling stories on porches and at country stores, preachers and lawyers using language to win souls and make their legal cases, professional humorists making listeners chuckle, or writers and singers, who have epitomized the region's styles for so long, crafting language to enthrall readers and fans. "When one Southern character speaks," O'Connor notes, "regardless of his station in life, an echo of all Southern life is heard" (199). But the South has also presented its observers with a compelling visual landscape, and creative people have responded to it. The land itself offers an often lush image, with flora and fauna that seem exotic to outsiders and that can stimulate a gothic imagination among writers and artists.

The Bible has been an essential source for the visual culture of the South, with an amalgamation of written words, oral delivery, and visual representations making southerners familiar with the images coming out of the scriptures. Even in a society with relatively high rates of illiteracy for the United States, southerners knew Bible characters and stories. "It takes a story to make a story," O'Connor noted, a story of "mythic dimensions, one which belongs to everybody, one in which everybody is able to recognize the hand of God and its descent." In the South, "the Scriptures fill this role." Note that O'Connor uses a compelling story, which presents a dramatic visual image, in explaining why the Bible plays a major role in making the South a storytelling place: "Our response to life is different if we have been taught only a definition of faith than if we have trembled with Abraham as he held the knife over Isaac" (202–3). In her novel *Wise Blood*, O'Connor herself has presented one of the most powerful visual images about the pervasiveness of religion in southern culture. The novel's main character, Hazel Motes, attempts to found a church without Christ, as a way to escape the inescapable meaning of the demands of a redeemer, yet Christ pursues him relentlessly. O'Connor takes the central biblical narrative of Christ and uses it in surprising ways to lead the reader to recognize the power of salvation.

O'Connor makes one additional point about the religious imagination in the South that can serve as further background for consideration of the cultural context that has provided fertile ground for the region's creative artists. She was highly aware of changes in the South after World War II, changes that meant "every day [southerners] are getting more and more like the rest of the country, that [they] are being forced out not only of [their] many sins, but of [their] few virtues" (28–29). She felt that the southern writer needed to "observe [their] fierce but fading manners in the light of an ultimate concern" (29). She used a visual image, suggesting the writer's gaze should go beyond looking at the surface, "beyond mere problems, until it touches that realm which is the concern of prophets and poets" (45). To do this, the writer had to "descend far enough into himself to reach those underground springs that give life to his work." That descent into self would also be a descent into region. "It will be descent through the darkness of the familiar into a world where," O'Connor writes with a biblical analogy, "like the blind man cured in the gospels, he sees men as if they were trees, but walking. This is the beginning of vision, and I feel it is a vision which we in the South must at least try to understand if we want to participate in the continuance of a vital Southern literature" (50). The South's self-taught artists lived through the changes of the twentieth century and were visionaries who descended into the darkness of the familiar to produce a distinctive tradition but one comparable to the literature and music of the region. O'Connor again uses an image to suggest the role of the creative artist in using the visual sense to exact deeper meanings: "The image of the South, in all its complexity, is so powerful in us that it is a force which has to be encountered and engaged. The writer must wrestle with it, like Jacob with the angel, until he has extracted a blessing" (198).

This complex image of the South, given to creative people as part of their southern birthright, includes a sense of loss. With black artists, it has surely been the horrors of slavery and the brutalities of racial segregation. For many southerners, it has been grueling poverty, the generations of economic deprivation and the threat of spiritual numbness resulting from such a reality. O'Connor saw poverty as one of the wellsprings of her own creativity as well as that of her region, representing as it did "the experience of human limitation" (131). The historical existence of poverty in the South gave the writer the images and stories to make it real to readers to understand its broader human meaning. O'Connor also mentioned defeat in the Civil War, in particular, which was the region's fall: "We have gone into the modern world with an inburnt knowledge of human limitations and with a sense of mystery which could not have developed in our first state of innocence – as it has not sufficiently developed in the rest of the country" (59). This sense of human limitation came not only out of specifically southern history but also out of scripture, out of the region's word. The biblical metaphor for loss that reverberated through southern culture was the Fall of man in the book of Genesis, but other biblical images struck southern creative people as appropriate as well.

O'Connor was a writer who worked with words but who understood how the visual and the oral intertwined in the South as part of the region's creativity. Artists in the region have not all had a religious imagination, as she did, but evangelical Protestantism has been so strongly imprinted on the landscape that they have had to wrestle with it often indeed. The South produced creative people who were sometimes skeptics and sometimes true believers, but they made use of religious images, characters, and stories as part of their work.

Anyone growing up in the South in the early twentieth century – when southern creativity began to blossom in new ways among so many of the region's writers, musicians, self-taught artists, and others – lived in the shadow of the Baptist and Methodist steeples. A 1906 religious census of the white South, including the former Confederate states east of the Mississippi River, showed that 96.6 percent of the population had Protestant affiliations, with 90 percent of church members joining Baptist and Methodist churches. Both had been regionally organized churches since before the Civil War, and the next largest popular denomination, Presbyterian, was also organized in a separate regional denomination that began during the war. Black Baptists and Methodists had differing histories and missions from white evangelicals but shared much theology, moralism, and liturgical practice.[2]

As embodied in these denominations, southern evangelicalism, as we've seen in previous chapters, insists that religious experience is the essence of faith – a key distinction in understanding how creative people could find inspiration in a tradition that also was fixated on orthodoxy to such an extent as to sometimes discourage the free play of the mind. Calvin was a patron saint of southern theology, with southerners taking to heart his dim view of human nature. John Wesley was another theological saint, though one who highlighted the centrality of grace. This combination made the dominant style of religion in the South one of sin and salvation, the belief in each profoundly held. Evangelicalism does not prioritize theology, though, but rather the personal relationship with the Redeemer. Sinners have to be born again, seeking God's grace through either patient study or the flash of immediate personal revelation, depending on denominational tradition. Justification by faith represents the workings of the supernatural in the life of the wicked, leading to conversion and a new relationship with God. The assurance of redemption then promotes a reformed lifestyle, with a deliberate effort to overcome the self and serve God. A prime aspect of that service is evangelism, sharing the good news of Christ with others, not as one part of faith but as a driving imperative. The coming millennium and heavenly reward provide future meaning to this vision of human history.

Holiness and Pentecostalism emerged around the turn of the twentieth century as sectarian groups outside the mainstream of southern religious life, but they injected a new infusion of the Holy Spirit into southern working-class evangelicalism, one with profound significance for musical and artistic creativity.[3]

The Bible occupied a position of peculiar religious authority in the South, dominated as it has been by evangelical Protestantism, unchallenged as a guide to faith and personal behavior. While other faiths and denominations may rely on historical traditions, communal experiences, theological exegesis, the episcopacy, or combinations of these factors, southern evangelicalism validates the Bible as the revealed word of God. Although fundamentalists and moderates in the region have long disputed the boundaries of interpretation of the scriptures, they typically have agreed that the Bible has the answers to life's questions. Additionally, the individual's interpretation of the scriptures gives coherence to the Christian message. The Bible gradually acquired special meanings in the South's public culture as well, as defenders of slavery and later racial segregation justified those peculiar institutions through citations of particular passages of the scriptures, ignoring others that spoke of more egalitarian impulses.[4]

The Bible and the workings of the Holy Spirit are seen as interwoven in the South, among people who believe in the active workings of the supernatural, providing a fertile spiritual soil for the creative soul. Both the Bible and the spirit were matters of everyday concern. One Tennessee Holiness preacher who was recently interviewed conveyed the connection. "I believe that all of the Bible is real," he explained. "If this book isn't the book of God, you'd better throw in the towel, for there is nothing else that will stand the test like this book." At the same time, he noted the intimacy of his experience with the Son of God: "I'll tell you frankly that I have been talking with Jesus, and His word lives in my heart." A Baptist minister from Cumberland County, Tennessee, passionately affirms the scriptures: "I believe with all my heart that the Bible is the holy Word of God, that He inspired men through the Holy Spirit to write the Word in order that they, not only in that bad time, but in the day in which we live, in this instant of time, might be able to receive the Word of God." The scriptures are not just a historical document, though, but one with continuing meaning through direct contact with Jesus, the central figure of the Christian scriptures: "Now, the Word of God is Jesus. Jesus was the Word. He was the light, and He brought light unto all men that we would believe upon Him." The Bible, the Savior, and the spirit, then, are all familiar figures on the southern landscape. For some religious leaders – fundamentalist theologians, guardians of denominational traditions, and ascetic moralists – the Bible and the spirit may conflict; for creative people, they are both inspirations, peculiarly well rooted in a South given to flashes of the spirit that are biblically based.[5]

One of the formative ethnic groups in the South, African Americans, reflected the mood and style of evangelical Protestantism, but they added distinctive approaches that provided further inspiration to southern artists living in a place where both the Bible and the Holy Spirit worked wonders. Laws prevented slaves from learning to read, which denied them access to the Bible and gave the Good Book a profound symbolic meaning at the foundation of black spirituality. Some slaves did learn to read and studied the scriptures, taking away messages different from those that white ministers tried to teach them. They studied the Bible for messages of hope, and reading the scriptures became a main incentive for literacy. African Americans especially prized stories from the Old Testament, showing God assisting the oppressed Hebrews and punishing their Egyptian oppressors. Protestantism validated their searching the scriptures to find meaning, and slave preachers fastened on passages that told of liberation not just in heaven but in this world as well. Moses, Daniel, and Joseph embodied the promise of deliverance; stories of Jonah, Elijah, and Abraham and Isaac showed God's hand in everyday life. The inheritance of African religions in African American culture added a receptivity to the supernatural, with ancestral spirits, conjure figures, and crossroads devils reverberating through black spirituality. The spirituals became the great musical expression of black creativity under slavery, and slaves drew from biblical narratives in projecting the hope of deliverance. The Old Testament themes of the Promised Land and God's chosen people resonated with enslaved people looking for messages of hope.[6]

For blacks and whites, the 1920s was the decade when creativity seemed to make a quantum leap in the South. The Southern Literary

Renaissance and the Harlem Renaissance brought unheard of production of novels, poetry, fiction, theater, memoirs, song lyrics and performances, paintings, sculptures, and other forms of creative expression. The stirrings of modernization – economic development, consumerism, urbanization, modern thought – now affected more southerners than ever before and nurtured a perception of a changing region. At the same time, a deeply rooted folk culture continued to provide the context for most southerners, with a deep well of stories, legends, myths, attitudes, and practices that nourished southern culture. Popular culture entered a new stage, with southern entertainers drawing from the folk culture for their songs and stories. New technology – radio, recordings, and electronic public address systems – encouraged the popularization of southern music. Movies brought the exploitation of southern themes and new opportunities for southerners in the film industry. When we consider the writers, singers, artists, and other creative people in the twentieth century South, when we acknowledge the formative influence of African Americans on southern culture, we need to recognize that a Southern Cultural Renaissance took place, with religion providing the inspiration for much of it.

Southern self-taught artists have been intimately related to the writers and musicians of the region, absorbing the biblically informed evangelical culture. One sees, first of all, generational relationships among writers, musicians, and self-taught artists. The earliest well-documented artists, such as Bill Traylor and William Edmondson, came to maturity in the late nineteenth and early twentieth centuries, growing up, like the writers and musicians who became prominent in those years, in a region with tangible ties to slavery and the Civil War. More self-taught artists appeared in the years between the two world wars, at the same time that writers and blues, jazz, gospel, and country musicians began recording careers that converted the South's folk music into popular music. The self-taught artists conveyed the most-stunning religious imaginations of all of these creative people. One could find doubt about religion among them, surely, but they were not well-educated literary figures struggling with modernist-generated religious skepticism. While the self-taught artists sometimes fell victim to the temptations of the secular world, they were mostly true believers. They had more in common in this regard with musicians than with writers. The world of self-taught artists was often one poor in material goods.

The poverty that O'Connor saw as being fundamental to the human condition and also as being a source of creativity was a lived experience for many self-taught artists. They often began producing their works not only out of compelling creative spirits but also for practical reasons – to supplement jobs and earn needed money. Mass culture, an important component of modernization, had a profound impact on self-taught artists, becoming a source of images, styles, and stories they set beside the Bible in creating a distinctive aesthetic that nonetheless resonated with that of the region's writers and musicians.

The southern religious context was the common background for the region's self-taught artists. They were more likely to be actual church leaders than the region's writers and musicians, yet one needs to understand what that meant in the context of the rural South. Some of the self-taught artists, such as J. L. Hunter, who attended Southern Bible College in the 1930s, became ordained ministers and then pastors of local congregations; many more of the artists, however, were "called" preachers, not theologically trained nor formally ordained but responding passionately to God's call to spread the Gospel. They harked back to an evangelical tradition of the frontier, an egalitarian one where ministers were not separated from their flocks by training but held other jobs and vocations while leading their local churches as well. These self-taught artists were also self-taught preachers like their rural predecessors. Georgia's R. A. Miller, for example, was a farmer and textile mill worker but also a minister in the Free Will Baptist Church. East Texas's Johnnie Swearingen grew up the child of migrant workers, attending school and church only periodically. In the early 1960s, at age 53, while working on a farm, he heard and obeyed God's command to preach – and eventually to make art. Benjamin Perkins, from north Alabama, was a part-time Church of God minister who made his living working at a variety of jobs before building his own church called the Original Church of God.[7]

Whether ministers or not, southern self-taught artists witnessed for their faith, showing throughout the region's history a capacity for the most primal expression of southern religiosity – the confidence among many evangelicals in their direct access to the Bible and the Holy Spirit.

Self-taught artists testified to their divine inspirations by recounting their visions in ways that writers and musicians seldom did. Those visions, from their evangelically based direct access to the Bible and the Holy Spirit, figured in their art as witness as well. Anderson Johnson, born in 1915 and raised in Virginia, had a vision in his father's cornfield at age eight to preach the Gospel. He gained little formal schooling but knew his Bible well – a must for a called preacher. Johnson began preaching at age twelve and left home to become an itinerant street corner preacher at sixteen. After his recovery from a paralyzing disease – attributed to God's healing – he converted the first floor of his living space to a mission, which he adorned with colorful biblical and historical paintings to attract worshippers. Jesse Aaron, of African American and Seminole Indian ancestry, can date precisely his visitation of the spirit to the early 1960s, when, praying to God for work, he was inspired to create images of animals – his "handiwork of God." William Edmondson was a middle Tennessee Primitive Baptist who had a vision in 1932 in which God told him to carve tombstones – which he did the rest of his life.[8]

Perhaps the most compelling stories of visionary inspiration among these artists are those of Elijah Pierce and Minnie Evans. The Mississippi-born carver Pierce created *Vision of Heaven*, a wood relief that portrays God's hand touching him as a young man, when he rejected the Bible to look at a Sears-Roebuck catalog. Pierce explains that "the good Lord laid his hand on [his] head, and [he] fell out of [his] chair." As a result of this inspiration, "every piece of work I carve is a message, a sermon," Pierce explained. "A preacher don't hardly get up in the pulpit without preaching some picture I got carved." Born in 1892 and raised by her grandmother in North Carolina, Minnie Evans powerfully illustrates how dreams and visions, along with the Bible, mythology, and the natural environment, could touch a creative spirit. She credits her dreams and visions with inspiring her, recalling going to bed once and seeing a beautiful light and a wreath: "I didn't see the wreath, but I saw the shadow of the wreath, and behind the shadow of this wreath is where God spoke to me. He said, 'I am Jehovah, your God.'" God promised that "this light that you see now shall shine around all of you." She insisted much later, "That's my daily food. He has given me that guarantee." She described her art as coming "from nations [that] might have been destroyed before the flood." While no one else knew about these lost places, "God [gave the responsibility] to [her] to bring them back into the world," which she surely did with a thousand drawings and paintings. She worked most of her life at an estate in North Carolina, one filled with extraordinary gardens of colorful flowers, birds, animals, trees, and water. She drew from images and characters from the Bible, but the florid colors and jungle of foliage in most of her works created, above all, a modern, unique vision of the Garden of Eden, often with a female face or faces looking out at the lush scenes.[9]

Self-taught artists convey the specifics of Bible-based faith and southern religious behavior. Jessie and Ron Cooper, from Kentucky, carve and paint biblical scenes and portraits of good and evil, full of preachers, snakes, devils, and ghosts. Josephus Farmer, a Pentecostal street corner evangelist, portrays reliefs with biblical subjects but also historical ones as well as dioramas conveying his memory of religion's place in rural life. But combined with biblical and other religious scenes for many self-taught artists were materials from mass culture, reflecting their role in a changing America, where images and ideas were just as directly accessible to them through radio, television, and film as the Bible and the Holy Spirit had always been within the context of southern religious practice. Mississippian O. W. "Pappy" Kitchens drew from the Bible but also from photographs, newspapers, magazines, television, and a crystal ball. South Louisiana's Prophet Royal Robertson studied the Bible, yet one finds in his art not only references to the scriptures but to girlie magazines, comic strips, and science fiction. Mississippian Mary T. Smith paid homage to God through her yard environment of artworks in the 1980s. However, she was watching television as well as reading the scriptures, and influences from both can be seen in her yard.

Death can be a spur to creative expression in any culture and that has surely been the case in the American South, where evangelical Protestantism views death as the time of moral judgment and the beginning of the afterlife as portrayed in the Bible. Nellie Mae Rowe grew up to be a field hand. She picked cotton in Georgia, married twice, and then, when her second husband died, she turned to her art for renewal. Her drawings and paintings did not often portray the stuff of religious life, but her symbols and images conveyed an imaginative spirituality, one that she attributed to God. "The Lord got me here for something," she once said. "I don't know, a lot of people say I preach." She preferred to think she taught, but under God's inspiration. "I just sees people crippled, and I drawed them to ask the Lord to help them through," she explained. When she learned in 1982 that she had terminal cancer, all of her remaining works portrayed images of death, such as tombstones, empty chairs, angels, dying plants, and butterflies. The roof in *Nellie's House at Night* is blue, a color that black southerners have long used to ward off evil spirits. Blue dogs are an ancestral symbol among the Kong in Zaire, and they appear in Rowe's work as well. She constructed an elaborate vision of heavenly redemption, one that drew from biblical inspiration as well as her own imagination. She recounted that when God called her "[she wanted] to be ready to fly all the way to Jesus." This world, she insisted "wasn't nigh ever home." The disinherited believer's sense of a better world to come infused her art. "They say this world don't stand," she said. "Nobody don't know how long it going to stand. I believe the time's at hand." She admitted she "had a hard time down here, struggling and tussling, folks is so mean to one another, Lord have mercy." Still, Judgment Day would come soon enough: "You be running but you can't hide. You run to the rock but you can't hide." Her hope remained in Jesus. "Yes, my Lordy," she prayed, "oh blessed, blessed be the name of the Lord." "I talk with him and he lets me know I still needs him," she allowed. "I still needs him to the very end. I just don't know nobody but my Lord."[10]

No theme of self-taught art revealed more about southern religious culture than millennialism, with its fearsome image of the Apocalypse featured in literature, music, and art. Indeed, artists' uses of the apocalyptic theme show more than any other theme the connections between the Bible and the spirit working to promote creativity among southern self-taught artists. Alabama's Myrtice West, for example, has produced two series of paintings inspired by the book of Revelation, which she began after entering a trance and ending up in the pulpit of a country church. "I'd never been in this church in my life," she explained, "and there I was, standing up in that pulpit, reading the Bible, and it was open to Revelations." She soon decided God was sending her a message, which she saw related to her natural abilities to paint. In an earlier depressed period of her life, "all [she] wanted to do was draw pictures of Jesus. It just seemed like the end of the world, like nothing was worth nothing." West's first Revelations paintings required months of Bible study, and her dreams and visions shaped the work as much as her study of the scriptures did. The book of Revelation was itself a vision of the biblical John, and "it seemed like John was putting these pictures in [her] mind, telling [her] the colors to use and everything."[11]

Another Alabamian who used the book of Revelation in powerful ways was Annie Lucas. She recounted that "Revelations was the first thing [she] did. [She] just started, you know, from the back of the Bible." Revelations talked about "the beasts and the devil, and [she] could just see in [her] mind how it was supposed to be, and [she] just started drawing." A seven-painting sequence portrayed what she had read – seven-headed beasts, locusts devouring everything on the land, angels, and the Devil. She read from the book of Revelation for inspiration before drawing each picture. Her work was intended to influence people to read the scriptures. Speaking of one particular painting she did, she says, "A lot of people see it, and they don't believe it's in the Bible. So they go to the Bible and then they read about it. So I feel like God's working through me."[12]

Two self-taught artists seem to suggest particularly strong connections with other creative spirits in the South's expressive culture and provide a final view of the range of their work, which balances tradition and innovation, the Bible and the spirit, and shows the geographical expanse of self-taught creativity from the Upper South to the Lower South, in a biracial culture. Gertrude Morgan is a good example of an artist in the years between the two world wars directly tied to the region's religious culture who used the word in diverse ways for evangelical purposes. Born in Lafayette, Alabama, she lived most of her life in New Orleans, where she was raised in a Baptist family. She later joined a Bible-based, spirit-filled sect whose members dressed only in black and sang and danced to connect with the Holy Spirit. By the 1930s, her singing, to the accompaniment of guitar and tambourine, was part of her evangelical approach to worship at the Everlasting Gospel Mission. Now she dressed only in white and had white furniture and white paint inside the church. She was a preacher whose paintings were part of her sermons. Speaking into a megaphone on the streets of New Orleans, she preached her message to those within earshot and had her paintings set up to illustrate her points. If she represents the evangelical nature of many self-taught artists, she also illustrates the importance of visionary inspiration to their work. On one of her paintings, *A Poem of My Own Calling*, she recalls when God spoke to her: "My heavenly father called me in 1934 on the 30th day of December or just about 38 years ago. The strong powerful words he said was so touching to me. 'I'll make thee as a signet for I have chosen thee go ye into yonders world and sing with a loud voice for you are a chosen vessel of mine to call men women boys and girls.'" Her example also reflects the same theme – millennialism – that was so important among other poor and working-class southerners. As in the later work of Myrtice West, the book of Revelation was a favorite inspiration for Morgan's sermons and paintings, including *Christ Coming in His Glory*, which portrayed a white-robed Jesus coming down from heaven. Although she dressed herself in pure white and adorned her mission church the same way, Morgan used vibrant colors in her art to convey the fiery nature of the Apocalypse. Like many self-taught artists, she used words, not just images, in her art, creating a spiritual calligraphy. On Morgan's *The Two Beasts of Revelations* she wrote: "Fear God and give glory to him: For the hour of judgment is come."[13]

Another artist, Kentucky's Edgar Tolson, was one of the most revealing self-taught artists in terms of the role of tradition, innovation, and religion in southern creativity. His father, James Perry Tolson, was a well-known lay preacher in Wolfe County, in eastern Kentucky, who for sixty years preached, prayed for the sick, comforted families of the dead, and laid on hands to heal. "Hell, he's cured cancer," Edgar Tolson once insisted. In the rural South, congregations of true believers were often unable to maintain full-time ministers or to have weekly worship services. Nonetheless, they met each Sunday to sing hymns and to "listen to a local, non-ordained preacher speak on the word of God as shown through the Bible." Although he was a Pentecostal, a member of the Church of God, James Tolson embraced the southern interdenominational religious tradition and took part in Baptist, Methodist, and Holiness meetings as well. The scriptures were common to all of these denominations. As Julia Ardrey has written, James Tolson "indoctrinated, one might almost say 'inoculated' his children with continual quotation from the King James translation of the Bible."

Young Edgar Tolson rebelled for awhile against the stern moral example of his father, but eventually he too began to preach. Between 1920 and 1950, he preached at house services, funerals, and revivals. Although a member of the Church of God, he normally identified himself as a Baptist. His private Bible study and evangelical faith, more than denominational labels, motivated his preaching. "You'd preach with the Methodists, Presbyterians, and all them," he said. "They all just mixed together and had a meeting." Edgar Tolson was conflicted, though, drawn to less holy activities, including drinking and womanizing. Eventually convicted of desertion of his children, he served two years in prison and divorced his wife. Worse yet, his preacher father condemned him with biblical passages. "My daddy got on him I don't know how many times," Tolson's brother Elvin said. "He told him, he says, 'The Bible says he that took hold of the plow handle and looked back is not fit for the kingdom of God,' and said, 'He's a dog turned again to his own vomit.'" His brother's judgment was that Edgar "loved the world, the cares of it, better than he did the word of God." Edgar Tolson's daughter, Mary, captured his conflict. "For years he's read the Bible," she said. "He'd come in from work, he'd sit with the Bible, he'd read till dark." She noted he wasn't drinking then, but "then all of a sudden, he doesn't read the Bible no more; and he drinks." Still, if you talked with him, "he'd always bring up the Bible, always referred to the Bible."[14]

Tolson found his great subject, an eight-piece series called *The Fall of Man*, about the biblical account of the beginning of time; like blues and gospel singers, he was drawn to the story of Adam and Eve. Rick Bell, a patron of Tolson's, once said after visiting him in Kentucky: "The story of Adam and Eve was so compelling, so obsessive with that group of people . . . and you could not talk long to Edgar . . . or any of those other people without the conversation coming around to Adam and Eve." In his series, he depicts eight episodes from the book of Genesis. Here the Adam and Eve narrative extends from the Garden of Eve through Eve's mourning of her dead son Abel, as his brother Cain departs. Biblical characters, a sense of human history, a tone of moral gravity, and an ultimately tragic vision haunt *The Fall of Man*, an important addition by a self-taught artist to the thematic concerns of the South's writers and musicians, one steeped in biblical and regional experience.

Tolson's carvings reflected eastern Kentucky's traditional culture but in a particular incarnation, one that evolved with new influences. Outsiders sometimes praised him for only using an old whittling knife and for his attachment to an old work bench. He was a traditional whittler, indeed, but one who did at times use power drills and who constantly purchased new knives rather than only use an inherited one. Responding to market demands for his work, he produced carvings that reflected the interests of patrons as well as those coming out of his own local culture. All of this suggests an artist poised between traditional ways and modern influences. He appreciated his own role as a tradition bearer, whether in the way he carved or in his attachment to the old-time gospel. Likewise, he was drawn to Old Testament subjects; explaining that to an interviewer, he said, "I was raised around the Bible. I like it." In 1980, he went even further, claiming, "I'm sort of a Bible historian."

One is drawn back to Flannery O'Connor's observation that the great writers in the twentieth-century South discovered they were "bound through the senses to a particular society and a particular history, to particular sounds and a particular idiom," all of which enabled the writer to use the specifics of place to gain broader "human perspective." Southern self-taught artists, like the region's writers and musicians, came out of a regional religious culture in which evangelical religion provided a dramatic background to spark creativity. Alice Walker has noted that Zora Neale Hurston's novel *Moses* resonates with black tradition because it invokes "the traditional Sunday morning sermon on Moses that all black people born before 1965 have heard at least once." Another writer, Reynolds Price, recalls that southern culture "provided [southerners] with a daily world in which religion played an omnipresent role," which was "immensely important" to those who would later become writers – and one might add to those who would become self-taught artists and musicians as well. Church services, Price says, gave southerners "a direct possibility of serious encounter with the center of things – the Creator," a different way to characterize evangelical faith's confidence in direct access to the meaning of the Bible, Jesus, and the Holy Spirit.[15] Southern self-taught artists, writers, and musicians grew up in a place that took religion seriously and that allowed its creative spirits to pursue their visions.

PART THREE

Spirituality

9

Apocalypse South
McKendree Long and
Southern Evangelicalism

In a "Sermon on St. Peter," recorded around 1950, the Reverend McKendree Robbins Long preached on the need for revival during a wicked time. "A great Southern preacher once said, 'There are plenty more Pentecosts in the sky,'" Long noted. He added, however, that while that might be true for "mere revivals," the times required a new kind of awakening, "the foundation of faith in terms of infinite power." He feared that "not a handful really believe we can have one," and yet he insisted on the need to look beyond "the apostasy about us" and to rely on the "loving-kindness of the Lord" to bring about a revival. A revivalist for almost three decades at that point, Long realized he faced new, unsettling times in the 1950s. His sermon came not long after the Soviet Union exploded its first nuclear weapon, bringing thoughts of the end times to believers rooted in biblical authority. He would soon begin painting his series of works based in the Revelation to John, using his artistry to try to alert the world to the imminence of doom without repentance.

People who had known the young McKendree Long would have likely been surprised that he had spent his life preaching an evangelical-fundamentalist faith and that he would now use his artistic talents to deliver the apocalyptic message that he visualized. Long, and the southern region from which he came and in which he preached his gospel, traveled a long road from the post-Reconstruction era of his birth into the atomic age. He was born into a world whose people had every expectation of Victorian-era certainty and stability. His father was a member in good standing of the commercial-civic elite that emerged in the South after the Civil War to direct its fortunes into a New South period that would promote progress for the region. Long grew to become a creative artist, trained in the formal techniques of Western art. Eudora Welty once described herself as a "privileged observer" of life who made art, and that description fits Long as well. He attended art schools, studied overseas in London, Amsterdam, and Madrid, and became accomplished, if not recognized as he wished. He came to maturity as modernism emerged as the driving artistic movement in the early twentieth century. But modernism was the problem for him, suggesting a morally confused and turbulent outlook that led ultimately, in the 1920s, to his rebellion, to his drastic change of course to enter evangelical ministry, and eventually to his decision to use his artistic abilities to express a profound vision of end times.

Long remained very much the southerner throughout his changes, but they indicate the complexity of identity for those people living in the South as the region entered the modern world. The post–Civil War South, though, had its own turbulence, while the twentieth-century South inherited social attitudes, economic realities, and political arrangements that would be the backdrop for Long's religious and artistic development. Reconstruction had been a violent and unsettling time, with intense conflicts among newly freed African Americans, defeated Confederate whites, and northerners bent briefly on attempting serious changes in the region's social system. The 1890s witnessed economic disaster and renewed political conflict, centered on the Populist rebellion, with its attempt to raise economic issues and make them more central than the racial issues that had emerged as the dividing line in southern life after the Civil War. The Populists failed, however, to overturn the political establishment, thanks to considerable intimidation, electoral chicanery, and outright violence. Out of these dramatic developments came a restricted electorate, a racially segregated society, and the triumph of a New South ideology that sought economic development, segregated but harmonious race relations, improved education, and sectional reconciliation with the rest of the United States. McKendree Long came to maturity as the South entered the Progressive Era of the early twentieth century, and Progressive reformers had considerable impact in the South, bringing governmental reforms, educational improvements, scientific realism, and business efficiency to government and public policy – making a society that surely seemed closer to modern ways than it had been only a few decades earlier. Long was the talented son of a well-off and respected family, a mainline Presbyterian – the religion that was the driving force behind many of the successful business people of North Carolina. He was well positioned to play a leading cultural role in this New South.

The change from a middle-class, Victorian sensibility into a modern one was part of the context of Long's decisions on religion and art. Like other places in the Anglo American world where Victorianism influenced, the South of the late nineteenth century prized order and stability, and the accompanying regional ideology of New South commercial industrialism lauded progress and rationality. The supposed line between civilization and savagery was clear to Victorian southerners. There was a right and a wrong, and Long would have grown up seeing "culture" as a vital part of the South's attempt to maintain a civilized life despite the catastrophe, for white southerners, of Confederate defeat. The Lost Cause sacralized the Confederacy in memory, and young McKendree Long surely heard stories of the war from his grandfather, a Confederate veteran. His mother exemplified women's role in nurturing cultural activities in the region, among which was her active role as a founder of the local chapter of the United Daughters of the Confederacy.

Writing in 1941, Piedmont journalist Wilbur J. Cash could talk of the mind of the South, suggesting the sense of unity that grew among whites out of the experiences of Confederate defeat and racial solidarity in a biracial society. The term "solid South" expressed this unity and continuity with the past, revealed especially through the dominance of the Democratic Party in the region. The South gained a common identity from its folk culture, which rested in the long persistence of rural living and small-town ways for most southerners, as well as an enveloping poverty that touched countless families and familiarized all social classes in the region with its miseries, breeding a unifying hope for economic development that would ease the desperate experiences of all too many southerners.

Long pursued his dream of artistic achievement in this southern society through the first two decades of the twentieth century, but religion began to focus his discontent in the 1920s. Not coincidentally, the pace of social change in the region increased perceptibly in that decade. Cities and larger towns now played a leading role in the region, harboring an expanding middle class of business people, professionals, and white-collar workers. Rural areas, by contrast, now seemed like places of hicks and hillbillies, not the repository of virtuous living, which earlier southern spokesmen had once idealized. Urban consciousness came to epitomize the fashionable in the South, and many southerners came to see "progress" resting with the promotions of the chamber of commerce and the Rotary Club.

As though in reaction to these signs of a quickened embrace of materialism by southerners, a politics of morality also appeared in the 1920s, and it came to sweep up McKendree Long's plans for his future. Defenders of moral values in the region identified them with evangelical Protestantism and rural and small-town life. Rural-based politicians emerged in a factionalized, disorganized political system focused often around charismatic personalities, such as Huey Long in Louisiana and Eugene Talmadge in Georgia. They reflected southern fears that powerful economic concerns from outside the region were reshaping the South, disregarding regional ways and local popular will. This political fundamentalism was more than matched by religious fundamentalism; in fact, the two often overlapped. Support for prohibition of alcoholic beverages was a virtual crusade of Baptists, Methodists, Presbyterians, and other orthodox Protestants, and many southern Evangelicals deserted the Democratic Party in the 1928 presidential election because of discomfort over Al Smith, the big-city, Roman Catholic presidential nominee who opposed Prohibition. Mainstream southern churches experienced conflict over denominational control between liberals and fundamentalists, and the antievolution movement found fertile ground in the region, with the Scopes trial in the summer of 1925 as a dramatic illustration of the conflict between traditionalism and modernism in the South. It was no wonder that H. L. Mencken coined the term "Bible Belt" to describe the region in the 1920s.

McKendree Long abandoned his artistic dreams in the 1920s, amid the conflict between traditionalism and modernism in the South, becoming first a Presbyterian minister and later a Baptist revivalist. While his socially prominent family would likely have been startled at this turn of events, Long was embracing an age-old regional tradition. Since the Great Revival of the early nineteenth century, evangelical Protestantism had dominated the South, and Baptists, Methodists, and Presbyterians were the region's religious establishment, judging by cultural and moral influence. Evangelical religion prizes religious experience over other aspects of faith, offering a tangible way to deal with the burdens of sin and guilt that its Calvinist-inspired view of human nature often inculcates as well; believers can claim God's freely given grace and rest in the assurance of salvation. This appeal of certainty, the blessed assurance of redemption, has always been a compelling quality of evangelicalism for people in times of social change and individual stress. Conviction of redemption often brings a commitment to personal morality and aspirations toward an upright life and work for the common social good. The Bible was the icon of faith for evangelicals like Long, the authoritative source for inspiration and daily living.

Evangelicalism inspires believers to share the faith, placing a premium on proselytizing, and Long's decision to become not just a minister but a revivalist must be seen in this context. Southern culture has been an expressive one, and southern life has long included a familiarity with evangelical Christianity. In Long's day, roadside signs cried out "Jesus Saves" and "Get Right with God," and homes and the airwaves were filled with the singing of gospel songs, a common body of which united evangelicals in many specific denominations. Traditional southern culture was an oral one, producing talkers – whether storytellers, lawyers, singers, or preachers. Advocates of the Gospel not only preached but also witnessed, one-to-one, to lost souls. Evangelistic campaigns were familiar to southerners of the 1920s, included among the major rituals of regional life. Frank Dixon, a northern observer of the South in 1900, noted that Southern Baptists had regarded "evangelism as the be-all and end-all of religion," and his observation held true long afterward. Methodist Sam Jones was the most famous southern revival preacher of the late nineteenth century, establishing the model from which Long drew for citywide, interdenominational services of southern communities. Mass revivals became even more popular in the 1920s than before; southerners could have heard not only Long preach but such well-known traveling revivalists as Mordecai Ham and Billy Sunday, as well as lesser known figures, such as J. C. Bishop, the "Yodeling Cowboy Evangelist."

Long came to his role as a revivalist slowly. While studying art in London, he attended services at the Metropolitan Tabernacle, an evangelical-fundamentalist haven founded by one of the most famous Baptist ministers of the nineteenth century, Charles Spurgeon. Long was rebaptized in 1912, reaffirming his Christian faith but with a new evangelical focus. He returned to North Carolina after that, though he worked first as a painter, proselytizing for southern cultural advancement more than religion. He advertised an exhibit of his work in Raleigh as that of "McKendree Long, Southern Painter," and he told the audiences viewing his work that the region needed a first-class museum and greater understanding of high art.

Gradually, as the dramatic conflicts of the 1920s developed, Long turned to evangelicalism in charting a new course for his creativity. After announcing his decision in the mid-1920s to become an evangelist, he preached high-profile revivalistic campaigns, such as the seven-week revival at Lumberton, North Carolina, in 1930. The *Charlotte Observer* reported that the campaign resulted in 675 professions of faith and repentance, "placing [Long] in a class with the best of the nationally known evangelists of the last twenty years." The revival began in Lumberton's downtown Methodist church, moved to the grade school auditorium when it grew in numbers, and relocated to a large tobacco warehouse, where it became a true community service. The *Observer* concluded from the revival that Long was "launched upon a career of great usefulness and success as a minster." Revealingly, the paper also noted the town's financial generosity toward Long, providing substantial contributions when it became clear he needed support. This generosity came despite "boll weevil conditions existing and mills running only on part time" in

Lumberton. Long also noted that he sold sixteen of his paintings locally, earning the equivalent of two months of a preacher's salary.

Long went through a personal crisis of sorts shortly after this revival, writing in November and December of 1930 about facing a decision whether to continue his revivalistic work or turn once again to art. He noted in his journal that he prayed God would help him discern what to do. "I was assured after this prayer," he wrote, "in which God's presence seemed to fill both the room and my own soul that I should know this, too, by Christmas, 1930." He hoped that God would allow his ministry, "since the whole evangelistic ministry is well-nigh on the rocks, through Modernistic persecution, and, alas, indiscreet methods by the evangels themselves in some cases."

By this time, the Great Depression had struck hard at the South. Even before the Depression, the South had faced serious economic problems, with chronic overproduction of its staple crops and an abundance of landless sharecroppers and tenant farmers; its leading industry, textiles, faced dim prospects in the late 1920s because of increasing competition and overproduction, and bad conditions were made worse by the collapse of export markets and declining incomes once the Depression began. On one day in 1932, authorities sold a quarter of the agricultural land in Mississippi; in the same year, a quarter of the labor force in Birmingham was unemployed. Such extreme conditions swept across the entire region, which Franklin D. Roosevelt pronounced "the nation's No. 1 economic problem."

Long noted in his journal on December 17, 1930, that eight banks had failed in North Carolina the previous day. "Want is a lean angel," he observed, "but the only one which can guide this land to betterment of soul." He confessed that it was "mournful indeed to hear men of the street, [his] brothers, and men of the artisan class, [his] brothers, and men of the professional class, [his] brothers, all, affirm that it is 'revivial [sic] or revolution,' in this our land." He concluded that "the very thought should rive all men to prayer and fasting." The only solution was "to pray for a revival."

Long continued to practice his preaching throughout the coming decades. World War II was an even greater disruption to the illusion of stability and permanence in southern life than the Depression had been;

New Deal farm programs had taken land out of production and forced sharecroppers and tenants to leave the land, while the war effort provided jobs and higher income, promoted industrialization, and concentrated population in urban areas. Newcomers came in huge numbers to train in the South, and southerners left the region as part of overseas military forces. Diverse changes led to the nationalization of southern life in the 1930s and 1940s as never before. Such technological innovations as the automobile, airplane, electricity, and agricultural machinery changed everyday life, and higher incomes nurtured a consumer culture that made national goods easily accessible in once isolated and provincial places. Political centralization and bureaucratization came to characterize the region's public policy, with an accompanying decline in regional and local control.

The South was very much a part of the nation's burgeoning prosperity after World War II, when the region moved closer to the mainstream of American economic prosperity. The economy continued to diversify, and federal dollars flowed into the South in a steady stream. By 1960, only 10 percent of southerners worked in agriculture, and between 1940 and 1960 the region's population went from 65 percent rural to 58 percent urban. The most distinguishing feature of southern culture, its Jim Crow segregation laws, remained in effect at the end of the war, but white southerners soon faced organized and eloquent challenges to its racial customs from the region's African American population and from the federal government. The "solid South" in which Long matured must have seemed like another world by this time.

When McKendree Long decided in the late 1950s to paint a series of visionary religious scenes, drawing especially from the biblical text of the Revelation to John, he did so having lived through dramatic events in the wrenching transformation of the traditional South into a modern society. The process was not complete by any means, and traditional culture abided in the region, with his embrace of millennialism as a main theme for his new visionary paintings a good example of his continued absorption in the region's traditional evangelical faith.

Millennialism is the conviction that human history will end in a golden age. Chapter 20 of Revelation predicts a thousand-year earthly reign by Christ, during which evil and human suffering will end and a utopian society will emerge. Christians have believed that Christ's Second Coming may occur before the millennium (premillennialism) or just afterward (postmillennialism). In the United States, millennial symbols helped to form the notion of the country as a redeemer nation with a special destiny in human history, perhaps the site of Christ's return, and they spawned sectarian movements and evangelical reform movements and revivals. Furthermore, Americans in the North and South saw the Civil War as the possible beginning of the millennium ("Mine eyes have seen the glory of the coming of the Lord").

After the Civil War, postmillennialism became an easy, progressive outlook accompanying the New South ideology, justifying gradual reform and development. But more relevant to Long's later attitudes was the strident premillennialism that grew in the South as part of the fundamentalist movement of the early twentieth century. This movement included a dispensational aspect, which drew from biblical prophecy to divide human history into epochs, culminating in the Second Coming. Ever since then, American evangelicals inclined to strong biblical literalism, like Long, have read the signs of human history for indications of end times. Indeed, the 1950s and 1960s, when Long painted his visionary scenes, must have seemed like years verging on the Second Coming. The South had witnessed dramatic economic and social changes through the twentieth century, and those middle decades would see the overturning of Jim Crow laws, an event accompanied by violence, unrest, and anxiety about the postsegregation South among the region's people.

Even more dramatically, the end of World War II saw the beginning of the nuclear age, with the explosion of the first atomic bombs. The cold war added an ongoing, unresolved conflict with the Soviet Union and communism, the dreaded symbol of atheism to Christians. American popular culture soon spread fears of an imminent doomsday and internal subversion. In addition, the early 1950s saw the publication of books designed to bring comfort to troubled minds, with such titles as *How to Stop Worrying and Start Living, Peace of Mind,* and *A Guide to Confident Living.* The South, however, did not easily embrace this popular psychology of "confident living." Evangelical fundamentalists, especially, dwelt in the soul-terror of doomsday, seeing newly relevant biblical meanings in the threat of nuclear war or communist dominance. Billy Graham was the exemplar of post–World War II revivalism, a preacher whose own experiences can, perhaps, shed light on McKendree Long and his turn toward apocalypticism in the early 1950s. Like Long, he was a North Carolinian, and he also grew up Presbyterian, joining the Southern Baptist Convention in the late 1930s. Graham preached the fundamentalism that Long embraced: "If by fundamentalism you mean a person who accepts the authority of the Scriptures, the virgin birth of Christ, the atoning death of Christ, His bodily resurrection, His second coming, and personal salvation by faith through grace, then I am a fundamentalist." In 1945, Graham began work as an organizer for Youth for Christ, a group that fought juvenile delinquency and communism. He soon staged his own revivals, becoming a national figure because of his attacks on communism and calls for nationwide revival. He preached that communists were the "agents of Satan, and the struggle between Communism and capitalism was a 'battle to the death' between 'Christ and the anti-Christ.'"

Graham's sermon on September 25, 1949, expressed evangelical-fundamentalist beliefs at a crucial point in history. Two days earlier, President Harry Truman had announced that the Soviets had exploded their first atomic bomb, crystallizing the potential for nuclear conflict. Graham believed that God had spared the United States from the worst impact of World War II because he must have hoped to "still use America to evangelize the world." In this new, terrifying circumstance, God was "giving us a desperate choice, a choice of either revival or judgment." "An arms race," he preached, "unprecedented in the history of the world, is driving us madly toward destruction!" The world was "divided into two sides": Western culture, founded in religion, and communism, which was against all religion. Revival would occur if people recognized the signs of the times, repented of their sins, prayed, and had faith. Graham combined the traditional revivalist's call for individual repentance with the doomsday possibility that the nuclear bomb now symbolized in the 1950s.

Southern gospel music dramatized such sentiments through songs that used images of nuclear war to remind listeners of the need to "get right with God." The popularity of these songs indicated a southern worldview that McKendree Long must have shared, attuned as he was to seeing modern developments through the lens of traditional belief. Kentucky bluegrass singer Jimmy Martin, for example, in "God, Guide Our Greatest Leader's Hands," asked divine guidance for national leaders so they would understand "that a war with these mighty destructive weapons could destroy us all upon this earth and land." Martin sang of "living in the days the Bible tells us," days "with hate and evil destroying each other's nations." He portrayed graphic imagery of the end of the world, picturing the time when people would "feel this old earth begin to tremble," "hear the mighty roaring in the sky," and see "a blinding flash of fire and destruction." His solution was to "pray for a great worldwide revival," rather than allowing countries to "see who's the strongest man."

"The Great Atomic Power," by the Louvin Brothers, white gospel performers from north Alabama, conveyed the uncertainty of the time. They personalized it, asking if hearers feared "this man's invention that they call atomic power." They asked, "Are we all in great confusion, do we know the time or hour" when a "terrible explosion may rain down upon our land, leaving horrible destruction, blotting out the works of man"? The song evoked the Rapture, the sweeping up of God's faithful before the terrible battle of Armageddon, when it asked: "Will you rise and meet your Savior in the air?" It would be a time when "fire rains from on high." The Louvin Brothers' solution to this terrible fate was to "be prepared to meet the Lord" and to offer "[their] heart and soul to Jesus," who would be a "shield and sword." Those who abided in Jesus would "never taste of death, for [they'd] fly to safety and eternal peace and rest," even if "the mushroom of destruction falls in all its fury great." Such a juxtaposition of ideas and images from the Bible and from contemporary nightmares perfectly captured the times that led Long to undertake his paintings of end times.

These southern gospel songs could have been the soundtrack to McKendree Long's paintings of millennial scenes from the book of Revelation. He himself wrote hymns, many of which spelled out similar sentiments regarding the Apocalypse. One hymn, written March 5, 1950, talked of men with their "lethal weapons, which furnish Hate its play!" He intimated his anticipation of Christ's return, writing that "rival despots" might rule for a day, but God still reigned on high, holding despots in derision "and soon will make it known!" Referring even more overtly to the new atomic age, Long continued:

> Though fission, fusion, both unite to make their monstrous bomb,
> Though universal Death may threat from out hell's fearful womb:
> To make men live, or make men die, lies only in Christ's breath,
> Who rising from the dead, brought back the keys of Hell and Death!

The Lord will return, "in flaming wrath they'll see," and he will punish "man's iniquity." The age might be new and threatening, but the old-time evangelical solution was the same: "Let hydrogenic bombs be piled as high as Everest's wrack," Long wrote in his hymn. "They'll be the jest of Jesus Christ, when Jesus Christ comes back!"

The years when Long painted his scenes of Revelation saw other southern visionary artists turn to the last book of the Bible for inspiration in understanding the terrible nuclear threat that imperiled humanity. Harrison Mayes, a coal miner from Middleboro, Kentucky, made massive concrete signs (some two thousand pounds) in the 1950s and 1960s, most of them saying, "Jesus Is Coming Soon" or "Get Right with God." In the mid-1950s, Sister Gertrude Morgan received a divine revelation in New Orleans and started dressing completely in white as a bride of Christ. She began to paint for the first time, believing that God moved her hands to evangelize the world through her paintings. She always painted biblical stories and scenes, but soon she concentrated on images from Revelation and her visualization of New Jerusalem, the utopian paradise that Revelation says will follow Christ's return. Howard Finster, the most renowned of visionary artists, painted works which combined traditional biblical beasts and devils, as well as quotes from prophetic books, with images of guided missiles, airplanes, naval vessels, and spaceships – all suggesting a specifically 1950s imagining of end times.

The Reverend McKendree Robbins Long's paintings from the Revelation series show the stages of civilization's decline and its salvation through the fires of the Apocalypse. In his epic painting *Apocalyptic Scene with Philosophers and Historical Figures*, Long depicts Hitler, Stalin, and Mussolini in the lake of fire and brimstone, while Descartes, Darwin, and Einstein observe. Few images could better represent the terrors, and perhaps some hopes, of the twentieth century that Long had lived through.

A southerner reared on the post–Civil War memory of the Civil War, he had lived through dramatic changes that had drawn the South into a global nexus. He still found comfort, though, in dwelling in the word of the Lord as he knew it. The Apocalypse portended doom for the wicked, but it would be followed by paradise for the righteous. All of his considerable artistic talent and religious passion went into imagining glory that would redeem the faithful.

10 "Just a Little Talk with Jesus"

Elvis Presley, Religious Music, and Southern Spirituality

In December 1956, Elvis Presley dropped in at Sun Studios in Memphis, just as a Carl Perkins recording session was ending. Presley was now a national star, having transcended during that year his previous status as a regional rockabilly performer. But that December afternoon turned into a special day, one that came to be known as the "Million Dollar Session," because of the supposed "million dollars" worth of talent that included Presley, Perkins, Jerry Lee Lewis, and briefly, Johnny Cash. An open microphone recorded a lively jam session. For the student of southern religious music, it was an especially revealing moment. In addition to improvising with country, blues, and early rock songs, the group sang from the common body of religious songs from the region, some of them gospel songs that dated from nineteenth-century revivals, others African American spirituals, others popular gospel quartet songs. All of these young performers who had grown up in the countryside near Memphis knew the songs, and when one started singing, the others easily fell into providing supporting lines. They had all come out of church backgrounds and would have been familiar with "Farther Along," "When God Dips His Love in My Heart," "Blessed Jesus (Hold My Hand)," and "As We Travel Along on the Jericho Road."

Elvis sang "Peace in the Valley," an old classic written by black composer Thomas A. Dorsey, which was the song Presley sang on the *Ed Sullivan Show* to defuse public concerns that he was an immoral renegade destroying America's youth. Between songs, the boys talked about the white gospel quartets who were so active around Memphis, an epicenter of white and black gospel traditions.[1]

"Just a Little Talk with Jesus" was an especially revealing expression of southern spirituality that day in Sun Studios in 1956, two years after the Brown decision and the year before the start of the Montgomery Bus Boycott and the launch of the Soviet satellite Sputnik, during a decade that saw the beginning of extraordinary cultural changes in the South. Elvis knew the song profoundly, singing a lively version and then slowing down the pace to fit the mood of the lyrics. The song's narrator tells the essential evangelical story of a person "lost in sin" but not without hope because "Jesus took [him] in." When that happened "a little light from heaven" filled his soul. Redemption was seen in the next lines, which say God "made [the sinner's] heart in love" and "wrote [his] name above." Despite "doubts and fears" and even though "[his] eyes be filled with tears," the song's narrator knows "Jesus is a friend who watches day and night." In the end, "just a little talk with Jesus gonna make it right."[2]

The Million Dollar Session is an appropriate introduction to consideration of the importance of Elvis Presley to understanding the role that music played in defining a distinctive southern spirituality and to look at the impact on that relationship of the dramatic changes in the South over the roughly two decades between that December day in Sun Studios in 1956 and Presley's death in Memphis in 1977. Charles Wolfe, Peter Guralnick, and others have written about Presley's relationship to the gospel music tradition. The concern of this chapter, however, is with a different but related issue – namely, how Presley can help open up the unexplored issue of southern spirituality. The lively field of southern religious history has examined, among other issues, the interdenominational evangelical tradition in the South, the cultural captivity experienced by its churches and religious leaders due to the influence of the Southern Way of Life, and religion's social role in sanctifying slavery, the Confederacy, and Jim Crow segregation. More recently, scholars are exploring the progressive elements of religion in the South, including ways the churches, even within constraints, helped provide needed leadership to reform efforts. But scholars have so far neglected to analyze the development of spirituality within the region's distinctive religious patterns. Neither the *Encyclopedia of Religion in the South* nor the *Encyclopedia of Southern Culture* included entries on "spirituality," and a survey of classic works by Sam Hill, Ed Harrell, Wayne Flynt, and others suggest they have seldom dealt directly with "spirituality" in the context of a southern regional religious tradition.[3]

A recent article on "Spirituality in the South," prepared for the second edition of *The New Encyclopedia of Southern Culture*, has intentionally opened up the topic for analysis, but the article stresses that "there are as many 'spiritualities' . . . as there are individual seekers." While undoubtedly true, I want to explore what a study of Elvis Presley's inherited and evolving spirituality might suggest about predominant regional patterns. While young Presley can easily be seen as a representative southerner of his time and place, it is hard to make that argument for the last two decades of his life, dominated as they were by extraordinary success and celebrity that moved him beyond the regional to national and international contexts. Nonetheless, I do want to suggest that his relationship to religious music and southern spirituality make him a revealing and perhaps even an emblematic figure in southern culture.[4]

The "spirituality" that I am exploring originally came more out of Catholic tradition than the Protestant faith that has dominated the American South. The *Oxford Dictionary of the Christian Church* (1997) defines the term as referring to "people's subjective practice and experience of their religion, or to the spiritual exercises and beliefs which individuals or groups have with regard to their personal experience with God." This definition might include prayer, meditation, contemplation, and mysticism. It notes that certain groups have "a characteristic set of spiritual practices and beliefs" such that "they may be regarded as constituting a 'school of spirituality,'" such as Cistercian spirituality, Carmelite spirituality, or Jesuit spirituality." The dictionary notes that this usage, reflecting recent changes, is now more generalized, "so that there is an increasing interest in 'lay spirituality,' 'married spirituality,' etc." In this context, religious music should be seen as the essence of a distinctive southern school of spirituality, a particularly important spiritual exercise and devotional practice rooted in organized religion but reflecting the reality that southern culture was infused by religion far beyond the church doors.[5]

Gladys Presley's favorite singing group was the Louvin Brothers, the harmonizing country music duo steeped in the South's religious music, and their experience suggests something of the traditional southern school of spirituality, based in religious music, which Elvis inherited. Born in the 1920s, they grew up at Sand Mountain, an isolated area of north Alabama, less than two hundred miles from Presley's hometown of Tupelo but part of the same hill country, which had a predominantly white folk culture. Music was an essential part of individual, family, and community life. In addition to dances and fiddling contests, such specifically religious gatherings as all-day church singings and sacred harp singings characterized the culture of the area. Their grandfather, Colonel Loudermilk, was a traditional frailing banjo picker, and their mother sang old, unaccompanied folk ballads like "Knoxville Girl" that went back to the British Isles. Their mother's family in general was active in sacred harp singing, a traditional form of religious singing based on songs from a popular songbook of the same name from the 1840s. It used shape notes – notes whose shapes, not the position on the staff, determined pitch. Once popular in New England and other areas of the United States, sacred harp singing came to be associated mostly with southern rural communities. Churches moved beyond its use as worship music, but periodic singings, often in church buildings, created a "second church" experience as people renewed a traditional Calvinist-inspired faith by singing the old songs the old way. Sacred harp singing, then, helped to perpetuate a strong strain of Calvinism in the rural South, even as churches themselves softened Calvinism's rigors through a theology of redemption.

The Louvins grew up singing sacred harp songs, and they participated in other activities that gave structure to the southern school of spirituality. Rural singing schools became pervasive in the hill country South, for example, taught by traveling teachers who would instruct students in religious and other forms of music. The singing convention also anchored southern spirituality. It gathered together those people who wanted to sing new songs published in small, paperback religious songbooks, which became an important form of devotional practice as well, making accessible older and newer religious songs. Companies in Lawrenceburg, Tennessee, and Chattanooga, not far from either the Louvins or the Presleys, used modern, aggressive sales practices to promote their books, including sponsoring professional gospel quartets who sang from the new songbooks.[6]

The Louvins lived through the modernization of southern religious music, and the publishing companies are one example of that process. Another factor was the coming of radio in the 1920s, and electrification of much of the rural South in the 1930s made religious music even more accessible and important to a changing culture. The Louvins heard Sunday morning preaching and everyday hymn singing on their radios. Phonograph records also became an important source for the Louvins and other southerners in the evolving spiritual culture in the decades between world wars. When their father visited Knoxville, he would go to the music store and bring home approximately a dozen albums, which the family would listen to long into the night, including the mournful songs of the Carter Family and the up-tempo religious songs of the Chuck Wagon Gang – both enormously popular early southern recording artists who drew from the traditional musical culture and defined it for a new generation of listeners. Once they started performing, the Louvins themselves became a force in the school of southern spirituality. Charlie Louvin remembered, "We were always running into people who said that Louvin Brothers music caused them to live in a Christian home. I run into people constantly that make you feel like you're a preacher." Listening devoutly to Louvin Brothers records became an embedded practice for those seeking not only entertainment but spiritual enlightenment rooted in the old ways of southern religion.[7]

Hank Williams, the immediate predecessor to Elvis as reigning musical giant in the South, grew up in central Alabama not far south of the Louvin Brothers' home on Sand Mountain, and his experiences also reveal much about the southern school of spirituality that Elvis Presley inherited. Hank's mother Lillie played organ at the Mount Olive West Baptist Church, and Hank sat beside her and sang "louder'n anybody else," as he put it. Lillie wanted him to shout for the Lord, so she scraped together the money to send him to a shape-note singing school in Avant,

Alabama. There Williams learned hymns and gospel songs that music critic Colin Escott says influenced his approach to music in general more than anything else.

However, with Hank Williams, we encounter a version of southern spirituality that is different from what Presley's would be. Williams's is a dark spirituality, based not in the spirit-filled religion of Holiness-Pentecostalism that influenced Presley; rather, Williams grew up in the Baptist church, inheriting a strong feeling of Calvinist sinfulness, reinforced by the temptations he faced in his life as a working-class-born entertainer. His favorite song was "Death Is Only a Dream," a song filled with morbid images and supernaturalism:

Sadly we sing with tremulous breath
As we stand by the mystical stream,
In the valley and by the dark river of death
And yet 'tis no more than a dream.

Williams's moralistic spirituality appeared in his narrative recordings as the fictitious singer Luke the Drifter, which included titles such as "Pictures from Life's Other Side," "Too Many Parties and Too Many Pals," "The Funeral," and "I've Been Down That Road Before." He bragged that "Men with Broken Hearts," which he wrote, was "the awfulest, morbidest song you ever heard in your life." The song he had on the charts at the time of his death was "You'll Never Get Out of This World Alive." Hank Williams came out of a hardscrabble working-class world; he came out of a hard-shell religious world as well. The broken bodies and broken hearts of this poor South nurtured a demanding, rigorous faith that included a religious music that could be morbid, otherworldly, and unforgiving, but it was pervasive and articulated the frustrated spiritual strivings and dislocations of white working-class southerners encountering the transition from a world of sharecropping to that of a modern South. The religious music tradition that Hank Williams inherited and with which he found commercial success was an important aspect of southern spirituality in its time and place.[8]

Elvis Presley grew up in the Assembly of God Church, a Pentecostal denomination that included a fundamentalist theology and rigorous expectations about moral behavior, as was the case in Hank Williams's

Baptist church, but Pentecostals also sought the gifts of the spirit that could bring a transcendent experience of spiritual ecstasy to people who often suffered the traumas of this vale of tears. Gladys took young Elvis to church in east Tupelo, and she reported that the singing and the service left her feeling "renewed and restored." When Presley was two years old, he jumped out of her lap and ran down to the front of the church to sing with the choir, foreshadowing his musical preoccupations as well as his draw to religious music. As a child, he listened to country gospel records his mother favored – the Louvin Brothers, the Bailes Brothers, and James and Martha Carson, for example. Charles Wolfe describes this formative recorded religious music he heard as "urgent, passionate, straining harmonies born in the Pentecostal church." Elvis's spirituality was formed not only through these recordings but also by hearing the same songs at church revivals and Friday night gospel singings in Tupelo, which were regularly attended by Vernon, Gladys, and Elvis. Such listening to "urgent, passionate, straining harmonies," attending communal singings, and being exposed to everyday singing of religious music by his mother constituted the family devotional context for Elvis's developing spirituality, akin to countless southerners before and after him.[9]

Elvis was eleven when his family moved to Memphis, a musically vibrant urban community with particularly powerful gospel singing communities. Sunday afternoon singings in church were typical, and gospel quartets often held song battles to gain fame and respect. In 1950, the Mississippi-born Blackwood Brothers, the most famous white gospel quartet in the nation, moved to Memphis, where they presided over two daily shows on WMPS, developed their own record label, and initiated concerts at Ellis Auditorium. A new institution within the school of southern spirituality developed in the 1940s, when promoter Wally Fowler popularized packaged all-night gospel singings that soon spread across the region, and Memphis welcomed them. Elvis heard dignified older groups like the Speers and the Chuck Wagon Gang, whose songs grew out of shape-note influences, and he heard the soaring harmonies of the Blackwood Brothers, who adapted songs from black quartets such as the Soul Stirrers and the Golden Gate Quartet. While extending the centrality of music to southern spirituality, these singings were commercial performance events and expressions of popular culture featuring a new flashy showmanship. As Charles Wolfe notes, "It was the hottest and most exciting fad in gospel music at the time: the dynamic young quartets, clicked up in their white coats, bow ties, and pencil-thin mustaches, backed up by pumping piano players that owed as much to Art Tatum as to Liberace, framed by sky-high tenors and booming bass voices, throwing the old stand-up mikes back and forth like batons." He adds that "it was a different kind of spirituality, but spirituality nonetheless," with a new vigor of movement. It represented show business to Elvis and others at the all-night singings, yet these performances still reinforced the function of religious music by teaching tenets of predominant southern evangelical culture, such as a familiarity with biblical characters and stories, moralistic expectations expressed in song lyrics, and the peculiar dynamic of sin and salvation at work in evangelical faith. The increasingly slick world of gospel music, then, nonetheless reinforced older, familiar messages for religious southerners.[10]

Presley was also able to experience black religious music in Memphis, making that distinct tradition another formative part of his developing spirituality. He listened to daily radio shows aired over WDIA, which dominated the black gospel scene, with its disc jockey Theo "Bless My Bones" Wade daily broadcasting nationally known black gospel groups, as well as local groups like the Spirit of Memphis, the Brewsteraires, and the Dixie Nightingales. The radio station sponsored Goodwill Revues at Ellis Auditorium, the mother church of Memphis gospel music. Presley also went to East Trigg Baptist Church to hear the preaching and singing of the Reverend Herbert W. Brewster, one of the greatest of African American gospel songwriters, and his lead soloist, Queen C. Anderson. Elvis later remembered that he enjoyed Brewster's frequent preaching on the idea that a better day was coming, one in which all men could walk together as brothers. Brewster himself recalled when Elvis and other young whites came to the church to not only worship but sing: "I knew that it wasn't going to hurt whether I said 'Must Jesus Bear the Cross Alone,' whether I say it with one beat or two or high or low. I told them to come in here and put your stuff together. They came in here and it was a glorious experience and Elvis was in that group."[11]

Young Elvis, the Elvis before Sun Studios, continued developing an identifiable religiosity. In 1954, he began attending an Assembly of God church in south Memphis, whose preacher denounced films and dancing and encouraged "ecstatic demonstrations of faith," such as speaking in tongues. He attended a Bible study group on Sunday mornings; yes, he was one of the Christ Ambassadors. The Blackwood Brothers were also members of this congregation, and he grew increasingly involved in attending their gospel singings, becoming a frequent presence backstage. Soon, quartet singing became, as Peter Guralnick says, "the center of his musical universe. Gospel music combined the spiritual force that he felt in all music with this sense of physical release and exaltation for which, it seemed, he was casting about." As a teenager, then, religious music came particularly to embody a "spiritual force" that was linked with the exaltation he must have first felt when singing religious music with his family and as part of spirit-filled Pentecostal services.[12]

When Presley entered the national stage upon achieving early rock success, he faced criticism from ministers about his lewd performances, and a friend at the time said Elvis cried when he read a newspaper story that claimed he was ignoring the religion with which he had grown up. In an interview, he admitted that his travel schedule did not permit his attending church, but he insisted: "I believe in God. I believe in Him with all my heart. I believe all good things come from God. . . . And the way I feel about it, being religious means that you love God and are real grateful for all He's given, and want to work for Him. I feel deep in my heart that I'm doing all this." He was defensive about the Assemblies of God and charges that his energetic performance style came from the church. Furthermore, he objected with uncharacteristic vehemence to the label "holy rollers" for the Assemblies of God. While he labeled his denomination a Holiness church, Elvis stressed, "I have never used the expression Holy Roller." He insisted also that "[he] always attended church where people sang, stood up, and sang in the choir and worshiped God." In a separate interview, a reporter asked him about his "unique style," and he admitted that he had "landed upon it accidentally." He continued, "More or less I am a pretty close follower of religious quartets, and they do a lot of rockin' spirituals." When a story then appeared that quoted Elvis as saying he "got the jumping around from my religion," he denied it. "My religion has nothin' to do with what I do now because the type stuff I do now is not religious music," he asserted, making an important distinction that would be true throughout his career. For Presley, religious music remained in a different category than rock, one that expressed his spiritual strivings above and beyond the material success he attained. Despite his enormous success with rock 'n' roll, he insisted on recording his first gospel album, *Peace in the Valley*, in 1957, early in his national career.[13]

Through the coming decades, religious music remained an anchor for him, despite the successes and temptations of such places as Hollywood and Las Vegas and frequent touring in the last years of his life. Like the South itself in the 1960s and early 1970s, Presley experienced enormous changes that took him far beyond the spirituality that a spirit-filled Pentecostal faith and the power of gospel music embodied. By the mid-1960s, for example, Presley was using LSD at Graceland and reading about Timothy Leary, although, as one scholar has noted, he did so in typical Presley fashion – turning on the television and ordering a pizza to go with his LSD. Larry Geller became his spiritual guru, directing Presley to explore much new spiritual reading and practice. It began with Presley reading Joseph Brenner's *The Impersonal Life*, a 1917 volume that taught that God was in each human, a message that Presley responded to immediately, having long before embraced the belief that his extraordinary success had been a gift from God with some purpose he had to discover. He later read *Autobiography of a Yogi* by Indian holy man Paramahanse Yogananda, and he read New Thought treatises by Madame Blavatsky and Krishnamurti. This type of spiritual exploration was, to be sure, an extraordinary change for the unlettered Presley, and one that disrupted his life. His buddy Joe Esposito recalled that he would get up in the morning only to find Elvis "sitting there reading a book and asking questions about religion." Bemoaning his friend's transformation, Esposito continued, "Hey, what about the football game that happened last weekend? We used to sit and watch football games. All that stuff was gone." In March 1965, Presley had a profound religious experience in the desert near Flagstaff, Arizona, where he said he saw the face of God in the clouds over the desert. He began visiting the Self-Realization Fellowship Lake Shrine Retreat in California, telling one friend he wanted to become a monk. He found a new serenity through the leader of the Self-Realization Fellowship, Sri Daya Mata. She recalled later that "he wanted to be a great spiritual influence on all these young people – that was at the basis of his desire." He told her, "I want to awaken in all these young people a closer relationship to God."[14]

What can one make of this increasingly experimental spirituality, dating to the mid-1960s and after? For purposes of considering southern spirituality, it obviously is a wild departure from the norms with which he had grown up, reflecting perhaps his struggles to come to terms with fame and its demands upon him. Part of Elvis surely became unhinged from formerly reliable foundations. Presley was getting caught up, though, in changing patterns of American spirituality and should not be seen as idiosyncratic. Asian religions acquired a new influence and relevance in 1960s America, and transcendental meditation in particular became prominent in popular religion. Indeed, Elvis had moved from traditional evangelical-based spirituality into new forms of popular religion. He represented countless southerners who now had access to previously unavailable schools of spirituality through television, the movies, inexpensive paperback books, popular magazines, and especially perhaps tabloids that told of psychic phenomena, the possibility of communicating with the dead, UFOs, Ravi Shankar's spiritual influence on the Beatles, and other phenomena that would appear outrageously unorthodox to members of the traditional evangelical denominations. Elvis thus joined countless southerners and other Americans as participants in new forms of popular spirituality.[15]

At the same time, those traditional denominations continued to dominate the southern religious scene in these years, becoming even more powerful forces in politics, whether for liberal civil rights causes or conservative New Right issues, and gaining increased economic clout as the region's economy boomed in the years of the Sunbelt. Similarly, despite his early New Age instincts, Presley still held fast to religious music as his anchor amid other changes in both his material and spiritual life. Gospel music continued to represent the legacy of the southern spirituality with which he had grown up and which now saw him through the transitions in his life in the 1960s and 1970s. Back in Memphis in the mid-1960s, after an extended stay in California, Presley visited his mother's grave weekly and sent flowers three times a week. His mother symbolized his earlier faith, and his return to Memphis seemed to trigger a new concern for his roots in the region's traditional spirituality. He told a reporter that he wanted to start going to church again, recalling that church had been, in his words, "our way of life since I can remember." He admitted that the last time he had attended church services "there was so much confusion, and auto-graph seeking, that out of respect [he] stayed away." Still, he saw his religious needs and contributions expressed in his music: "I've been working on religious songs for an album. I feel God and his goodness, and I believe I can express his love for us in music."[16]

Spirituality is by definition about the interior life and the spiritual exercises to cultivate it, but Presley saw his spirituality as also having a public dimension, reaching as he did countless people through his music. He recorded four gospel albums, and the songs and arrangements he selected revealed much about his spirituality in the 1960s and 1970s. His second gospel album, *His Hand in Mine*, recorded in the fall of 1960, included seven songs by the Statesmen, the white gospel group that influenced him so much in general. Among the songs was "Milky White Way," a black gospel standard, with the arrangement modeled on the Trumpeteers, a Baltimore quartet of the 1940s; "Mansion over the Hilltop," a country gospel number based on an old preacher's story; "Swing Down Sweet Chariot," a quartet number recorded by one of Presley's favorite black gospel groups, the Golden Gate Quartet, but with an arrangement from the Blackwood Brothers; and "If We Never Meet Again," written by one of the great white gospel songwriters, Albert Brumley. His third gospel album, *How Great Thou Art*, was not a tribute to classic gospel quartet singing as much as it was a collection of "church specials," numbers popular in revivals and the churches themselves. Again, it was a mix of songs popularized by black and white gospel groups. Among the songs on the album were "Farther Along," a country gospel classic that first appeared in the Stamps-Baxter songbook in 1937; "Where Could I Go But to the Lord," another songbook tune that a singing school teacher from Mississippi had written; "Run On," which had been popularized by the Golden Gate Quartet; and "Stand By Me," which Charles Albert Tindley, another prolific African American songwriter, published in 1905.[17]

Presley's fourth gospel album appeared in 1971 and reflected changes in gospel music and the evolution of his spirituality. California-centered Jesus music, exultant praise music, and the beginnings of Christian rock were well represented, as Elvis moved beyond the southern origins of gospel. Likewise, new gospel songwriters such as Andrae Crouch and Ralph Carmichael had songs on the album. Carmichael, a California-based songwriter who added strings and large orchestras to his gospel compositions, was a particularly significant change. One sacred song on the album stood out even more than the others: "Miracle of the Rosary" explored a Catholic sensibility more than anything Presley had previously recorded, again suggesting that his spiritual journey through music was not just an exploration of new forms of popular religion prominent in 1960s America but also of a traditional Catholic spirituality that now resonated with him.[18]

Presley's public spirituality included an active promotion of religious music. He incorporated gospel songs into his movie soundtracks, as when he included "Swing Low Sweet Chariot" in *Trouble with Girls.* He even introduced gospel music to Las Vegas – no mean feat, featuring religious numbers in his performances there. Additionally, wherever he performed in the 1970s, Presley showcased the Jordanaires, the Stamps Quartet, and other gospel groups. Such promotion conveyed his personal spirituality to audiences that were not expecting such open religiosity in an entertainment venue, even if they were often receptive to it. Taken as a whole, he saw his actions as essential parts of his growing efforts to witness his faith through religious music. The mix of private and public spirituality appears on the tape of a 1970s concert, when Presley asks the audience to listen to the Stamps Quartet singing "Sweet, Sweet Spirit." Presley lets them sing, while he appears transported by listening to the music, his eyes closed, his head gently shaking, and then his entire face smiling along with a certain lyric and musical notes – the image of his private spirituality written on his public stage.[19]

In this stress on musical evangelism, he reflected the abiding evangelical impulse toward conversion as the essence of religious faith, which Samuel Hill has called the central theme of southern religion. For southern evangelicals, despite the importance of theology, doctrine, ritual, and morality, the experience of God's saving grace is essential – have you seen Jesus and been born again was the imperative question driving the dynamic of sin and salvation. Presley's personal life in the mid-1970s became increasingly tortured, with abuse of prescription drugs the best symbol of a life that strayed far from the notably ascetic demands of his early Pentecostalism. He used religious music as a counterweight in nurturing his private spirituality and in trying to influence his fans toward an increased appreciation of God's goodness. J. D. Sumner, the legendary gospel singer who became his close friend, has said that he thought in the last five years of his life Presley was returning to his roots in music, to the gospel music that even preceded his rockabilly classics. Sumner suggested that if Presley had lived another six months, he would have become a full-time gospel singer.[20]

Even before then, one can see the centrality of religious music for Presley's spirituality in these last years of his life through an informal jam session caught on film in March 1972, for the documentary *Elvis on Tour.* Like the Million Dollar Session in 1956, this spontaneous sing-along was spirited and relaxed, showing the ease with which Presley sang gospel music in private. This session, which happened to be filmed, reflected others that had long been typical of his quest for quiet moments with the music. Early in his career, while performing on the road with the Louvin Brothers, he sat at the piano and began playing gospel songs, telling them, "This is really my favorite kind of music." When he performed on stage, he said, "I do what they want to hear; when I'm back here, I do what I want to do." In his last years of performing, he always wanted the Stamps Quartet to come to his suite after his shows to relax by singing gospel music with them all night. At the 1972 jam, he joined in singing old quartet numbers, spirituals, "Nearer My God to Thee" (which goes back to the 1840s), and a 1922 hymn, "Turn Your Eyes Upon Jesus." As he said in an interview for the film, gospel music "more or less puts your mind to rest. At least it does mine, since I was two."[21]

This chapter has been a tentative exploration of southern spirituality, arguing that religious music was a traditional spiritual exercise in the South, one that individuals cultivated privately, at church singings, and in a variety of institutions – sacred harp singings, singing schools, singing conventions, all-night gospel singings, and other distinctive contexts. Presley's experience revealed the changes in spirituality in the South as the region modernized and its religious and musical institutions began to use technology as well as promotional techniques adopted from the modern entertainment industry to extend the old-time message of evangelical spirituality. Like many Americans, Presley explored new forms of popular religiosity in the 1960s. Samuel Weber, in his *New Encyclopedia of Southern Culture* entry on "Spirituality in the South," concludes that in the past three decades, "for many, 'spirituality' has become synonymous with 'finding the true self' and 'unleashing the potential for truth and love,' as well as terms such as 'serenity' and 'peace of heart.'" This describes Presley's spiritual questing perfectly. His attraction to the Self-Realization Fellowship in the 1960s represented a new expression in a long journey that grew out of the intensity of his Pentecostal background and was expressed in his religious music. His traditional southern spirituality rested on the hope of redemption, even for a sinner, stemming from a personal relationship with the divine. Elvis's aunt Lorene recalled that when Elvis was a young boy he disappeared one day, and when he returned, he began crying and said that "he had been talking to Jesus." As the lyric to one of his favorite songs says, Elvis appears to have continued to believe, as most people in his native region did in his lifetime, that "Just a Little Talk with Jesus Gonna Make It Right."[22]

11 Richard Wright's *Pagan Spain*

A Southern Protestant Abroad

When Richard Wright arrived in Seville in the spring of 1955 to observe Holy Week in the Spanish city, the first thing he commented on were shop windows filled with "tiny robed figures with tall, pointed hoods that gave [him] a creepy feeling, for these objects reminded [him] of the Ku Klux Klan of the Old American South." He surmised that "it must have been from here that the Ku Klux Klan regalia had been copied." Wright may or may not have been correct that the Seville Catholic symbolism was the source for the Klan's ceremonial dress, much of which came instead from the assumed mysteries of a Celtic religion. The Klan, in any event, would hardly have admitted to borrowing from Catholics. Nonetheless, Wright's book *Pagan Spain* is a powerful expression of connections between Spain and the American South.[1]

This chapter argues that Wright saw the Spain he visited in the 1950s through the lens of the American South in which he was raised and developed his purpose as a writer. That South was a Jim Crow, white supremacist society; but it was also a hegemonic evangelical Protestant culture that suffused both white and black life with certain forms of spirituality. In Spain, he recognized some of those similarities with the South;

others he portrayed in his text but without self-consciously naming them. A careful study of *Pagan Spain* suggests the importance of civil religion and popular religion as the defining traditions connecting the American South and Spain.

To raise religion rather than race as a central issue for *Pagan Spain* seems surprising. Wright's memoir *Black Boy* outlines the brutal and demeaning education he received as a black southerner living at the apogee of racial segregation. While we know to be careful in using that memoir as the full story of his childhood and youth, the book's undeniable power comes from its single-minded focus on the tragic results of the Jim Crow system. But Wright finds that race is not an issue in the Spain of the 1950s, noting "they had no racial consciousness whatsoever" after his first encounters with Spanish youth.[2]

Wright's career in the 1950s has become a subject of increasing interest, mostly because of studies of the literature of the African diaspora. His other nonfiction writings of the 1950s, *Black Power* (1954) and *The Color Curtain* (1956), are about non-Western cultures and his explorations of race in Africa and Asia in postcolonial times, as he struggled to position his experience, and those of African Americans in general, in relation to these worlds. Yet little of this perspective enters *Pagan Spain*. From the beginning, religion is Wright's key focus. On his first visit, he is awakened by "the melancholy tolling of churchbells." Two young men befriend him, taking him to their cathedral. Wright is impressed by their religiosity. "To these boys it was unthinkable that there was no God and that we were not all His sons," he writes. As he walks down the aisle of the cathedral, he admits to feeling "a mood of awe." That feeling turns more skeptical, if Wright is not downright offended, when he sees a mummified corpse of a bishop displayed in a glass coffin.[3]

Wright's daughter Julia once observed that "the very aspects of suffering, oppression, and religious mysticism Wright is most sensitive to in Spain are those which molded his own oppressed youth in the American South." And yet Wright himself confesses, "I have no religion in the formal sense of the word." I want to go deeper into the religious context of the South that produced Wright to explore how he reads Spain through the South.[4]

In *Black Boy*, Wright recounts several formative religious experiences. One is exposure to the millennialist faith of his grandmother, who attended the Seventh-day Adventist Church. This denomination was not a mainstream church among either white or black Protestants in the South, but it was part of a culture of apocalypse that was deeply rooted among poor and working-class southerners. It was a world-denying faith that taught of the wickedness of human society and the need to retreat from it and build enclaves of faith from which to wait for the end of the world. Wright recalled that the church he attended "expounded a gospel clogged with images of vast lakes of eternal fire, of seas vanishing, of valleys of dry bones, of the sun burning to ashes, of the moon turning to blood, of stars falling to the earth, of a wooden staff being transformed into a serpent, of voices speaking out of clouds, of men walking upon water, of God riding whirlwinds, of water changing into wine, of the dead rising and living, of the blind seeing, of the lame walking." He appreciated "the vivid language of the sermons" and was "pulled toward emotional belief"; full emotional commitment and intellectual belief, however, never came.[5]

Popular religion figures prominently in both *Black Boy* and *Pagan Spain* as dramatic experiences. Popular religion rests in the belief in supernatural outcroppings that people see outside the church doors, in everyday life. In the South, devils can instigate sinful behavior, angels may appear to give hope, and doomed lives may be saved by faith. Writer Frances Mayes, who grew up in Georgia before earning fame as author of *Under the Tuscan Skies*, recalls the JESUS IS COMING signs tacked on trees in the South of her childhood. Another said REPENT. These signs marked the southern landscape as a sacred one because common folks were claiming it as such with religious signs. Just as COLORED and WHITE signs became a powerful part of the visual landscape of white supremacy, GET RIGHT WITH GOD signs claimed the land for a rigorous and spirit-filled religion.[6]

The spirituality Wright experienced in his grandmother's house was a hard and demanding one. "There were prayers at sunup and sundown, at the breakfast table, followed by a Bible verse from each member of the family," he recalled. When someone in Spain is impressed with a biblical reference Wright makes, he notes that "[he] was weaned on it," meaning the Bible. As a child, he also had to attend ritualistic all-night prayer meetings and religious revivals. Out of this experience, he came to appreciate "the hymns for their sensual caress," but this memory

allows him to connect the religion of his childhood to sexuality, an interpretation of religion and sexuality that he would explore more fully and
somewhat luridly in *Pagan Spain*. "It was possible," he wrote in *Black Boy*,
"that the sweetly sonorous hymns stimulated me sexually, and it might
have been that my fleshly fantasies, in turn, having as their foundation
my already inflated sensibility, made me love the masochistic prayers."
He went on to wonder if "the church's spiritual life" was "polluted by
my base yearnings, by the leaping hunger of my blood for the flesh,"
because he gazed yearningly for hours at the elder's wife during prayer
meetings. He converted his desires into "a concrete religious symbol": it
was "a black imp with horns; a long, curving, forked tail; cloven hoofs, a
scaly, naked body; wet, sticky fingers, moist, sensual lips; and lascivious
eyes feasting upon the face of the elder's wife."[7]

Wright's sexual fantasies in church provided an unorthodox, if life-
affirming, memory of his time in the southern black millennial world and
softened the rigor of the demanding spirituality around him. In addition
to experiencing Adventist religion, he also attended a black Methodist
church, a denomination that was one of the mainstream church groups
among southern blacks; more broadly, Methodism was part of an evangelical hegemony among whites and blacks. Two points are worth noting
in terms of his later observations of Spain, and both relate to a revival he
attended. The congregation had targeted young men like Richard, hop-
ing they would respond to the revival's emotional drama of salvation
seeking. "We young men had been trapped by the community, the tribe
in which we lived and of which we were a part," he observed. To say no
to conversion was to reject the community's feelings, "placing ourselves
in the position of moral monsters." The second point to highlight is the
role of mothers in this ceremonial scene, who ringed the young men targeted for conversion. "Now," the minister preached, "you good sweet
mothers, symbols of Mother Mary at the tomb, kneel and pray for your
sons, your only sons."[8] Wright's mother, the symbolic biblical mother,
emerges as a central spiritual figure in the essential southern religious
drama of redemption.

Wright's experience in the South's Jim Crow society ultimately raises
an issue profoundly rooted in religion, albeit not in the church, and it
also centered around his mother. Wright's mother was debilitated during

his youth, often enduring enormous pain, with young Richard holding her hand. "I merely waited upon her knowing that she was suffering," he remembered. The word *suffering* reverberates through *Black
Boy* and *Pagan Spain* as the key link between the Jim Crow South and
Franco's Spain. "My mother's suffering grew into a symbol in my mind,"
he writes, "gathering to itself all the poverty, the ignorance, the help-
lessness; the painful, baffling, hunger-ridden days and hours; the rest-
less moving, the futile seeking, the uncertainty, the fear, the dread; the
meaningless pain and the endless suffering."[9]

Wright admits in *Black Boy* that his mother's life, her suffering, "set the
emotional tone of [his] life," determining his attitude toward events that
had not yet happened," including trips to visit Spain. Wright insisted,
"The spirit I had caught gave me insight into the sufferings of others,"
making him analyze every circumstance "and lay it open to the core of
suffering." When someone in Spain asks Wright what his book will say,
he responds: "I shall tell them that the people of Spain are suffering." In
recounting a conversation with a barber, he writes of telling him, "The
thing that worries me about Spain is the suffering." This reaction was a
logical conclusion from the trajectory he outlined for his life's work in
Black Boy. He portrays the poverty and backwardness of Spain, the pervasiveness of deprived young women openly serving as prostitutes, the
oppression of Protestants, and the authoritarianism of General Francisco
Franco. But he singles out the Roman Catholic Church as a fellow trav-
eler with the latter – a source and cause of suffering because of its collab-
oration with a tyrannical political state.[10]

Here we encounter Wright's major insight in *Pagan Spain*: Spain sees
itself as a sacred state. He does not use the term, but he in fact ana-
lyzes a conservative Spanish civil religion that saw transcendent meaning in national experience. Early in the book, he tells of meeting a young
woman named Carmen who shares with him a political catechism from
the Falangists, the fascist political authority that gave ideological meaning to Franco's regime; it was intended to inculcate the principles of
fascism in girls from age nine upward. Wright effectively used excerpts from the catechism to show the sacred sanction given to the state.
The catechism begins with references to Spain's destiny to influence the
world. Spain is "our Motherland," the catechism intones, "because we

feel ourselves incorporated in its destiny in the world." What was that destiny? The Falangist answer was "to include all men in a common movement for salvation." Spain would achieve its destiny through "the influence it exercises over other nations and also by conquest." This is messianic Christianity, and Wright shows readers evidence of its reach into Spanish society. The civil guard openly displays machine guns in all public places, and Wright seems especially bothered that armed guards surround the statue of the Virgin in Seville's Holy Week processions. He sees churches across Spain with the names of Fascist leaders etched in stone on them. The Valley of the Fallen displays the monumental tributes that express a civil religion's ability to project religious-political connections on a grand scale. Loyalist prisoners during the Spanish Civil War built this huge granite shrine on a mountainside, with a large crypt topped by a five-hundred-foot cross. Christian icons, statues, and artwork are displayed in a triumphal mix, and the basilica here was built to be Franco's burial spot.[11]

Wright understood the power of blurred lines between the state and the sacred and did not always see them as so negative as he did in Spain. He went to the Gold Coast in Africa in the 1950s, at the invitation of Kwame Nkrumah. Wright observed that Nkrumah's popular nationalist movement had "fused tribalism with modern politics," creating "a new kind of religion." He saw this new form as necessary as Africa went through the transition from traditionalism, as represented by premodern tribal structures, to modernity. His writings on Africa advised Nkrumah that "it's a secular religion that you must slowly create," a phrase that might be another name for civil religion.[12]

Spain in the 1950s seemed to Wright more trapped by traditionalism than on a road to modernity. As Richard King has recently noted, Wright saw little future for folk cultures but was "a confirmed member of the party of enlightenment." The Spanish Civil War had ended less than two decades before *Pagan Spain* appeared and is the context of the civil religion and popular religiosity that Wright sees as a Spanish burden. He meets one woman who suffers from having seen soldiers in the civil war kill her father. Wright notes that the Catholic Church used such traumas to teach acquiescence to the Spanish masses. "It's the same everywhere," said a relative of the woman. "Father Rubio was telling us that only last week. It's the same all over the world." Wright's insight is that "to negate this horror, the church had to make it the normal lot of man. If this horror were the heritage of all men, then rebellion was senseless, was sinful."[13]

Despite making some analogies between the totalitarianism of Jim Crow segregation and Franco's tyranny, Wright does not note an important point: the American Civil War was the background for a southern civil religion just as the Spanish Civil War was the context for Franco's society. Southern whites had sacralized their history after the Civil War, making Robert E. Lee a saint and Stonewall Jackson a martyr. Ministers were at the forefront of explaining a theology of defeat in a holy war – God had punished his chosen people to prepare them for a redemptive future. In 1917, Southern Baptist Convention leader Victor I. Masters published *The Call of the South*, which explained, in words that Falangists would have understood, that the South had a special mission. Having suffered through Confederate defeat and wandered symbolically in the Lost Cause wilderness afterward, white southerners by the early decades of the twentieth century saw themselves as the last bastion in the Western world for an evangelical Zion, with a mission under God's Providence to embody traditional Christian spirituality and, in fact, go out to convert the world.[14]

Wright was born around the time of Masters's call to southern missionary arms, and he grew up in a southern world of civil religion's messianic Christianity. Monument dedications to Confederate heroes were key community events; Confederate Memorial Day reminded southerners, black and white, of a cult of the dead that empowered the Confederate ghosts with moral and spiritual authority; the song "Dixie" was heard at public events, no matter what the occasion; and waving Confederate battle flags were visual reminders of the Confederate sacrificial ethos that fought to redeem the South from Yankee rule. Wright's sensitivity to issues of civil religion that he saw in Spain and in Africa surely reflected walking through, seeing, and listening to the symbolic representations on the southern landscape in which he grew of age.[15]

Expressions of popular religion – those supernatural outcroppings in everyday life that blur lines between the sacred and the secular – often embodied sacralization of the state in Spain and the South and showed ways that this religiosity, for Wright, expressed a primitive sensibility. His close observation of a bullfight and the famous shrine to the Virgin at Montserrat reveal these connections.

A building outside the bullfight arena displayed a giant Falangist emblem, a representation of the Yoke and Arrows that had been a historical Spanish symbol dating back to Ferdinand and Isabella. This image provides a sacred-state framing as Wright contemplates the drama of the bullfight. He quotes Juan Belmonte, one of the most famous Spanish bullfighters, who said that bullfighting was "fundamentally a spiritual exercise and not merely a sport." The Falangist catechism claimed that the Spanish republic had collapsed because it scoffed at religion, and this "cut the Spaniards to the quick." The bullfight, then, becomes a primal expression of Spanish religiosity in Franco's postwar sacred state. Matadors kneel before images of the Virgin before the contest, pray and cross themselves. Furthermore, the cruelty of the fight scene itself "hinted at terrible torments of the heart," and the ceremonial slaying of the bull brought resolution.[16]

Sacrifice is another keyword in the popular religiosity of the bullfight. An American who went to Spain to become a bullfighter tells Wright that the bullfight "has the intensity of religious emotion," and the bullfighter must "offer to sacrifice his life to the bull." Wright does not explicitly evoke the lynching of southern blacks while discussing the ritual slaying of the bull and the bullfighter's confrontation with death in this spectacle, but the analogy is clear. He sees the bull as "a creature of our common fantasy, a projected puppet of our collective hearts and brains, a savage proxy offered by us to ourselves to appease the warring claims that our instincts were heir to." Wright is deeply troubled by the cruelty of the crowd, who wanted the bull "slain in a manner that would be unforgettable." After the bull is dead, crowd members attack the bull's testicles, kicking and stomping them "while their eyes held a glazed and excited look of sadism." They attacked the part of the dead bull's body that somehow "symbolized for them and poured out the hate and frustration and bewilderment of their troubled and confused consciousness." This description could have been one for the spectacle lynchings of blacks in the South, which often involved mutilation of victims. Wright's short story "Big Boy Leaves Home" portrayed such a lynching, with the victim hanged from a tree and burned alive as a white mob chants in an emotional frenzy and takes souvenirs from the body. Religious historian Donald Mathews has recently argued that inherent in southern Protestantism has been a dynamic of atonement, seeking to purge society of sin, which expressed itself not only in such church rituals as individual conversion and baptism but also in the violent sacrifice of blacks considered the dark embodiments of sin for the southern body politic. As Wright says of the sacrifice of the bull in the bullfight, "Death must serve as a secular baptism of emotion to wash the heart clean of its illegal dirt."[17]

Wright is grounded in Freudian psychology throughout *Pagan Spain*, as he was in *Black Boy* a decade earlier. His emphasis on sexuality and gender often reflects this interest, which we see clearly in his account of another site of popular religiosity – visiting the Black Virgin shrine at Montserrat. He admits to feeling "a hint of the mystical" in the rugged physical landscape, pointing toward the heavens. Religiosity and sexuality become tied together in the following description of the setting of the shrine: "More and more nations of seriated granite phalluses, tumefied and turgid, heaved into sight, each rocky republic of erections rising higher than its predecessor, the whole stone empire of them frozen into stances of eternal distensions, until at last they became a kind of universe haunted by phallic images."[18] Wright emphasizes the paganism of Spanish culture, suggesting that traditional male-female gender roles hark back to a primitive faith that invests women with a special authority but with complex expressions. Here again he makes explicit connections between the American South and Spain. Just as the southern white woman is idealized and placed on a pedestal, so the young Spanish virgin is worshipped as untouchable by Spanish men. And just as southern black women could be sexually exploited by white men, so Spanish prostitutes, often poor and with few alternatives and deeply religious, were a public presence everywhere Wright went. The Catholic Church, he writes, with its stress on the inevitability of sinfulness, was "a religion whose outlook upon the universe almost legitimizes prostitution."[19]

Wright admits that his interpretation of the Spain he saw was shaped by the Protestantism he grew up with in the South. "I was born a Protestant," he notes at one point. "I lived a Protestant childhood." At another point, he wants "to be clear about" his own deep non-Catholic sensibility, "[his] undeniable and inescapable Protestant background and conditioning." Of course, by the 1950s, he was far beyond this childhood Protestant upbringing and confessed no religion; but he was right that his southern Protestant background clearly influenced his reading of Spain. For one thing, it made him especially sensitive to the plight of Protestants. He lamented "the needless, unnatural and utterly barbarous nature of the psychological suffering that the Spanish Protestant was doomed to undergo at the hands of the Church and State officials and his Catholic neighbors." He notes that such "psychological suffering" was his experience, "stemming from [his] previous position as a member of a persecuted racial minority," linking again his southern experiences and his Spanish observations.[20] Wright's Protestant background, moreover, surely explains in part some of his revulsion at specifically Catholic practices. His disgust at the public display of the mummified bishop, noted earlier, was typical. He could have even been a Protestant reformer given his sometimes notable physical reactions against seeing the crucifix. Similarly, he complained of all the gold displayed in religious icons, again like a Protestant reformer wanting to topple the Catholic altars.

Wright captures Spanish popular religion, noting that "the boundaries of Spanish religiosity went beyond the church," and we see its shrines, rituals, processions, pilgrimages, festivals, icons, relics, sacred virgins, weeping angels, suffering saints, magic symbols, and catechisms. He does not always tell us, though, what these experiences mean to the faithful. He is disturbed by the Holy Week processions in Seville, for example, but does not explain their purpose in recreating the Via Dolorosa of Christ's path to his destiny. We don't find out what the "tortured Christs and weeping Virgins" mean to the crowds of passionate worshippers. For Wright, popular religion is a diversion for these suffering people, causing him to portray their popular religiosity in the context of a culture of poverty and backwardness, a judgment he makes according to Western standards. He dismisses, moreover, not only this religiosity but other renowned aspects of Spanish culture as well. For instance, he ridicules Grenada's Alhambra as "this monstrous pile of dead glory," while his lurid account of flamenco dancing among Andalusian gypsies evokes images of what he calls "sexual animality," not acknowledging the ancient heritage, craft, and beauty of this art.[21] Similarly, Wright seldom commented positively on the South's cultural achievements, other than the blues. The social realist in him, the skeptic and iconoclast, kept him focused on the social problems that humans faced and needed to confront in order to address the suffering that resulted.

Near the end of *Pagan Spain*, Wright concludes that he had learned that Spain was "a holy nation, a sacred state." The Falangist catechism reinforced the conservative Spanish civil religion, and popular religiosity worked to distract Spaniards from confronting the need for change. "All was religion in Spain," he ultimately decides. Wright's spirituality, formed in southern black churches, attuned him to a basically religious insight on life that he kept with him as he left the South for new experiences, including his time in Spain. Wright admits in *Black Boy* that "the religious symbols" of the southern black churches "appealed to [his] sensibilities," giving him a grounding in spirituality that remained with him. Evangelical Protestantism instills an unusual awareness of mortality, which stayed with him all his life. He responded to "the dramatic vision of life held by the church, feeling that to live day by day with death as one's sole thought was to be so compassionately sensitive toward all life as to view all men as slowly dying, and the trembling sense of fate that welled up, sweet and melancholy, from the hymns blended with the sense of fate that [he] had already caught from life." Significantly, the first two sections of *Pagan Spain* are "Life after Death" and "Death and Exaltation." The evangelical Protestant image of a dying Christ that he sang about in churches and the centrality in evangelical Protestant religion of overcoming death through salvation remained an active memory for Wright, and his stress on suffering – a central religious concern – made him indeed "compassionately sensitive" toward the Spanish people he met and about whom he wrote.[22]

In *Black Boy*, Wright comes to realize, in the end, that despite "that southern swamp of despair and violence," he had gained "in [his] personality and consciousness . . . the culture of the South." He projected the hope that he was "taking a part of the South to transplant in alien soil" to hopefully bloom.[23] Perhaps his hard won and skeptical spirituality, on vivid display in *Pagan Spain*, was his own distinctive take on southern culture that indeed survived to allow him to compassionately survey the Spanish people in their sufferings under a sacred state.

12 A Journey to Southern Religious Studies

My journey to the study of southern religion began as a child in Nashville, Tennessee, took me to Texas, and brought me to Mississippi. It began in the Church of Christ, led to years outside any church orbit, and has brought me now to Episcopalianism. I am a historian but easily see ways to use the theories and methods of other disciplines to illuminate the study of southern religion in context. I have had many mentors, both actual teachers and intellectual figures whose works have shaped me. Looking back on my life, I see how spiritual issues have been enduring influences, if sometimes oblique, on my academic work.

My roots and raising were in Tennessee, as part of a very close-knit southern family. My parents were from small towns in middle Tennessee, tobacco-growing country north of Nashville. They were what historians would call the "plain folk" – not wealthy, not the stereotypical "poor whites," but, in my father's case at least, poor in worldly goods. My father's people were burdened with a hardscrabble life as sharecroppers who had lost family land in the early twentieth century. By contrast, my mother's life was more sheltered in the small town of Springfield, though again life was not extravagant for her as the daughter of a barber.

Their spiritual lives may have been constrained, as with so many others, because of the austere context of their material lives.

I inherited from my parents pronounced churchly orientations. My mother was a Southern Baptist, my father a member of the Church of Christ. My father's parents were, it seemed to me, faithful members of the Coopertown church, and my memories of church there are of hard pews, lean preachers, and the groaning tables of fine dinners on the grounds. My grandparents on my mother's side were religious but less churchly. My grandmother betrayed an insecurity, perhaps, in judging weekly services as too much of a social occasion, with the congregation more interested in what she was wearing than in her soul. Perhaps this suggested insecurity, but perhaps it showed that her religious beliefs were more important to her than her appearance. My grandfather Charlie Ward, for whom I am named, was a gentle man, a model Christian it seemed to me, although he was not in church that often. I do remember going with him to the Ebenezer Baptist Church, in Greenbrier, Tennessee, and sitting through innumerable invitation calls.

My father would not attend any church but the Church of Christ, so my mother switched to that church when she married, even being rebaptized as this demanding new faith required. She reserved the right, nonetheless, to give an occasional Baptist critique of the Sunday sermon on the way home from services. I attended the Church of Christ regularly as a child, along with my brother, Martin, who was two years younger than I. In visiting relatives, though, we might attend Baptist or Methodist services as well as those of the Church of Christ. I thought of them as interchangeable experiences at the time, which suggests that preachers were not fully communicating the complexities of the differing theological traditions of those churches to the young. The Church of Christ is a Restorationist church that strives to re-create the early Christian church, based on the books of the New Testament. Growing up in it gave me a thorough grounding in the scriptures, the stories and characters and wisdom of, in fact, the Old Testament as well as the New. I recall reading the King James Version around the kitchen table with my mother, father, and brother, and I can still see in my mind the graphic, sometimes gory illustrations of our edition. I absorbed more lessons in Sunday school and vacation Bible school, that southern summer ritual of childhood. Familiarity with the Bible surely has benefited my studies of southern religion, grounding me in specific biblical incidents that I recall in reading historical texts and also providing tropes for my own conceptualization of southern sacred experiences.

The Church of Christ, I would later discover, is not an evangelical church; it remains grounded in theological inheritances from its early influences in Presbyterianism and Scottish Common Sense Realism. It shares much with its southern evangelical neighbors, though, as I remember from childhood – not only the familiarity with the Bible that one would expect in a fundamentalist faith but also that wide body of hymns and gospel songs that unite believers across denominational lines. My mother was surely a character from rural folk tradition, knowing by heart innumerable songs and keeping the church hymnal around for others, as she sang to my brother and me throughout our youth and beyond. I learned from her and from those songs, more than from ministers, about the grace of Jesus. "I come to the garden alone, while the dew is still on the roses," says one of the most comforting of those songs, portraying what a friend we have in Jesus, as another of my favorites says. The singing in the Church of Christ is without musical accompaniment, though, which sounds odd to nonmembers, but I remember the compelling quality of the spare sounds. The bass voices coming in on "Up from the Grave He Arose," which we sang each Easter morning, still electrifies my memory. I consciously weave references to these religious songs into anything I write.

When I was nine years old, in 1957, we left Tennessee to move to El Paso, Texas, a move occasioned by my mother's worsening health in the wet and humid Southeast. The uprooting severed me from an extended kin of grandparents, aunts and uncles, and cousins, but it bound me even closer to my nuclear family. I grew up in a very cosmopolitan, suburban place – El Paso, a city with a mobile military population, strong cultural influences from Southern California (we watched the Los Angeles Dodgers on cable TV), and the intriguing Anglo-Hispanic culture of a Mexican border town. One of my strongest memories is of walking past a church not long after moving to Texas and seeing men dressed in long robes and white collars sprinkling water on animals, a menagerie of cats and dogs and birds and others – the blessing of the animals on St. Francis Day, although I did not realize what I had observed until much later.

At the time, I simply realized I was not in Tennessee anymore, or at least the Tennessee in which I had grown up as part of a Protestant family seldom exposed to other religious traditions. In any event, I now was in a spot to observe a bright world of Hispanic Catholicism, living in a borderland that exposed me in ways I did not even realize to the sights and sounds of a multireligious culture.

After we moved to Texas, my brother and I, with our mother and father when he could get away from work, would return to small-town Tennessee every summer, spending it with grandparents in Greenbrier. I loved much of that life, but my high school years were more preoccupied with the Beatles and fear of the Vietnam War than with any icons of the South. Indeed, I positively repudiated the ugliness in the South's resistance to social change as I was coming of age in the early 1960s. For me, religion was about the brotherhood of man, and I did not see much of it in the South of my roots and raising.

The death of my grandfather, my mother's father, was a jolting event that led to a loss of faith. He was a sweet, funny, endearing man who played old-time tunes on his fiddle – as perfect a grandfather as one could have created. True, by the time he died, I had heard his stories one too many times, and as a teenager, part of me rebelled against him as a symbol of the traditional South I could not embrace in the 1960s. My grandfather remained, though, a powerful embodiment for me of a good, decent man, and his death shook my faith; unresolved questions about suffering and death focused emotional and intellectual doubts I had already developed about my fundamentalist upbringing. His death came in the summer of 1966, the same year that I began college at the University of Texas at El Paso (UTEP), which until that year had been called Texas Western College. There I learned new ideas and viewpoints, many of which challenged my inherited Church of Christ beliefs, and my inability to come to terms with what I then saw as the injustice of my grandfather's death added to my spiritual turmoil. I drifted away from the church, from religion, with intellectual activity replacing it. I had as a young teenager even aspired to preach, although I feared I could never achieve the moral level I had heard sketched endlessly from the pulpit. Now, a secular aspiration replaced the ministerial one – I would be a professor, a historian.

In college, I discovered my fascination with ideas and with history in particular. I remember taking a course titled the Philosophy of Civilization, during which we read and reread only one book, Alfred North Whitehead's *Adventures of Ideas*, which led me to Whitehead's other books – a body of work that intimated a very individualistic vision of spirituality requiring no institutional church. I worked with Carl T. Jackson, a scholar of Asian religions in the United States, on my master's thesis at UTEP, flirting at first with a topic involving Asian religions in America before writing about the portrayal of Native Americans in American popular magazines. I included a long chapter on Indian spirituality, which became one of my first published articles and reflected my interest in writing about religious issues in history.[1]

I pursued my doctorate at the University of Texas at Austin, where I discovered what I wanted my life's work to be – the study of the South and its religious history. My work at UTEP with another outstanding mentor, Kenneth K. Bailey, one of the first scholars to publish a major work on southern Protestantism, had first set me on this path. From him, I learned rigorous standards of scholarship and how to take religion seriously as a subject of historical research. In Austin, I now immersed myself in studying the South's complex history, a project that raised issues that seemed to call forth to me religious understandings. I had absorbed Reinhold Niebuhr's work and, like others, found his use of historical irony most applicable to the southern story I wanted to tell. C. Vann Woodward's "The Irony of Southern History" pointed me to the theme, and I saw a chance to explore its religious meanings, which Woodward did not develop. What interested me was the post–Civil War period, when spiritual issues related to defeat, poverty, a mean-spirited moralism and racism, and an uncritical longing for the past nurtured the Lost Cause.

I then discovered the seminal work of Samuel S. Hill, and I still work within his intellectual orbit. *Southern Churches in Crisis* (1966) in particular had a profound influence upon me. It defined a distinctive interdenominational southern religious system that gave coherence to my other readings on the South and resonated with my experiences as a native southerner. His work made me see that southern religion had intellectual substance and cultural meaning, that its complexities were worth grappling with. Additionally, his insights about southern Protestant worship services made me see what I had lived through in a new light. Hill's tone of moral outrage over religious racism hit the deepest chord in me. The book was simultaneously an objective study, bringing a wide perspective of European theological and church historical understanding to southern religion, and also a passionate subjective treatise calling the southern churches to task for moral failures.[2]

I had not gone to Austin intending to study southern religion, though. I worked with William H. Goetzmann in American intellectual and cultural history. Those areas were clearly my main interests, and I was surely already a regionalist, but I went to Austin expecting to study the West with Goetzmann, a Pulitzer Prize–winning historian of western exploration. Goetzmann himself had studied with the preeminent Yale southernist David M. Potter, and he reacted positively when I told him of my desire to study the South instead of the West. He gave me my original dissertation topic, which was "Fundamentalist Attitudes toward the Civil War." Upon investigation, I discovered that the early twentieth-century fundamentalist movement had little to say about the Civil War, but when I looked at southern religious life after the Civil War, I refined my topic to focus on that subject. The library at the University of Texas is one of the nation's best for studying the South, thanks to the Littlefield Fund, and I happily researched church records, the files of *Confederate Veteran* magazine, annual meetings of denominational assemblies, ministerial memoirs, and other primary sources. I traveled elsewhere, to the Presbyterian archives in Montreat, North Carolina, discovering there a genteel researcher's world where nice ladies not only brought you church records but also served tea and cakes in the afternoon. I also visited the United Daughters of the Confederacy Museum in Austin and was welcomed as, in the words of my elderly hostess, the only "gentleman caller" of the day.

Out of my research came my dissertation and eventual first book, *Baptized in Blood: The Religion of the Lost Cause* (1980). At the heart of its conceptualization was the idea of civil religion, a still debated but useful idea that sees spiritual significance in nationalism or, in my case, regionalism. G. Howard Miller, who taught American religious history at Texas, introduced me to the concept and directed my reading about it, although he himself was skeptical of it. Robert N. Bellah's seminal article in 1969 argued that religion existed not just in churches but in cultural institutions and in such social rituals as holiday celebrations, patriotic commemorations, and political ceremonies. Bellah suggested that civil religion had prophetic as well as celebratory features, citing figures such as Lincoln, who brought the nation under divine judgment.[3]

The idea of civil religion was an odd one for me to embrace. Growing up in the Church of Christ gave me no sense of the history of religion in general and certainly not an understanding of how religion could exist away from the church's sanctuary. As a Restorationist church, the Church of Christ skipped over centuries, millennia even, to reach back to the original communities of Christianity as models to re-create. Although Alexander and Thomas Campbell were iconic figures in the church, they were disembodied for me as actual historical actors associated with any time or place. I grew up also without a sense of the church's wider role in society. Instead, I mainly recall hearing preaching on individual sin, moral standards, individual redemption, and the necessity of contending for the faith. Yet, in graduate school, I was fascinated with civil religion's positing that society, not just the individual, could have religious significance. Bellah saw the country's democratic ideals as embodying for Americans a sacred cause throughout history.

My understanding of how religion fits more broadly into southern culture was deepened when I worked as a fellow with John Shelton Reed in his 1980 National Endowment for the Humanities Summer Seminar on Continuity and Change in Southern Culture. Reed exposed me to new approaches to the interdisciplinary study of the South, especially showing me how social science research could be useful. I began thinking how my historical studies of southern religion related to his findings of much continuity of southern religion into the contemporary era. His own engaging lecturing and writing style also made me realize the value and pleasure of academic essays, where one could even use a phrase that might make a reader smile.

I conceived in his seminar, nonetheless, a still ongoing, somber research project, "The Southern Way of Death." Anthropologist Christopher Crocker used that title for a case study in the 1970s, but I am studying how death beliefs, rituals, symbols, and customs can be a window into larger issues – the behavioral and ideological dimensions of the Southern Way of Life. Embarking on this study of such cheerful topics as funerals, cemeteries, and mortality rates undoubtedly revealed my continuing interest in the suffering side of life. When I told my mother that

I was following up my study of the South's Lost Cause of defeat with a study of death, she looked at me and said, "Can't you find something happy to write about?"

I came to the University of Mississippi in the fall of 1981 to coedit the *Encyclopedia of Southern Culture* with William Ferris and to teach in the Department of History.[4] I have lived in Mississippi twenty-eight years now, teaching, among other things, courses on American religious history and southern religion. When my course enrollments were very high the first time I taught the latter course, my departmental chair, Robert J. Haws, suggested students thought they were signing up for a devotional hour. Often, though, the biggest challenge in teaching religious history courses is to persuade students to take all religions seriously. Most of my students are middle class, and anything too emotional or unorthodox simply will not do. I show them films of Appalachian snake handlers but try to make the students see how they are part of the same religious culture as snake handlers, those exaggerated fundamentalist believers who take biblical passages literally.

Teaching at the Center for the Study of Southern Culture enabled me to see the folk and popular dimensions of the southern evangelical culture that has dominated the region for so long. Bill Ferris, our founding director, documented African American religious and musical traditions in the Mississippi Delta of the late 1960s and 1970s, and his films have a timeless, primitive quality that still gives an intimate view of those traditions. Lisa Howorth taught a folk arts course in the southern studies curriculum, and I learned much from her about the images and styles of rural folk art. Likewise, Tom Rankin's documentary fieldwork and photography opened my mind to new visual perspectives on southern religiosity. While working single-mindedly during the 1980s on the *Encyclopedia of Southern Culture*, I found myself still reflecting on southern religion, gravitating toward interest in the South's popular religion and its relationship to the larger evangelical culture.

My intellectual interest in the symbols, rituals, imagery, and icons of popular religion emerged at the same time as I began attending the Episcopal Church in the mid-1980s. Friends had invited me to attend St. Peter's Episcopal Church in Oxford, and I had been drawn to its liturgical ceremony, the beauty of its services, the sense of community in the small church, and, the more I studied it, the middle way of Anglican theology, drawing from both Protestantism and Roman Catholicism. This was a dramatic departure, of course, from my religious raising. As I had known it, the Church of Christ had been an austere visual and liturgical experience, but I now discovered that those dimensions would be important in any new spiritual commitments I made. Episcopal aestheticism is far from popular religion, of course, but I sensed that my academic and spiritual aspirations were somehow converging with the need for both experiential and intellectual understanding of the mythic and ritual.

I had the good sense to marry a Mississippi woman, Marie Antoon, in 1985, at the Episcopal Chapel of the Cross, located north of Jackson, Mississippi. Marie is Roman Catholic, not always a churchly one but one in spirit. The ancient church grabs hold of its young early and leaves its mark, or at least that is so in the case of Catholics I have known. She is introspective and sometimes intense, my temperamental opposite. Our marital separation in the early 1990s became a metaphor in my self-understanding of the divided life I had often led. I had worked hard on teaching and scholarship, sometimes to the detriment of both my marriage and my spiritual life. Through my renewed relationship with Marie, seen in our marital reconciliation, I discovered the need to bring more closely together the intellectual and emotional sides of my personality, a realization that is far from achieved but that has contributed in turn to my increasing personal interest in spirituality and my continuing academic fascination with the mythic and ritual.

Out of all these developments and reflections in the late 1980s and early 1990s came *Judgment and Grace in Dixie: Southern Faiths from Faulkner to Elvis* (1995). A collection of essays that had been previously published, the book summarized my thinking on southern popular religion and its relationship to broader regional culture. Some of the essays extended my thinking on the civil religion concept as it related to the South; in particular, I argued that the seemingly unrelated agrarian literary movement of the early twentieth century and the civil rights movement in the mid-twentieth century both saw the South as having a transcendent meaning – namely, as a region still under divine judgment and expectation. I was countering the idea that the South no longer had distinctive regional meanings, showing that different southerners had invested different meanings in the region. Despite the extraordinary social changes in recent years in the South, I believe southern culture still is associated with a worldview rooted in the past and specifically in re-ligion. While the social and economic foundations of the South have surely shifted, southern cultural forms are yet adjusting, with religion itself an anchor as the South continues modernizing. I also suggested that the region's civil religion was not only seen in ideology but also bubbled up from below, in such modern southern rituals as beauty con-tests and college football games. The book looks at the recent South in the long perspective of southern history, and I made conscious compari-sons between the Lost Cause I had studied and the recent commemora-tion of the civil rights movement.[5]

My academic work had begun with *Baptized in Blood,* a study of the white southern cultural identity rooted in religion. *Judgment and Grace in Dixie,* by contrast, explored the biracial context of southern identity. I had long before discovered James McBride Dabbs, a white South Carolina farmer and social activist, whose mid-twentieth-century writings, such as *Haunted by God* (1972), had analyzed the complexities of black-white rela-tions in the South and their deeper spiritual significance for people of faith, and his work has deeply influenced my conceptualization of south-ern culture. Folk art, literature, and music especially seemed to embody this theme, and my examination of those topics in *Judgment and Grace* enabled me to look at biracial cultural interaction in the South and at simi-larities and differences in cultural styles. The essays in the book came out of lectures I had given that often related to broader monographic studies on which I am working, analyzing the relationships between the socially constructed, racially exclusive identity of white southerners and the bi-racial, behavioral features of a southern culture that represented an alter-nate regional identity. Religion has been crucial to each, sacralizing the white southern identity yet providing the shared evangelical culture that has nurtured blacks and whites throughout hard southern times.[6]

Oxford, Mississippi, was a stimulating community context for me in the early 1990s as I pondered these matters. I joined St. Peter's Episco-pal Church in 1992, entering into the church's educational, spiritual, and outreach activities. I went through an Education for Ministry program that deepened my understanding of church history and theology; I began contemplative prayer sessions each Tuesday morning and continued with them for some seven years. Again, I am constantly struck by these depar-tures from my religious raisings. Contemplative prayer, especially, rests in the profound legacy of Roman Catholic mysticism and such modern exemplars of it as Father Thomas Keating. The Church of Christ has an intellectually activist tradition, contending sharply for points of belief, but with little sense of the need for meditation. The church aspires to consensus, although it has often been forced to deal with schism and controversy because points of faith do not always turn out to be so obvious when interpreted. The assertive, and argumentative, Paul of New Testament letters would be the patron saint of the church, if it had saints. Yet, in meditating, I find that I do draw from less contentious scenes evoked from the southern gospel music I grew up with – the peaceful garden, the friend of Jesus, even the green pastures of heaven. My earlier church tradition did include prayerful devotionalism, with which I find continuities now, even though the disciplines and conventions of contemplative prayer and Protestant devotionalism remain so distinct.

St. Peter's has been significant during the last decade and a half for its involvement in a biracial religious effort, which is still unusual for a small southern town. Duncan Gray III, rector of St. Peter's, and Leroy Wadlington, pastor of Second Baptist Church, grew up in Oxford, coming of age in the 1960s and both living through the turbulent violence and social instability in Oxford during James Meredith's entrance as the first African American student at the University of Mississippi. Yet, as part of racially segregated communities, they never knew each other growing up. In 1992, the two began intentionally bringing their churches together for carefully planned activities, both religious and social. The two preached at each other's churches, with their congregations hospitably listening to very different styles than what they were used to hearing. After Wadlington's lively Baptist sermon, the associate rector, representing the congregation, thanked him, noting that even though he was an Episcopalian, he had almost yelled out "Amen." Several of us met afterward in small groups at neighborhood houses to reflect on the experience. No one had prepared the Baptists to rely on the Episcopal Book of Common Prayer to guide them through the service. Some members of Second Baptist had been surprised, moreover, to taste real wine in the Episcopal communion, rather than the grape juice they were accustomed to taking. Since then, the congregations have had joint summer picnics in the town park, visited each other's services, sponsored youth retreats, and even tailgated together before football games in the once all-white Grove at the University of Mississippi.

I played a minor role as a supporter of this exchange, participating in its activities and in a racial self-awareness workshop the church sponsored and also chronicling the story in an article for *Christian Century* – all of which represented the most recent way that my own grappling with religious issues has influenced my study of religion. My mentor here was Duncan Gray III, rector at St. Peter's from 1985 until he became bishop in 2000. He articulated for me a model of the Christian faith that I found shaping my intellectual and spiritual life. The son of Episcopal bishop Duncan Gray II, who achieved renown for his courage as a racial moderate in Mississippi during the 1960s, Gray led the contemplative prayer sessions in which I participated but also insisted that spirituality is not a phenomenon disengaged from society. He understands the challenge of nurturing a just society that overcomes the continuing racial divide, which still symbolizes a division in the human psyche rather than the wholeness that his Christian faith represents in ideal. As a native Mississippian, he comprehends the special burden and opportunity his home state has in addressing this concern.[7]

Although not a native of Mississippi, I too understand the special responsibilities regarding race relations facing the state in which I live and especially my home institution, the University of Mississippi. I was chair of the advisory board that worked with the William Winter Institute for Racial Reconciliation on campus, whose director, Susan Glisson, is my former student. In my own work, I became increasingly drawn to the issue of civic society and what the South may have to offer the emerging national discussion of that concept, which I see growing out of the idea of the civil religion. Southern conservatives have long articulated a regional tradition of community concern, a belief that laissez-faire economics and the ruthless individualism of capitalism are insufficient bases for the good society. White southerners interpreted their Confederate and agrarian heritages as foundations for spiritual meanings to "southernness." Socially progressive southerners have had a similar belief that American individualism is inadequate for civic life. Since the 1960s, they have esteemed the cultural values and achievements of traditional southern rural society while at the same time urging reform in economic and social institutions, often motivated themselves by the Judeo-Christian ethic of brotherhood. The shared value placed on religious sentiments and a religious worldview in the South may provide a common ground for new ideals of civic renewal. Certainly, regional belief in the value of civility in social discourse seems a contribution the nation desperately needs at this point in its political life. As director of the Center for the Study of Southern Culture, I worked with others to gain funding for the Endowment for the Future of the South, whose mission is to advance the goal of civic renewal in the region.

Students of southern religion have represented a distinct field for several decades now. My first book followed shortly after early works by Kenneth K. Bailey, Samuel S. Hill, John Lee Eighmy, and others gave legitimacy to the field. One of the most promising signs of its continued vitality is the appearance of insightful new studies by such young scholars as Paul Harvey, Beth Schweiger, and Daniel Stowell, among others. Back in 1984, I directed a symposium titled "Religion in the South," which brought together Bailey, Hill, John B. Boles, Wayne Flynt, C. Eric Lincoln, Edwin S. Gaustad, and David E. Harrell Jr. For Bailey, it was an opportunity to return to the Mississippi in which he had grown up, and amid his scholarly observations he had perhaps the best line of the symposium. In the old days, he said, southern ministers had known not only their church traditions but also "how to thump a watermelon." That evocative image neatly conveyed how important the regional context had been in understanding religion in the South. I am old enough to have a memory of the rural religion of my grandparents, a religion that surely connected them to generations of earlier southern worshippers. My own life since then has moved me through personal experiences linking the academic world with broader southern society. I have moved away from the fundamentalist church of my childhood, but I know it planted in me a seriousness with which I take religion, both personally and in my apprehension of its role in southern society. St. Peter's Episcopal Church in Mississippi, in which I now make my spiritual life, remains also, of course, a very southern church, albeit far from the "southern" church of Mississippi Episcopalianism half a century ago; it has been the institution through which I have glimpsed possibilities of combining personal and societal spirituality, which I believe will continue to form the backdrop to my own scholarly work.

AFTERWORD

Constructing and Experiencing the Spirit

This book has examined ways that "the spirit" has informed understandings of the South. We have looked at writers, musicians, vernacular artists, preachers, politicians, policy makers, journalists, and others in an attempt to capture something of the breadth of meanings of the spirit in the South. Scholarly analysis reveals that spirit-based narratives are constructed, but participants in spirit worlds nonetheless know the physical, mental, and emotional effects of the spirit. This book is meant to be suggestive, to point the attention of scholars of southern studies to the relationship between the workings of the spirit and southern identity, which is seen not just in self-conscious reflections on that identity but in enactments of regional identity and performances of cultural traditions deeply rooted in the region. Sometimes the southern spirit can be a patriotic, celebratory one; chapters on invented tradition, self-conscious regional identity, a regional sense of mission, and the American and the Southern Ways of Life reveal specific examples of such celebratory spirits. Eric Hobsbawm and Terence Ranger note that invented traditions proscribe "the values, rights and obligations of the group membership they inculcate," and they mention such examples as "school spirit," along with patriotism, loyalty, duty, and "playing the game." The focus on group "values, rights, and obligations" suggests the importance of community, but some observers argue that the force of historical change disrupted organic community in the twentieth-century South, and its celebrations rang hollow. Hobsbawm and Ranger mentioned "school spirit," and Marion Montgomery satirizes such a spirit, quoted from an imagined "Spirit Galore in '74" Committee, that, he writes, "is making every effort to cover our stadium with Red & Black. Please try to make your football clothes our colors so that our boys can not only hear your spirit – but hear your spirit!" Montgomery sees this "spirit" as representing a "dissolution of community through its loss of a vision of reality, the chief burden of modernism." Nonetheless, celebrating the spirit of southern icons has often been intended to inculcate social unity. In 1920,

Lucian Lamar Knight toasted the southern woman's "silent influences, eternal vigil, and gentle spirit." As Anne Goodwyn Jones points out, the ideological purpose of such a statement was "to unify the South in its difference" while at the same time keeping "women elevated into perpetual silence and passivity."[1]

At other times, the "spirit" evokes specifically religious meanings, with the workings of the Holy Spirit long noted by observers of the South. Folklorist Glenn Hinson has documented spirit work in African American sanctified churches. He confesses to having been moved by "the transformative power of the holy touch," a power experienced both physically, by a bodily "feeling" that participants have, and emotionally, through an infusion of joy. Hinson concludes that even more noticeable is "the Spirit's power to move the soul, to touch that mysterious wellspring that grants being its experiential essence." Members of the spirit-filled black churches "say that soul is the domain not of body or mind, but of spirit. And when the Spirit touches spirit, the soul rejoices in an epiphany of truth and knowledge." Southern white religious traditions are not the same as those of blacks, but deep in evangelical Protestantism is a profound biracial supernaturalism that welcomes the workings of the spirit. Samuel S. Hill has noted the recent changes in the South's predominant Protestant churches, with increased religious diversity and a new concern among the largest churches for enforcing doctrinal and moralistic creeds; but he also draws us back to that faith's foundation, noting that the revivalistic evangelicalism of the past shares with "the doctrinal rationalism" of recent years "the conviction that everything about the churches' message and mission is supernatural." Whether by the workings of the Holy Spirit or of the scriptures, seekers look for "the revelation of God's truth" that is unavailable from naturalistic and materialistic philosophies. This "radical and consistent supernaturalistic worldview" differentiates the South from even many other Christian communities around the world in the post-Enlightenment period, providing a fertile grounding for workings of the spirit in southern places and among southern social groups.[2]

Constructions of the southern spirit give a particular resonance to ideas of the South that are not only narrated but also, as we have seen, performed and enacted in everyday life. Spirit matters because ideas

of the South attached to divine spirits provide a metaphysical grounding for regional traditions and creativity. As Hinson notes, these spirit-
grounded traditions and innovations extend "the web of emotional connectedness that links people to communities, places, animals, things, and
the encompassing environment by including the supernatural and the
divine." Cultural critic Houston A. Baker Jr. suggests that spirit is behind
what he calls "Afro-America's classical performances," from the blues
and jazz to women's vernacular quilting and literary production. Spirit
has been at work among whites as well as blacks in the South, where,
along with other southerners, they have shared, at times, not only space
but the spirit. Baker has recently identified a new southern studies, and
cross-cultural, multidisciplinary work on the region is indeed producing new insights. Few of these new, self-consciously revisionist studies
are including "spirit" among their topics; yet the "spirit work" of the
region offers opportunities for moving beyond the stress on discourse
and narrative in much of the new literary and historical southern studies
to understand spirit's movements in the region.[3]

NOTES

Preface. Spirit and a New Southern Studies

1. Houston A. Baker Jr. and Dana D. Nelson, "Preface: Violence, the Body and 'The South,'" *American Literature* 73 (June 2001): 231–44.

2. Michael Kreyling, "Toward 'A New Southern Studies,'" *South Central Review* 22 (Spring 2005): 4–18.

3. Kathryn McKee and Annette Trefzer, "Preface: Global Contexts, Local Literature: The New Southern Studies," *American Literature* 78 (December 2006): 677–90.

4. Richard Maxwell Brown, "The New Regionalism in America, 1970–1981," in *Regionalism and the Pacific Northwest*, ed. William G. Robbins, Robert J. Frank, and Richard E. Ross (Corvallis: Oregon State University Press, 1983), 137–96.

5. Tara McPherson, *Reconstructing Dixie: Race, Gender, and Nostalgia in the Imagined South* (Durham, N.C.: Duke University Press, 2003), 8–11. See also Suzanne W. Jones and Sharon Monteith, eds., *South to a New Place: Region, Literature, Culture* (Baton Rouge: Louisiana State University Press, 2002); Jon Smith and Deborah Cohn, eds., *Look Away! The U.S. South in New World Studies* (Durham, N.C.: Duke University Press, 2004); James C. Cobb, *Redefining Southern Culture: Mind and Identity in the Modern South* (Athens: University of Georgia Press, 1999); John Lowe, *Bridging Southern Cultures: An Interdisciplinary Approach* (Baton Rouge: Louisiana State University Press, 2005); and insightful review essays by Katherine Renee Henninger, "How New? What Place? Southern Studies and the Rest of the World," *Contemporary Literature* 45 (2004): 177–85, and Alfred Hornung, "'Unstoppable' Creolization: The Evolution of the South into a Transnational Cultural Space," *American Literature* 78 (December 2006): 859–67.

6. Showing the range of work in intentionally new approaches to the South are the titles published as part of the two book series. The New Southern Studies books include the following: Melanie R. Benson, *Disturbing Calculations: The Economics of Identity in Postcolonial Southern Literature, 1912–2002* (2008); Leigh Anne Duck, *The Nation's Region: Southern Modernism, Segregation, and U.S. Nationalism* (2006); James L. Peacock, *Grounded Globalism: How the U.S. South Embraces the World* (2005); Riché Richardson, *Black Masculinity and the U.S. South: From Uncle Tom to Gangsta* (2007). The New Directions in Southern Studies books include the following: Jessica Adams, *Wounds of Returning: Race, Memory, and Property on the Postslavery Plantation* (2007); Katherine Renee Henninger, *Ordering the Façade: Photography and Contemporary Southern Women's Writing* (2007); Wanda Rushing, *Memphis and the Paradox of Place: Globalization in the American South* (2009); Amy

Louise Wood, *Lynching and Spectacle: Witnessing Racial Violence in America, 1890–1940* (2009). Of course, many presses are publishing volumes that are contributing to the growing interest in a new southern studies, but they sometimes do not use the discourse of those scholars more self-consciously exploring this project. The first volume of *The New Encyclopedia of Southern Culture*, on religion, appeared in 2006, and fifteen volumes have been published through spring 2010: Charles Reagan Wilson, gen. ed., *The New Encyclopedia of Southern Culture* (Chapel Hill: University of North Carolina Press, 2006–10), vols. 1–15.

7. Celeste Ray, ed., *Southern Heritage on Display: Public Ritual and Ethnic Diversity within Southern Regionalism* (Tuscaloosa: University of Alabama Press, 2003).

8. Rushing, *Memphis and the Paradox of Place.*

9. Edward L. Ayers, *The Promise of the New South: Life after Reconstruction* (New York: Oxford University Press, 1992); W. Fitzhugh Brundage, *The Southern Past: A Clash of Race and Memory* (Cambridge, Mass.: Belknap Press of Harvard University Press, 2005); Matthew Pratt Gutterl, *American Mediterranean: Southern Slaveholders in the Age of Emancipation* (Cambridge, Mass.: Harvard University Press, 2008); Jack Temple Kirby, *Mockingbird Song: Ecological Landscapes of the South* (Chapel Hill: University of North Carolina Press, 2006); Ted Ownby, "Director's Column," *Southern Register* (Winter 2010): 2–3.

10. Paul Harvey, *Freedom's Coming: Religious Culture and the Shaping of the South from the Civil War through the Civil Rights Era* (Chapel Hill: University of North Carolina Press, 2005); Donald G. Mathews, "The Southern Rite of Human Sacrifice," *Journal of Southern Religion,* http://jsr.fsu.edu/mathews.htm; www.southern spaces.org.

11. Charles Reagan Wilson, *Southern Missions: The Religion of the American South in Global Perspective* (Waco, Tex.: Baylor University Press, 2005); Charles Reagan Wilson, "American Regionalism in a Postmodern World," *Amerikastudien* (1997); Douglass Sullivan-Gonzalez and Charles Reagan Wilson, eds., *The South and the Caribbean: Essays and Commentaries* (Jackson: University Press of Mississippi, 2001).

12. Martyn Bone's quote is found in "Discussion of Understanding the South, Understanding America," http://understandingthesouth.wordpress.com/discus sion, 6.

Introduction. "The Soul-Life of the Land"

1. Al Green, "Southern Soul," *Southern Magazine,* October 1986, 46.

2. W. E. B. Du Bois, *The Souls of Black Folk: Essays and Sketches* (Greenwich, Conn.: Fawcett Publications, 1961), 21, 43, 67–69.

3. Elizabeth J. Jewell and Frank Abate, eds., *New Oxford American Dictionary* (New York: Oxford University Press, 2001), 1644.

4. Lewis P. Simpson, "Southern Spiritual Nationalism: Notes on the Background of Modern Southern Fiction," in *The Cry of Home: Cultural Nationalism and the Modern Writers*, ed. H. Ernest Lewald (Knoxville: University of Tennessee Press, 1972), 203–4; Richard M. Weaver, "The South and the American Union," in *The Lasting South: Fourteen Southerners Look at Their Home*, ed. Louis D. Rubin Jr. and James J. Kilpatrick (Chicago: Henry Regnery, 1957), 63–64; Maurice Halbwachs, *On Collective Memory*, trans. and ed. Lewis A. Coser (Chicago: University of Chicago Press, 1992), 204.

5. W. J. Cash, *The Mind of the South* (New York: Knopf, 1941); James C. Cobb, *Away Down South: A History of the Southern Identity* (New York: Oxford University Press, 2005); Susan Donaldson and Anne Goodwyn Jones, eds., *Haunted Bodies: Gender and Southern Texts* (Charlottesville: University of Virginia Press, 1997), 1; Jay Watson, "Body," in *The New Encyclopedia of Southern Culture*, vol. 4, *Myth, Manners, and Memory*, ed. Charles Reagan Wilson (Chapel Hill: University of North Carolina Press, 2006), 30–33.

6. W. Fitzhugh Brundage, ed., *Where These Memories Grow: History, Memory, and Southern Identity* (Chapel Hill: University of North Carolina at Chapel Hill, 2000), 21.

7. Lillian Smith, *The Winner Names the Age: A Collection of Writings by Lillian Smith*, ed. Michelle Cliff (New York: W. W. Norton and Company, 1978), 136, 140; George W. Bagby, *The Old Virginia Gentleman and Other Sketches*, ed. Thomas Nelson Page (New York: Charles Scribner's Sons, 1911), 6; Joel Williamson, "The Soul Is Fled," in *New Perspectives on Race and Slavery in America*, ed. Robert H. Abzug and Stephen E. Maizlish (Lexington: University Press of Kentucky, 1986), 185; White quoted in Paul Harvey, *Freedom's Coming: Religious Culture and the Shaping of the South from the Civil War through the Civil Rights Era* (Chapel Hill: University of North Carolina Press, 2005), 116.

8. Charles Hudson, *The Southeastern Indians* (Knoxville: University of Tennessee Press, 1976), 169–73; Alan Gallay, *The Indian Slave Trade: The Rise of the English Empire in the American South, 1670–1717* (New Haven, Conn.: Yale University Press, 2002), 29, 120.

9. Frank Owsley, "The Irrepressible Conflict," in *I'll Take My Stand: The South and the Agrarian Tradition* (Baton Rouge: Louisiana State University Press, 1977, originally 1930), 66; Wilson Gee, "The Distinctiveness of Southern Culture," *South Atlantic Quarterly*, April 1939, 124–25.

10. Laura Martin Rose, *The Ku Klux Klan* (New Orleans: L. Graham, 1914), 75–76; Emily Herbert Glaze quoted in South Carolina Division of the United Daughters of the Confederacy, *Recollections and Reminiscences, 1861–1865 through World War I* (Columbia, S. C.: Southern Carolina Division of the United Daughters of the Confederacy, 1992), 3:572–73; *Spirit of the South: The Sculpture of Alexander Galt, 1827–1863* (Williamsburg: Joseph and Margaret Muscarelle Museum of Art, 1992), 1, 55.

11. Wolfgang Schivelbusch, *The Culture of Defeat: On National Trauma, Mourning, and Recovery* (New York: Metropolitan Books, 2001), 18–21; Hodding Carter, *Southern Legacy* (Baton Rouge: Louisiana State University Press, 1950), 23–24.

12. Rhys Isaac, *The Transformation of Virginia: Community, Religion, and Authority, 1740–1790* (Chapel Hill: Published for the Institute of Early American History and Culture, Williamsburg, Va., by the University of North Carolina Press, 1982); Christine Leigh Heyrman, *Southern Cross: The Beginnings of the Bible Belt* (New York: Knopf, 1997).

13. Carter, *Southern Legacy*, 27, 37; Frederick L. Gwynn and Joseph L. Blotner, eds., *Faulkner in the University: Class Conferences at the University of Virginia, 1957–58* (Charlottesville: University Press of Virginia, 1959), 190.

14. Albert Raboteau, *Slave Religion: The "Invisible Institution" in the Antebellum South* (New York: Oxford University Press, 1978); Sylvia R. Frey and Betty Wood, *Come Shouting to Zion: African American Protestantism in the American South and British Caribbean* (Chapel Hill: University of North Carolina Press, 1998).

15. Robert Farris Thompson, *Flash of the Spirit: African and African American Art and Philosophy* (New York: Random House, 1983), xiii, 132–45.

16. Ibid.; Eudora Welty, *The Wide Net and Other Stories* (New York: Harcourt Brace Jovanovich, 1971), 15; Robert Palmer, *Deep Blues* (New York: Viking, 1981), 116; Anne Moody, *Coming of Age in Mississippi* (New York: Dell, 1976), 129.

17. Richard Wright, *Native Son,* (New York: Harper and Row, 1940), 437; Zora Neale Hurston, *Dust Tracks on a Road: An Autobiography* (Urbana: University of Illinois Press, 1984), 20–21.

18. Bertram Wyatt-Brown, *Southern Honor: Ethics and Behavior in the Old South* (New York: Oxford University Press, 1986), 141, 144; Paul Harvey, *Redeeming the South: Religious Cultures and Racial Identities among Southern Baptists, 1865–1925* (Chapel Hill: University of North Carolina Press, 1997), 82; Ted Ownby, *Subduing Satan: Religion, Recreation, and Manhood in the Rural South, 1865–1920* (Chapel Hill: University of North Carolina Press, 1990), 11, 14.

19. Harvey, *Redeeming the South,* 95, 104.

20. Thomas Merton, "'Baptism in the Forest': Wisdom and Initiation in William Faulkner," in *The Literary Essays of Thomas Merton,* ed. Patrick Hart (New York: New Directions Books, 1981), 103–5.

21. James McBride Dabbs, *Haunted by God: The Cultural and Religious Experience of the South* (Richmond: John Know Press, 1972), 136–45.

22. Harvey, *Freedom's Coming,* 49.

23. Martin Luther King Jr., *Why We Can't Wait* (New York: Harper and Row, 1964), 116; Charles Marsh, *God's Long Summer: Stories of Faith and Civil Rights* (Princeton: Princeton University Press, 1997), 5, 6, 194; Smith, *The Winner Names the Age,* 91, 93, 133, 136.

24. Marsh, *God's Long Summer,* 26, 193.

25. Robert Coles, "God and the Rural Poor," *Psychology Today,* January 1972, 33–40.

26. Marsh, *God's Long Summer,* 5, 12, 22, 193.

27. Vincent Harding, "I Always Wanted to Be Free," in *Souls Grown Deep: African American Vernacular Art of the South,* ed. Paul Arnett and William Arnett (Atlanta: Tinwood Books; in association with the Schomburg Center for Research in Black Culture, the New York Public Library, 2000), 1:16–23.

28. William Dean, *The American Spiritual Culture and the Invention of Jazz, Football, and the Movies* (New York: Continuum, 2002), 27–28; Lee Atwater quoted in "Comment: Going Positive," *The New Yorker,* May 5, 2008, 24.

29. Heyrman, *Southern Cross;* Ownby, *Subduing Satan,* 103–21; Anne Goodwyn Jones, *Tomorrow Is Another Day: The Woman Writer in the South, 1859–1936* (Baton Rouge: Louisiana State University Press, 1981); Evelyn Brooks Higginbotham, *Righteous Discontent: The Women's Movement in the Black Baptist Church, 1880–1920* (Cambridge: Harvard University Press, 1993), 70; Grant Wacker, *Heaven Below: Early Evangelicals and American Culture* (Cambridge, Mass.: Harvard University Press, 2001).

30. Alice Walker, *In Search of Our Mothers' Gardens: Womanist Prose* (New York: Harcourt Brace Jovanovich, 1983), 231–43; Tara McPherson, *Reconstructing Dixie: Race, Gender, and Nostalgia in the Imagined South* (Durham: Duke University Press, 2003), 198–99; Valerie Wells, "Feminist-Retreat Founder Dies," *Jackson Clarion-Ledger,* February 13, 2008, 3B; Wendy Reed and Jennifer Horne, *All out of Faith: Southern Women on Spirituality* (Tuscaloosa: University of Alabama Press, 2006).

31. Mark Salber Phillips and Gordon Schochet, eds., *Questions of Tradition* (Toronto: University of Toronto Press, 2004), x, 3–10; Charles Joyner, *Shared Traditions: Southern History and Folk Culture* (Urbana: University of Illinois Press, 1999); Eugene D. Genovese, *The Southern Tradition: The Achievement and Limitations of an American Conservatism* (Cambridge, Mass.: Harvard University Press, 1994).

32. Richard Westmacott, *African-American Gardens and Yards in the Rural South* (Knoxville: University of Tennessee Press, 1992), 109; Paul Gilroy, *Against Race: Imagining Political Culture beyond the Color Line* (Cambridge, Mass.: Belknap Press of Harvard University Press, 2000), 120; McPherson, *Reconstructing Dixie,* 30. See also Simon J. Bronner, *Creativity and Tradition in Folklore: New Directions* (Logan: Utah State University Press, 1992).

33. Robert Wuthnow, *After Heaven: Spirituality in America since the 1950s* (Berkeley: University of California Press, 1998); Charles H. Lippy, in *Religion in the Contemporary South: Changes, Continuities, and Contexts,* ed. Corrie E. Norman and Don S. Armentrout (Knoxville: University of Tennessee Press, 2005), 128–34.

34. Samuel S. Hill, *Southern Churches in Crisis Revisited* (Tuscaloosa: University of Alabama Press, 1999), xxiii.

Chapter 1. The Invention of Southern Tradition

1. Thanks to Tom Rankin for bringing the Hazelhurst mural to my attention. See also Sue Bridwell Beckham, *Depression Post Office Murals and Southern Culture: A Gentle Reconstruction* (Baton Rouge and London: Louisiana State University Press, 1989).

2. Eric Hobsbawm and Terence Ranger, eds., *The Invention of Tradition* (Cambridge: Cambridge University Press, 1983).

3. C. Vann Woodward, *The Strange Career of Jim Crow* (New York: Oxford University Press, 1955). William A. Blair uses the idea of invented traditions to explore the political meanings of post–Civil War commemorative rituals in *Cities of the Dead: Contesting the Meaning of the Civil War in the South, 1865–1914* (Chapel Hill: University of North Carolina Press, 2004).

4. E. Merton Coulter, "What the South Has Done About Its History," *Journal of Southern History* 2 (February 1936): 3–28.

5. William Garrett Piston, *Lee's Tarnished Lieutenant: James Longstreet and His Place in Southern History* (Athens: University of Georgia Press, 1987), 118.

6. Thomas L. Connelly, *The Marble Man: Robert E. Lee and His Image in American Society* (New York: Alfred A. Knopf, 1977).

7. Thomas Nelson Page, "The Want of a History of the Southern People," in *The Old South: Essays Social and Political* (New York: Charles Scribner's Sons, 1903), 253.

8. Ibid., 254–66, 269.

9. Ibid., 268.

10. D. H. Hill Jr., *Southern Histories: A Paper Read before the Southern Educational Association at Chattanooga, Tenn., July 1, 1891, by D. H. Hill Jr.* (Raleigh, N.C.: Edwards and Broughton, printers, 1892), 5.

11. Herman Hattaway, "Clio's Southern Soldiers: The United Confederate Veterans and History," *Louisiana History* 12 (Summer 1971).

12. Ibid.

13. Susan Pendleton Lee, *Lee's Advanced School History of the United States* (Richmond: B. F. Johnson Publishing Company, 1899). See also Ruth Miller Elson, *Guardians of Tradition: American Schoolbooks of the Nineteenth Century* (Lincoln: University of Nebraska Press, 1964), 34, 93, 94, 170, 173–79; and Karen Cox, *Dixie's Daughters: The United Daughters of the Confederacy and the Preservation of Confederate Culture* (Gainesville: University Press of Florida, 2003).

14. David D. Van Tassel, "The American Historical Association and the South, 1884–1913," *Journal of Southern History* 23 (November 1957); Joseph J. Mathews, "The Study of History in the South," *Journal of Southern History* 31 (February 1965).

15. For my general approach to analyzing the artifacts of nationalism, see Wilbur Zelinsky, *Nation over State: The Shifting Foundations of American Nation-*

alism (Chapel Hill: University of North Carolina Press, 1988). See also Cheryl Thurber, *"Dixie": The Cultural History of a Song and a Place* (PhD diss., University of Mississippi, 1993); and John M. Coski, *The Confederate Battle Flag: America's Most Embattled Emblem* (Cambridge, Mass.: Belknap Press of Harvard University Press, 2005).

16. Confederated Southern Memorial Association, *History of the Confederated Memorial Associations of the South* (New Orleans: Graham Press, 1904). Toni W. Terrett recounts Mississippi's celebration of the King-Lee holiday in "2 Men, Different Visions, Same Holiday," *Jackson Clarion-Ledger,* January 19, 2004, 1A, 7A.

17. Harnett T. Kane, *The Southern Christmas Book. The Full Story from Earliest Times to Present: People, Customs, Conviviality, Carols, Cooking* (New York: David McKay Company, 1958).

18. Gaines M. Foster, *Ghosts of the Confederacy: Defeat, the Lost Cause, and the Emergence of the New South* (New York: Oxford University Press, 1987), 41, 129–31.

19. Ibid.; Paul M. Gaston, *The New South Creed: A Study in Southern Mythmaking* (New York: Vintage Books, 1970); Charles Reagan Wilson, *Baptized in Blood: The Religion of the Lost Cause* (Athens: University of Georgia Press, 1980).

20. John Lesslie Hall, *Half-Hours in Southern History* (Richmond: B. F. Johnson Publishing Company, 1907), 21–22.

21. For the connections between various individuals and groups using the southern past in this period, see James M. Lindgren, "'Whatever Is Un-Virginian Is Wrong': The APVA's Sense of the Old Dominion," *Virginia Cavalcade* 38 (Winter 1989); and W. Fitzhugh Brundage, ed., *Where These Memories Grow: History, Memory, and Southern Identity* (Chapel Hill: University of North Carolina Press, 2000).

22. The discussion of southern oratory draws from Waldo Braden, *The Oral Tradition in the South* (Baton Rouge: Louisiana State University Press, 1983).

23. Ibid.

24. Ibid.

25. The discussion of Greek Revival architecture draws from Robert Gamble, "The White-Column Tradition: Classical Architecture and the Southern Mystique," *Southern Humanities Review* 11 (Special Issue 1977).

26. Ibid.

27. Ibid.

28. Anne Firor Scott, *The Southern Lady: From Pedestal to Politics, 1830–1930* (Chicago: University of Chicago Press, 1970); Anne Goodwyn Jones, *Tomorrow Is Another Day: The Woman Writer in the South, 1859–1936* (Baton Rouge: Louisiana State University Press, 1981); Jean Friedman, *The Enclosed Garden: Women and Community in the Evangelical South, 1830–1900* (Chapel Hill: University of North Carolina Press, 1985); John L. Underwood, *The Women of the Confederacy* (New York: Neale Publishing, 1906); "Tributes to Miss Winnie Davis," *Confederate Vet-*

eran 6 (October 1898): 467–69; Sarah H. Case, "The Historical Ideology of Mildred Lewis Rutherford: A Confederate Historian's New South Creed," *Journal of Southern History* 68 (August 2002): 599–628.

29. Steven Hahn, *The Roots of Southern Populism: Yeoman Farmers and the Transformation of the Georgia Upcountry, 1850–1890* (New York and Oxford: Oxford University Press, 1983); Lawrence Goodwyn, *Democratic Promise: The Populist Moment in American History* (New York: Oxford University Press, 1976); Samuel C. Hyde Jr., *Plain Folk of the South Revisited* (Baton Rouge: Louisiana State University Press, 1997).

30. For suggestive ideas on these points, see Charles Reagan Wilson, ed., *The New Encyclopedia of Southern Culture*, vol. 4, *Myth, Memory, and Manners* (Chapel Hill: University of North Carolina Press, 2006). See also Sheldon Hackney, *Populism to Progressivism in Alabama, 1865–1896* (Baton Rouge: Louisiana State University Press, 1970).

31. Foster, *Ghosts of the Confederacy*, 131.

32. Wayne Mixon, "The Ultimate Irrelevance of Race: Joel Chandler Harris and Uncle Remus in Their Time," *Journal of Southern History* 61 (August 1990): 457–80; Joel Williamson, *The Crucible of Race: Black-White Relations in the American South Since Emancipation* (New York and Oxford: Oxford University Press, 1984); David Glassberg, *American Historical Pageantry: The Uses of Tradition in the Early Twentieth Century* (Chapel Hill: University of North Carolina Press, 1990), 257.

33. David Blight, *Frederick Douglass' Civil War: Keeping Faith in Jubilee* (Baton Rouge and London: Louisiana State University Press, 1989), 228–31; Blair, *Cities of the Dead*, 6; W. Fitzhugh Brundage, *The Southern Past: A Clash of Race and Memory* (Cambridge: Belknap Press of Harvard University Press, 2005), 55–104.

34. Allison Davis, Burleigh Gardner, and Mary Gardner, *Deep South: A Study of Social Class and Color Caste in a Southern City* (Chicago: University of Chicago Press, 1941), 64. For black rejection of southern culture, see Neil R. McMillen, *Dark Journey: Black Mississippians in the Age of Jim Crow* (Champaign: University of Illinois Press, 1989).

35. Glassberg, *American Historical Pageantry*; William H. Wiggins Jr., *O Freedom! Afro-American Emancipation Celebrations* (Knoxville: University of Tennessee Press, 1987); William H. Wiggins Jr. and Douglas Denatale, eds., *Jubilation!: African American Celebrations in the Southeast* (Columbia: University of South Carolina Press, 1993).

36. Charles Reagan Wilson, "'God's Project': The Southern Civil Religion, 1920–1980," in *Religion and the Life of the Nation: American Recoveries*, ed. Rowland A. Sherrill (Urbana and Chicago: University of Illinois Press, 1990).

37. Glassberg, *American Historical Pageantry*, 251–58.

38. W. J. Cash, *The Mind of the South* (New York: Alfred A. Knopf, 1941).

39. Hobsbawm and Ranger, *The Invention of Tradition*, 98.

Chapter 2. The Burden of Southern Culture

1. The quote is from "An Old Flag Bedevils the New South," *Washington Post*, February 11, 2000. See also David Firestone, "South Carolina Acts on Goals, but N.A.A.C.P. Isn't Happy," *New York Times*, May 12, 2000.

2. Charles Reagan Wilson, "Unifying the Symbols of Southern Culture," in *Judgment and Grace in Dixie: Southern Faiths from Faulkner to Elvis* (Athens: University of Georgia Press, 1995), 159–63; James C. Cobb, *Redefining Southern Culture: Mind and Identity in the Modern South* (Athens: University of Georgia Press, 1999), 125–49; Kevin P. Thornton, "Symbolism at Ole Miss and the Crisis of Southern Identity," *South Atlantic Quarterly*, Summer 1987.

3. *Webster's Ninth New Collegiate Dictionary* (Springfield, Mass.: Merriam Webster, 1984), 188.

4. C. Vann Woodward, *The Burden of Southern History*, 2nd ed. (Baton Rouge: Louisiana State University Press, 1968), vii–xiii, 3–26.

5. Richard Maxwell Brown, "The New Regionalism in America, 1970–1981," in *Regionalism and the Pacific Northwest*, ed. William G. Robbins, Robert J. Frank, and Richard E. Ross (Corvalis: Oregon State University Press, 1983), 137–96.

6. See introduction to *The New Regionalism: Essays and Commentaries*, ed. Charles Reagan Wilson (Jackson: University Press of Mississippi, 1998), ix–xxiii.

7. See "General Introduction," in *The New Encyclopedia of Southern Culture*, ed. Charles Reagan Wilson (Chapel Hill: University of North Carolina Press, 2006), xi–xvi; Raymond Williams, *Keywords: A Vocabulary of Culture and Society* (New York: Oxford University Press, 1976), 76–82; and Terry G. Jordan, "The Concept and Method," in *Regional Studies: The Interplay of Land and People* (College Station: Texas A & M University Press, 1992), 8–24. For an example of cultural studies approaches applied to the South, see Tara McPherson, *Reconstructing Dixie: Race, Gender, and Nostalgia in the Imagined South* (Durham: Duke University Press, 2003); for an ethnographic study, see Celeste Ray, *Southern Heritage on Display: Public Ritual and Ethnic Diversity within Southern Regionalism* (Tuscaloosa: University of Alabama Press, 2003).

8. Clifford Geertz, *The Interpretation of Cultures* (New York: Basic Books, 1979).

9. Rhys Isaac, *The Transformation of Virginia, 1740–1790* (Chapel Hill: University of North Carolina Press, 1982); Ted Ownby, *Subduing Satan: Religion, Recreation, and Manhood in the Rural South, 1865–1920* (Chapel Hill: University of North Carolina Press, 1990).

10. Lewis P. Simpson, "Southern Spiritual Nationalism: Notes on the Background of Modern Southern Fiction," in *The Cry of Home: Cultural Nationalism and the Modern Writer*, ed. H. Ernest Lewald (Knoxville: University of Tennessee Press, 1972).

11. William R. Taylor, *Cavalier and Yankee: The Old South and American National Character* (New York: Harper and Row, 1961).

12. Christine Leigh Heyrman, *Southern Cross: The Beginnings of the Bible Belt* (New York: Alfred A. Knopf, 1997).

13. Charles Reagan Wilson, *Baptized in Blood: The Religion of the Lost Cause, 1865-1920* (Athens: University of Georgia Press, 1980).

14. Daniel Joseph Singal, *The War Within: From Victorian to Modernist Thought in the South, 1919-1945* (Chapel Hill: University of North Carolina Press, 1982); Fred Hobson, *Tell about the South: The Southern Rage to Explain* (Baton Rouge: Louisiana State University Press, 1983), 204–5.

15. Simpson, "Southern Spiritual Nationalism," 190, 206.

16. Leslie W. Dunbar, "The Annealing of the South," *Virginia Quarterly Review* (Autumn 1961): 507.

17. Martin Luther King Jr., *Why We Can't Wait* (New York: Harper and Row, 1963), 80, 116; Martin Luther King Jr., *The Wisdom of Martin Luther King: In His Own Words* (New York: Lancer/Bill Adler Books, 1968), 28, 41, 64, 75, 77.

18. David R. Goldfield, *Black, White, and Southern: Race Relations and Southern Culture, 1940 to the Present* (Baton Rouge: Louisiana State University Press, 1990); Cobb, *Redefining Southern Culture*, 125–49.

19. Benedict Anderson, *Imagined Communities: Reflections on the Origin and Spread of Nationalism* (New York: Verso, 1991). For a postmodern critique of "southernness," see Jefferson Humphries, "The Discourse of Southernness: Or How We Can Know There Will Still Be Such a Thing as the South and Southern Literary Culture in the Twenty-first Century," in *The Future of Southern Letters*, ed. Jefferson Humphries and John Lowe (New York: Oxford University Press, 1996), 119–33.

20. The quote is in David Firestone, "Bastion of Confederacy Finds Its Future May Hinge on Rejecting the Past," *New York Times*, December 5, 1999.

Chapter 3. Saturated Southerners

1. James Agee and Walker Evans, *Let Us Now Praise Famous Men* (1941; Boston: Houghton Mifflin, 1988), 300.

2. William Alexander Percy, *Lanterns on the Levee: Recollections of a Planter's Son* (1941; Baton Rouge: Louisiana State University Press, 1973), 149. For the image of the southern poor white, see Shields McIlwaine, *The Southern Poor White: From Lubberland to Tobacco Road* (Baton Rouge: Louisiana State University Press, 1939); Merrill Maguire Skaggs, *The Folk in Southern Fiction* (Athens: University of Georgia Press, 1972); and Sylvia Jenkins Cook, *From Tobacco Road to Route 66: The Southern Poor White in Fiction* (Chapel Hill: University of North Carolina Press, 1976). See also Michael O'Brien, *The Idea of the American South, 1920-1941* (Baltimore: Johns Hopkins University Press, 1979); and Daniel Singal, *The War Within: From Victorian to Modernist Thought in the South, 1919-1945* (Chapel Hill: University of North Carolina Press, 1982).

3. See chap. 1.

4. George Brown Tindall, "The Lost World of *Let Us Now Praise Famous Men*," in *James Agee: Reconsiderations*, ed. Michael A. Lofaro (Knoxville: University of Tennessee Press), 21–31; Jack Temple Kirby, *The Countercultural South* (Athens: University of Georgia Press, 1995); Wayne Flynt, *Poor but Proud: Alabama's Poor Whites* (Tuscaloosa: University of Alabama Press, 1989). See esp. chap. 9, "'Out of the Dust': Poor Folks' Culture," and chap. 11, "'We Didn't Know the Difference': The Great Depression."

5. John Shelton Reed, *Southern Folk, Plain and Fancy: Native White Social Types* (Athens: University of Georgia Press, 1986). See esp. chap. 3, "Common Men."

6. Walker Evans, "Foreword: James Agee in 1936," in Agee and Evans, *Let Us Now Praise Famous Men*, xlviii; Laurence Bergreen, *James Agee: A Life* (New York: E.P. Dutton, 1984), 4–11; Alan Spiegel, *James Agee and the Legend of Himself: A Critical Study* (Columbia: University of Missouri Press, 1998), 7–8; Mark A. Doty, *Tell Me Who I Am: James Agee's Search for Selfhood* (Baton Rouge: Louisiana State University Press, 1989), 5.

7. Agee and Evans, *Let Us Now Praise Famous Men*, xlvi, 11, 100–107.

8. Ibid., 27–31, 36, 39–43.

9. Ibid., 70, 76–77, 87, 214.

10. Ibid., 378–81.

11. Ibid., 70–72, 344, 391.

12. Evans, "Foreword," xli; John Hersey, "Introduction: Agee," in Agee and Evans, *Let Us Now Praise Famous Men*, xvii–xviii.

13. Agee and Evans, *Let Us Now Praise Famous Men*, 154, 206.

14. Ibid., 202–3, 210.

15. Ibid., 265–66.

16. Ibid., 9.

17. Roger M. Williams, *Sing a Sad Song: The Life of Hank Williams* (Urbana: University of Illinois Press, 1981); Colin Escott, *Hank Williams: The Biography* (New York: Little, Brown and Company, 1994).

18. "Get a radio or a phonograph capable of the most extreme loudness possible, and sit down to listen to a performance of Beethoven's Seventh Symphony or of Schubert's C-Major Symphony. But I don't mean just sit down and listen. I mean this: Turn it on as loud as you can get it. Then get down on the floor and jam your ear as close into the loudspeaker as you can get it and stay there, breathing as lightly as possible, and not moving, and neither eating nor smoking nor drinking." This same technique is quite effective in listening to Hank Williams's classic "I'm So Lonesome I Could Cry," although the part about not drinking anything should not be observed. Agee and Evans, *Let Us Now Praise Famous Men*, 15. For the importance of music to southern rural culture, see Bill C. Malone, *Southern Music/American Music* (Lexington: University Press of Kentucky, 1979).

19. Escott, *Hank Williams*, 3–5; David Anderson and Patrick Huber, "'The Log Train': Hank Williams's Last Song," *Tributaries: Journal of the Alabama Folklife Association*, Spring 1999, 20.

20. The text of "Countrified" is in Don Cusic, ed., *Hank Williams: The Complete Lyrics* (New York: St. Martin's Press, 1993), 13.

21. Ibid.

22. George Lipsitz, *Rainbow at Midnight: Labor and Culture in the 1940s* (Urbana: University of Illinois Press, 1994), 23–29, 318–19; Kent Blaser, "'Pictures from Life's Other Side': Hank Williams, Country Music, and Popular Culture in America," *South Atlantic Quarterly*, Winter 1985, 12–26. The text of "I'll Never Get out of the World Alive" is in Cusic, *Hank Williams*, 54.

23. Escott, *Hank Williams*, 6–9.

24. The text of "I Saw the Light" is in Cusic, *Hank Williams*, 43.

25. Anderson and Huber, "'The Log Train,'" 31. The text of "Pan American" is in Cusic, *Hank Williams*, 109.

26. The text of "The Log Train" is in Cusic, *Hank Williams*, 82.

27. Rufus Jarman, "Country Music Goes to Town," *Nation's Business*, February 1953, 51.

28. W. K. McNeil, "'Hillbilly' Image," in *Encyclopedia of Southern Culture*, ed. Charles Reagan Wilson and William Ferris (Chapel Hill: University of North Carolina Press, 1989), 504–5.

29. Clyde A. Milner II, "The View from Wisdom: Four Layers of History and Regional Identity," in *Under an Open Sky: Rethinking America's Western Past*, ed. William Cronon, George Miles, and Jay Gitlin (New York: W. W. Norton, 1992), 204; Wendell Berry, "The Regional Motive," in *A Continuous Harmony: Essays Cultural and Agricultural* (New York: Harcourt Brace Jovanovich, 1972), 67.

Chapter 4. Our Land, Our Country

1. William Faulkner, "On Privacy (The American Dream: What Happened to It?)," in *Essays, Speeches, and Public Letters*, ed. James B. Meriwether (London: Chatto and Windus, 1967), 73.

2. Wendy L. Wall, in *Inventing the "American Way": The Politics of Consensus from the New Deal to the Civil Rights Movement* (New York: Oxford University Press, 2008), challenges the idea of a mid-twentieth-century national consensus that the term "American Way" suggests. Wall shows how fears of fascism and communism promoted Americans rallying around the ideological construction of a singular American Way.

3. Mitford M. Mathews, ed., *A Dictionary of Americanisms on Historical Principles* (Chicago: University of Chicago Press, 1951), 1:26; Warren I. Susman, *Culture as History: The Transformation of American Society in the Twentieth Century* (New York: Pantheon, 1984), 302. See also Merle Curti, "The American Exploration of Dreams and Dreamers," *Journal of the History of Ideas* 27 (July–September 1966): 391–416.

4. Susman, *Culture as History*, 76–85.

5. Ibid., 156 (quote), 164–66; Warren Susman, "The Thirties," in *The Development of an American Culture*, ed. Stanley Coben and Loren Ratner (Englewood Cliffs, N.J.: Prentice-Hall, 1970), 227–31; Jackson Lears, "A Matter of Taste: Corporate Cultural Hegemony in a Mass-Consumption Society," in *Recasting America: Culture and Politics in the Age of Cold War*, ed. Lary May (Chicago: University of Chicago Press, 1989), 41; George V. Denny Jr., et al., "Can We Depend upon Youth to Follow the American Way?" in *Conversations with Richard Wright*, ed. Kenneth Kinnamon and Michael Fabre (Jackson: University Press of Mississippi, 1993), 22.

6. Susman, *Culture as History*, 155; J. Ronald Oakley, *God's Country: America in the Fifties* (New York: Dembner Books, 1986), 320.

7. Frances FitzGerald, *America Revised: History Textbooks in the Twentieth Century* (Boston: Little-Brown, 1979). See also Stephen Whitfield, *The Culture of the Cold War* (Baltimore: Johns Hopkins University Press, 1991), 57.

8. Will Herberg, *Protestant-Catholic-Jew: An Essay in American Religious Sociology* (1955; Garden City, N.J.: Anchor Books, 1960), 75.

9. For the South in the 1950s, see Numan V. Bartley, *The New South, 1945–1980* (Baton Rouge: Louisiana State University Press and the Littlefield Fund for Southern History of the University of Texas, 1995); Pete Daniel, *Lost Revolutions: The South in the 1950s* (Chapel Hill: Published for the Smithsonian National Museum of American History, Washington, D.C., by the University of North Carolina Press, 2000).

10. Twelve Agrarians, *I'll Take My Stand: The South and the Agrarian Tradition* (1930; Baton Rouge: Louisiana State University Press, 1977), xxxvii, xliv, 1.

11. Ibid., 35.

12. "Carry on the Fight," *Meridian (Miss.) Star*, August 26, 1964.

13. "Address to the Graduating Class of Pine Manor Junior College," *Essays*, 141–42; "On Privacy," 73.

14. "On Privacy," 62.

15. Ibid., 65–66.

16. "Address upon Receiving the National Book Award for Fiction," and "Address to the English Club of the University of Virginia," *Essays*, 144, 162.

17. William Faulkner, *Intruder in the Dust* (New York: Random House, 1948), 202; "On Privacy," 71.

18. Faulkner, *Intruder in the Dust*, 156.

19. "On Fear: Deep South in Labor: Mississippi," *Essays*, 94–95.

20. Ibid., 91, 93, 95. See also "Letter to a Northern Editor," *Essays*, 86–91.

21. "On Fear," 95–96, 105.

22. Ibid., 95.

23. James McBride Dabbs, *The Southern Heritage* (New York: Knopf, 1958), 24–36 (quotes from p. 24).

24. "On Fear," 101–2.

25. Ibid., 102–3.

26. Ibid., 104, 105. For background on this point, see Paul Carter, *Another Part of the Fifties* (New York: Columbia University Press, 1983); and William Manchester, *The Glory and the Dream: A Narrative History of America, 1932–1972* (Boston: Little-Brown, 1974).

Chapter 5. The Myth of the Biracial South

1. Charles L. Black Jr., "Paths to Desegregation," *New Republic,* October 21, 1957, 15.

2. Leslie W. Dunbar, "The Annealing of the South," *Virginia Quarterly Review* 37 (Autumn 1961): 507.

3. George B. Tindall, "Mythology: A New Frontier in Southern History," in *The Idea of the South: Pursuit of a Central Theme,* ed. Frank E. Vandiver (Chicago: University of Chicago Press, 1964), 1–15. For an overview of the South's mythic history, see Charles Reagan Wilson, ed., *The New Encyclopedia of Southern Culture,* vol. 4, *Myth, Memory, and Manners* (Chapel Hill: University of North Carolina Press, 2006). Jordan's quote is on page 151. See also Patrick Gerster and Nicholas Cords, eds., *Myth and Southern History,* 2 vols. (Urbana: University of Illinois Press, 1989).

4. Fred C. Hobson, "The Savage South: An Inquiry into the Origins, Endurance, and Presumed Demise of an Image," in Gerster and Cords, *Myth and Southern History,* 133–40 (quotes pages 145, 146).

5. Ibid.; George B. Tindall, "Mythic South," in *Encyclopedia of Southern Culture,* ed. Charles Reagan Wilson and William Ferris (Chapel Hill: University of North Carolina Press, 1989), 1098.

6. Joel Williamson, *The Crucible of Race: Black-White Relations in the American South since Emancipation* (New York: Oxford University Press, 1984), 6, 82–86, 507–10.

7. Thomas Nelson Page, *Social Life in Old Virginia before the War* (New York: Charles Scribner's Sons, 1897). The Grady quote is in Henry W. Grady, *The New South* (New York: Bonner's Sons, 1890), 146–152.

8. John Egerton, *Speak Now Against the Day: The Generation before the Civil Rights Movement in the South* (New York: Alfred A. Knopf, 1994); Morton Sosna, *In Search of the Silent South: Southern Liberals and the Race Issue* (New York: Columbia University Press, 1977).

9. Sosna, *In Search of the Silent South,* 173–74; McGill, *The South and the Southerner* (New Boston: Little, Brown, 1963), 58, 217.

10. Martin Luther King Jr., *The Wisdom of Martin Luther King in His Own Words* (New York: Lancer/Bill Adler Books, 1968), 23, 64, 75; Martin Luther King Jr., *Why We Can't Wait* (New York: Harper and Row, 1963), 80; *New York Times,* August 28, 1983, 16.

11. Willie Morris, introduction to *You Can't Eat Magnolias*, ed. H. Brandt Ayers and Thomas H. Naylor (New York: McGraw-Hill, 1972), xi. See also Karen McDearman, "L. Q. C. Lamar Society," in Wilson, *Myth, Memory, and Manners*, 242–43.

12. Ayers and Naylor, *You Can't Eat Magnolias*, 5, 19.

13. Stephen A. Smith, *Myth, Media, and the Southern Mind* (Fayetteville: University of Arkansas Press, 1985), 74–78; *Southern Journal* (Oxford, Miss.: Center for the Study of Southern Culture, 1980).

14. "Out of a Cocoon," *Time*, September 27, 1976, 40.

15. Busbee and Edwards quoted in Waldo W. Braden, "The Speaking of the Deep South Governors, 1970–1980," in *A New Diversity in Contemporary Southern Rhetoric*, ed. Calvin M. Logue and Howard Dorgan (Baton Rouge: Louisiana State University Press, 1987), 198. See also Smith, *Myth, Media, and the Southern Mind*, 62–93.

16. Braden, "The Speaking of the Deep South Governors, 1970–1980," 200; David R. Goldfield, *Promised Land: The South since 1945* (Arlington Heights, Ill.: Harlan Davidson, 1987), 173–74.

17. James C. Cobb, "Community and Identity: Redefining Southern Culture," *Georgia Review*, Spring 1996, 9–24.

18. Reuben Askew quoted in Smith, *Myth, Media, and the Southern Mind*, 89.

19. Larry King quoted in ibid., 89–90.

20. "The Spirit of the South," *Time*, September 26, 1976, 30–31.

21. Ibid.

22. Jack Temple Kirby, *Media-Made Dixie: The South in the American Imagination*, rev. ed. (Athens: University of Georgia Press, 1986), chapters 8 and 9.

23. Quoted material from David R. Goldfield, *Black, White, and Southern: Race Relations and Southern Culture, 1940 to the Present* (Baton Rouge: Louisiana State University Press, 1990), 220, 225–26.

24. Mary E. Mebane, "And Blacks Go South Again," *New York Times*, July 4, 1972, 17. For the black migration southward, see also Goldfield, *Black, White, and Southern*, 221; and "Race and the South," *U.S. News and World Report*, July 23, 1990, 22.

25. Curtis M. Graves, "Beyond the Briar Patch," in Ayers and Naylor, *You Can't Eat Magnolias*, 41–42.

26. Thadious M. Davis, "Expanding the Limits: The Intersection of Race and Region," *Southern Literary Journal* 20 (Spring 1988): 6–7; Alice Walker, "The Black Writer and the Southern Experience," in *In Search of Our Mothers' Gardens: Womanist Prose* (New York: Harcourt Brace Jovanovich, 1983), 21.

27. Paul Delaney, "A New South for Blacks?" in *Dixie Dateline: A Journalistic Portrait of the Contemporary South*, ed. John B. Boles (Houston: Rice University Press, 1983), 37–47. See also Charles Reagan Wilson, "Unifying the Symbols of Southern Culture," in *Judgment and Grace in Dixie: Southern Faiths from Faulkner to*

Elvis (Athens: University of Georgia Press, 1995), 159–63; and Kevin Thornton, "The Confederate Flag and the Meaning of Southern History," *Southern Cultures* 2 (Winter 1996): 233–45.

28. Wilson, "Unifying the Symbols of Southern Culture," 159–63; "In Virginia, King Shares His Day of Honor with Confederate Heroes," *Atlanta Journal-Constitution,* January 15, 1989, 14A.

29. Paul Greenberg, "Blacks, Whites Must Accept Common Past, Symbols," *Jackson Clarion-Ledger,* February 17, 1988, 7A.

30. Delaney, "A New South for Blacks?" 44–46; Nadine Cohodas, *The Band Played Dixie: Race and the Liberal Conscience at Ole Miss* (New York: Free Press, 1997).

31. Peter Applebome, "Columbia, South Carolina: Southern Partisans, Then and Now," in *Dixie Rising: How the South Is Shaping American Values, Politics, and Culture* (New York: New York Times Books, 1997), chap. 5, esp. 118–119 and 131.

32. See Ted Ownby, ed., *Black and White: Cultural Interaction in the Antebellum South* (Jackson: University Press of Mississippi, 1993) for a consideration of the South's biracial cultural history.

33. Oscar Carr Jr., quoted in "The Spirit of the South," 30.

34. William Raspberry, "Return Home Proves State of Mississippi Is, Finally, a Good Place To Be," *Jackson Clarion-Ledger,* November 21, 1991, 21A.

35. "Other Voices," *Time,* September 26, 1976, 99.

Chapter 6. Beyond the Sahara of the Bozart

1. Eudora Welty, *One Writer's Beginnings* (Cambridge, Mass.: Harvard University Press, 1983), 3–13, 22–23.

2. David Evans, *Big Road Blues: Tradition and Creativity in the Folk Blues* (New York: Da Capo, 1982), 42–43.

3. H. L. Mencken, *Prejudices: Second Series* (New York: Alfred A. Knopf, 1920), 70–73.

4. Richard Wright, *Black Boy: A Record of Childhood and Youth* (New York: A Perennial Classic, 1966), 282.

5. Classic studies of the Southern Literary Renaissance that deal with the issue of why it began when it did include Daniel J. Singal, *The War Within: From Victorian to Modernist Thought in the South, 1919–1945* (Chapel Hill: University of North Carolina Press, 1982); and Richard H. King, *A Southern Renaissance: The Cultural Awakening of the American South, 1930–1955* (New York: Oxford University Press, 1980). See also Michael Kreyling, *Inventing Southern Literature* (Jackson: University Press of Mississippi, 1998).

6. Michael O'Brien suggested bringing together southern musicians as well as writers in consideration of the renaissance in "A Heterodox Note on the Southern Renaissance," in *Perspectives on the American South: An Annual Review of Society,*

Politics, and Culture, vol. 4, ed. James C. Cobb and Charles Reagan Wilson (New York: Gordon and Breach Science Publishers, 1987), 5. John Egerton, in "Creative Expression and Regional Identity," in *Alternate Roots: Plays from the Southern Theater,* ed. Kathie deNobriga and Valetta Anderson (Portsmouth, New Hampshire: Heinemann, 1994), xi, xiv, mentions language as a source of widespread creativity in the South.

7. J. Richard Gruber, compiler, *The Art of the South, 1890–2003: The Ogden Museum of Southern Art* (New Orleans: Ogden Museum, 2004); William W. Frehling et al., *A Place Not Forgotten: Landscapes of the South from the Morris Museum of Art* (Lexington: University of Kentucky Art Museum, 1998).

8. Jack Temple Kirby, *Rural Worlds Lost: The American South, 1920–1960* (Baton Rouge: Louisiana State University Press, 1987); Pete Daniel, *Standing at the Crossroads: Southern Life in the Twentieth Century* (New York: Hill and Wang, 1986); Donald Davidson, *Why the Modern South Has a Great Literature,* Vanderbilt Studies in the Humanities, vol. 1 (Nashville, Tenn.: Vanderbilt University Press, 1951), 3–8; Katharine Jocher, Guy B. Johnson, George L. Simpson, and Rupert B. Vance, eds., *Folk, Region, and Society: Selected Papers of Howard W. Odum* (Chapel Hill: University of North Carolina Press, 1964), 202–21.

9. Eudora Welty, "Place in Fiction," in *The Eye of the Story: Selected Essays and Reviews* (New York: Vintage Books, 1975), 116–133; Patricia Yaeger, *Dirt and Desire: Reconstructing Southern Women's Writing, 1930–1990* (Chicago: University of Chicago Press, 2000); Yi-Fu Tuan, *Space and Place: The Perspective of Experience* (Minneapolis: University of Minnesota Press, 2001); Martyn Bone, *The Postsouthern Sense of Place in Contemporary Fiction* (Baton Rouge: Louisiana State University Press, 2005); James Peacock, *Grounded Globalism: How the U. S. South Embraces the World* (Athens: University of Georgia Press, 2007).

10. Ulrich Bonnell Phillips, *Life and Labor in the Old South* (Boston: Little, Brown, and Company, 1929), 3; Charles Reagan Wilson, gen. ed., *The New Encyclopedia of Southern Culture,* vol. 8, *Environment,* vol. ed. Martin Melosi (Chapel Hill: University of North Carolina Press, 2007).

11. Wright, *Black Boy,* 14–15, 283.

12. Alice Walker, *In Search of Our Mothers' Gardens: Womanist Prose* (New York: Harcourt Brace Jovanovich, 1983), 15–21, 231–43.

13. Evans, *Big Road Blues,* 42–43; Zora Neale Hurston, *Dust Tracks on the Road: An Autobiography* (1942; Urbana, Ill.: University of Chicago Press, 1984), 135.

14. Bill C. Malone, *Southern Music/American Music* (Lexington: University Press of Kentucky, 1979).

15. Pete Daniel, *Lost Revolutions: The South in the 1950s* (Chapel Hill: Published for the Smithsonian National Museum of American History, Washington, D.C., by the University of North Carolina Press, 2000), 137.

16. Charles Joyner, "A Single Southern Culture: Cultural Interaction in the Old South," in *Black and White: Cultural Interaction in the Antebellum South,* ed. Ted Ownby (Jackson: University Press of Mississippi, 1993), 3–22.

Chapter 7. Flashes of the Spirit

1. Susan Ketchin, *The Christ-Haunted Landscape: Faith and Doubt in Southern Fiction* (Jackson, Miss.: University Press of Mississippi, 1994), 347.

2. Lewis Simpson, "Southern Spiritual Nationalism: Notes on the Background of Modern Southern Fiction," in *The Cry of Home: Cultural Nationalism and the Modern Writers*, ed. H. Ernest Lewald (Knoxville: University of Tennessee Press, 1972), 203–4 ; Lisa Howorth, "Fear God and Give Glory to Him: Sacred Art in the South," *Reckon*, 1995, 40–50.

3. Alice Rae Yelen, *Passionate Visions of the American South: Self-Taught Artists from 1940 to the Present* (New Orleans: New Orleans Museum of Art, 1993), 137–38; Howard Finster, *Stranger from Another World: Man of Visions Now on This Earth* (New York: Abbeville Press, 1989), 52–53.

4. Charles Reagan Wilson, gen. ed., *The New Encyclopedia of Southern Culture*, vol. 1, *Religion*, vol. ed. Samuel S. Hill (Chapel Hill: University of North Carolina Press, 2006).

5. Yelen, *Passionate Visions*, 139; Albert J. Raboteau, *Canaan Land: A Religious History of African Americans* (New York: Oxford University Press, 2001).

6. Frederick L. Gwynn and Joseph L. Blotner, eds., *Faulkner in the University: Class Conferences at the University of Virginia, 1957–1958* (Charlottesville: University Press of Virginia, 1959), 41.

7. Ketchin, *Christ-Haunted Landscape*, 83–87,

8. Ibid., 135–36.

9. Ibid., 74–75; Yelen, *Passionate Visions*, 137; Gwynn and Blotner, *Faulkner in the University*, 41.

10. Miles Richardson, "Speaking and Hearing (in Contrast to Touching and Seeing) the Sacred," in *Religion in the Contemporary South: Diversity, Community, and Identity*, ed. O. Kendall White Jr. and Daryl White (Athens: University of Georgia Press, 1995), 13–22.

11. Joe York, *With Signs Following* (Jackson: University Press of Mississippi, 2008); Yelen, *Passionate Visions*, 175, 320.

12. Yelen, *Passionate Visions*, 137, 139.

13. J. F. Turner, *Howard Finster: Man of Visions* (New York: Knopf, 1989), 72.

14. Richardson, "Speaking and Hearing," 13–22.

15. Ketchin, *Christ-Haunted Landscape*, 84–85.

16. Ibid., 247.

17. Golden Gate Quartet, *Swing Down, Chariot* (Columbia Records CK47131, 1991).

18. Carol Crown, *Coming Home! Self-Taught Artists, the Bible and the American South* (Memphis: Art Museum of the University of Memphis, 2004).

19. Doris Betts, "The Christ-Haunted Psyche of the Southern Writer," *Books and Reading*, March 1985, 14.

20. Ketchin, *Christ-Haunted Landscape*, 70–71, 295.

21. Yelen, *Passionate Visions*, 141, 142.

22. Ibid., 137; Judith McWillie, "Writing in an Unknown Tongue," in *Cultural Perspectives on the American South*, vol. 5, ed. Charles Reagan Wilson (New York: Gordon and Breach, 1991), 103–118.

23. Yelen, *Passionate Visions*, 139, 143; Ketchin, *Christ-Haunted Landscape*, 284.

24. Flannery O'Connor, *Mystery and Manners: Occasional Prose*, ed. Sally and Robert Fitzgerald (New York: Farrar, Straus and Giroux, 1969), 132–34.

25. Robert Coles, "God and the Rural Poor," *Psychology Today*, January 1972, 33–40.

26. Ketchin, *Christ-Haunted Landscape*, 288.

27. Don Cusic, ed., *Hank Williams: The Complete Lyrics* (New York: St. Martin's Press, 1993), 43.

28. Ketchin, *Christ-Haunted Landscape*, 129, 283.

29. Yelen, *Passionate Visions*, 137; Ketchin, *Christ-Haunted Landscape*, 79.

Chapter 8. The Word and the Image

1. Flannery O'Connor, *Mystery and Manners: Occasional Prose*, ed. Sally and Robert Fitzgerald (New York: Farrar, Straus and Giroux, 1969), 31, 41, 124, 197. Quotations to this work are cited hereafter in the text.

2. Samuel S. Hill, *The South and the North in American Religion* (Athens: University of Georgia Press, 1980), 110.

3. Donald G. Mathews, "Evangelicalism," in *Encyclopedia of Religion in the South*, ed. Samuel S. Hill (Macon: Mercer University Press, 1984), 243–44. See also James Davison Hunter, *American Evangelicalism: Conservative Religion and the Quandary of Modernity* (New York: Holt, Rinehart and Winston, 1967).

4. Mark Noll, "The Bible and Slavery," in *Religion and the American Civil War*, ed. Randall Miller, Harry Stout, and Charles Reagan Wilson (New York: Oxford University Press, 1999), 43–73.

5. Loyal Jones, *Faith and Meaning in the Southern Uplands* (Urbana: University of Illinois Press, 1999), 106.

6. Theophus H. Smith, *Conjuring Culture: Biblical Formations of Black America* (New York: Oxford University Press, 1994).

7. Information on the self-taught artists comes from the following sources: Paul Arnett and William Arnett, eds., *Souls Grown Deep: African American Vernacular Art of the South*, vol. 1 (Atlanta: Tinwood Books; in association with the Schomburg Center for Research in Black Culture, the New York Public Library, 2000); Joyce Ann Miller, "In the Handiwork of Their Craft Is Their Prayer: African-American Religious Folk Art in the Twentieth-Century South" (master's thesis, University of Mississippi, 1992); Alice Rae Yelen, *Passionate Visions of the American*

South: Self-Taught Artists from 1940 to the Present (New Orleans: New Orleans Museum of Art, 1993).

8. Arnett, *Souls Grown Deep*, 1:308; Yelen, *Passionate Visions*, 323.

9. Yelen, *Passionate Visions*, 303, 307, 318, 328.

10. Arnett, *Souls Grown Deep*, 1:304.

11. Kathy Kemp, *Revelations: Alabama's Visionary Folk Artists* (Birmingham: Crane Hill Publishers, 1994), 212–14.

12. Ibid., 114.

13. Jane Livingston and John Beardsley, *Black Folk Art in America, 1930–1980* (Jackson: University Press of Mississippi and the Center for the Study of Southern Culture for the Corcoran Gallery of Art, 1982), 100.

14. Julia S. Ardery, *Temptation: Edgar Tolson and the Genesis of Twentieth-Century Folk Art* (Chapel Hill: University of North Carolina Press, 1998), 12–13, 18–19, 41.

15. Alice Walker, ed., *I Love Myself When I Am Laughing . . . And Then Again When I Am Looking Mean and Impressive: A Zora Neale Hurston Reader* (Old Westbury: Feminist Press, 1979), 176; Susan Ketchin, *The Christ-Haunted Landscape: Faith and Doubt in Southern Fiction* (Jackson: University Press of Mississippi, 1994), 86.

Chapter 10. *"Just a Little Talk with Jesus"*

1. Colin Escott's liner notes from *Million Dollar Quartet* (RCA Records, 1990), 1–3. Peter Guralnick discusses the Million Dollar Session in *Last Train to Memphis: The Rise of Elvis Presley* (Boston: Little Brown, 1994), 365–68. For background on southern gospel music, see James R. Goff Jr., *Close Harmony: A History of Southern Gospel* (Chapel Hill: University of North Carolina Press, 2002). For background on black gospel, see Kip Lornell, *Happy in the Service of the Lord: Afro-American Gospel Quartets in Memphis* (Urbana: University of Illinois Press, 1988).

2. Escott, *Million Dollar Quartet.*

3. See especially Charles Wolfe, "Presley and the Gospel Tradition," *Southern Quarterly* 18 (Fall 1979), 135–50; and Cheryl Thurber, "Elvis and Gospel Music," *Rejoice* 1 (1988), 6.

4. Samuel F. Weber, "Spirituality in the South," in *The New Encyclopedia of Southern Culture*, gen. ed. Charles Reagan Wilson, vol. 1, *Religion*, vol. ed. Samuel S. Hill (Chapel Hill: University of North Carolina Press, 2006). See also Bill Leonard, "Spirituality in America: Signs of the Times," *Religion and American Culture* 9 (Summer 1999), 152–57.

5. "Spirituality," in *The Oxford Dictionary of the Christian Church*, ed. F. L. Cross, 3rd ed. (Oxford: Oxford University Press, 1997), 1532. See also Gerald O'Collins

and Edward G. Farrugia, *A Concise Dictionary of Theology* (New York: Paulist Press, 2000).

6. Charles Wolfe, *In Close Harmony: The Story of the Louvin Brothers* (Jackson: University Press of Mississippi, 1996).

7. Ibid., 65.

8. Quote is from Colin Escott's liner notes from Hank Williams (as Luke the Drifter), *Beyond the Sunset* (Mercury Records 170184, 2001), 2. See also Colin Escott, *Hank Williams: The Biography* (Boston: Little, Brown and Company, 1994), 6–9; and Roger M. Williams, *Sing a Sad Song* (Urbana: University of Illinois Press, 1981).

9. Elaine Dundes, *Gladys and Elvis* (New York: Macmillan, 1985), 73, 82 (quote); Charles Wolfe's liner notes from Elvis Presley, *Amazing Grace: His Greatest Sacred Performances* (RCA Records 66421, 1994), 10. For the importance of the Assemblies of God to Presley, see Van K. Brock, "Assemblies of God: Elvis and Pentecostalism," *Bulletin of the Center for the Study of Southern Culture and Religion* 3 (June 1979).

10. Wolfe, *Amazing Grace*, 10 (quote). For the Memphis music context in the 1950s, see Michael T. Bertrand, *Race, Rock, and Elvis* (Urbana: University of Illinois Press, 2000).

11. *He Touched Me: The Gospel Music of Elvis Presley* (Coming Home Music, 1999), video (Brewster quote); Guralnick, *Last Train to Memphis*, 75 (Presley quote about Brewster); Wolfe, *Amazing Grace*, 11–12.

12. Guralnick, *Last Train to Memphis*, 47 (quote).

13. Jerry Osbourne, *Elvis: Word for Word* (New York: Harmony Books, 2002), 30, 52–53, 70.

14. Peter Guralnick, *Careless Love: The Unmaking of Elvis Presley* (Boston: Little Brown, 1999), 175–77, 195–96, 209, 363.

15. See Charles H. Lippy, *Being Religious, American Style: A History of Popular Religiosity in the United States* (Westport, Conn.: Praeger, 1994).

16. Guralnick, *Careless Love*, 222–23 (quotes). For the idea of Presley as a liminal figure in southern popular religion, see Charles Reagan Wilson, *Judgment and Grace in Dixie: Southern Faiths from Faulkner to Elvis* (Athens: University of Georgia Press, 1996).

17. Wolfe, *Amazing Grace*, 16–23.

18. Ibid., 24–26

19. *He Touched Me*, video

20. Wolfe, "Presley and the Gospel Tradition," 148 (quote).

21. Wolfe, *In Close Harmony*, 81 (quote with Louvin Brothers); *He Touched Me*, video (quote on gospel music). See also Wolfe, *Amazing Grace*, 26–28.

22. Weber, "Spirituality in the South"; Vester Presley, as told to Deda Bonura, *A Presley Speaks* (Memphis, Tenn.: Wimmer Brothers, 1978), 117.

Chapter 11. *Richard Wright's* Pagan Spain

1. Richard Wright, *Pagan Spain* (1959; New York: Harper Collins, 1995), 280.
2. Ibid., 15.
3. Ibid., 5, 11–12.
4. Ibid., xii, 21.
5. Richard Wright, *Black Boy: A Record of Childhood and Youth* (1946; New York: HarperPerennial, 1993), 113.
6. Frances Mayes, *Under the Tuscan Skies: At Home in Italy* (New York: Broadway Books, 1997), 262.
7. Wright, *Black Boy*, 122, 124–25; Wright, *Pagan Spain*, 49.
8. Wright, *Black Boy*, 166–69.
9. Ibid., 111.
10. Ibid., 111–12; Wright, *Pagan Spain*, 92.
11. Wright, *Pagan Spain*, 23, 68–69.
12. Quoted in Richard King, "Richard Wright: From the South to Africa – and Beyond," in *Look Away! The U.S. South in New World Studies*, ed. Jon Smith and Deborah Cohn (Durham, N.C.: Duke University Press, 2004), 238, 240.
13. Ibid, 229; Wright, *Pagan Spain*, 62.
14. Victor I. Masters, *The Call of the South* (Atlanta: Home Mission Board, Southern Baptist Convention, 1918), 17–18.
15. For a discussion of the post–Civil War Lost Cause as the South's civil religion, see Charles Reagan Wilson, *Baptized in Blood: The Religion of the Lost Cause, 1865–1920* (Athens: University of Georgia Press, 1980).
16. Wright, *Pagan Spain*, 131, 133, 118.
17. Ibid., 209, 112, 134, 156, 114; Richard Wright, "Big Boy Leaves Home," in *Uncle Tom's Children* (New York: Harper and Row, 1940), 17–53; Donald G. Mathews, "The Southern Rite of Human Sacrifice," *Journal of Southern Religion* 3 (2000), http://jsr.fsu.edu/mathews.htm.
18. Wright, *Pagan Spain*, 67–68.
19. Ibid., 151.
20. Ibid., 162, 231, 240.
21. Ibid., 196–98, 190.
22. Ibid., 229; Wright, *Black Boy*, 123–24.
23. Wright, *Black Boy*, 284.

Chapter 12. *A Journey to Southern Religious Studies*

1. Alfred North Whitehead, *Adventures of Ideas* (New York: Macmillan, 1933); Charles Reagan Wilson, "Attitudes toward the American Indian in Popular

American Magazines, 1865–1900" (master's thesis, University of Texas at El Paso, 1972).

2. Samuel S. Hill, *Southern Churches in Crisis* (New York: Holt, Rinehart and Winston, 1967).

3. Charles Reagan Wilson, *Baptized in Blood: The Religion of the Lost Cause, 1865–1920* (Athens: University of Georgia Press, 1980); Robert N. Bellah, "Civil Religion in America," in *American Civil Religion*, ed. Russell E. Richey and Donald G. Jones (New York: Harper and Row, 1974), 21–44.

4. Charles Reagan Wilson and William Ferris, eds., *Encyclopedia of Southern Culture* (Chapel Hill: University of North Carolina Press, 1989)

5. Charles Reagan Wilson, *Judgment and Grace in Dixie: Southern Faiths from Faulkner to Elvis* (Athens: University of Georgia Press, 1995).

6. James McBride Dabbs, *Haunted by God: The Cultural and Religious Experience of the South* (Richmond, Va.: John Knox Press, 1972).

7. Charles Reagan Wilson, "Church Burnings and Christian Community," *Christian Century*, 25 September–2 October 1996, 890–95.

Afterword. Constructing and Experiencing the Spirit

1. Eric Hobsbawm and Terence Ranger, eds., *The Invention of Tradition* (Cambridge: Cambridge University Press, 1983), 10; Marion Montgomery, *Possum, and Other Receipts for the Recovery of 'Southern' Being* (Athens: University of Georgia Press, 1987), 113; Anne Goodwyn Jones, *Tomorrow is Another Day: The Woman Writer in the South, 1859–1936* (Baton Rouge: Louisiana State University Press, 1981), 3–5.

2. Glenn Hinson, *Fire in My Bones: Transcendence and the Holy Spirit in African American Gospel* (Philadelphia: University of Pennsylvania Press, 2000), 2; Hinson, "Folklife," in *The New Encyclopedia of Southern Culture*, gen. ed. Charles Reagan Wilson, vol. 14, *Folklife*, ed. Glenn Hinson and William Ferris (Chapel Hill: University of North Carolina Press, 2010); Samuel S. Hill, "Thirty Years Later," in *Southern Churches in Crisis Revisited* (Tuscaloosa: University of Alabama Press, 1999), lv.

3. Hinson, "Folklife"; Houston A. Baker Jr., *Workings of the Spirit: The Poetics of Afro-American Women's Writing* (Chicago: University of Chicago Press, 1991), 74–75; Houston A. Baker Jr. and Dana D. Nelson, "Preface: Violence, the Body and 'The South,'" *American Literature* 73 (June 2001): 234; Kathryn McKee and Annette Trefzer, eds., "Global Contexts, Local Literatures: The New Southern Studies," *American Literature* 78 (December 2006).

INDEX

CPSIA information can be obtained at www.ICGtesting.com
Printed in the USA
LVOW101133030513

332057LV00002B/120/P